D0464818

# THE
# DAY I
# OWNED THE
# SKY

# THE
# DAY I
# OWNED THE
# SKY

Robert Lee Scott, Jr.,

Brigadier General, USAF (Retired)

BANTAM BOOKS

TORONTO · NEW YORK · LONDON · SYDNEY · AUCKLAND

To Kitty Rix and our daughter, Robin Lee

THE DAY I OWNED THE SKY
*A Bantam Book / March 1988*

BOMC offers recordings and compact discs, cassettes
and records. For information and catalog write to
BOMR, Camp Hill, PA 17012.

*All rights reserved.*
*Copyright © 1988 by Robert Lee Scott, Jr.*
*Book Design by Richard Oriolo.*
*No part of this book may be reproduced or transmitted in any form*
*or by any means, electronic or mechanical, including photocopying,*
*recording, or by any information storage and retrieval system,*
*without permission in writing from the publisher.*
*For information address: Bantam Books.*

LIBRARY OF CONGRESS
Library of Congress Cataloging-in-Publication Data

Scott, Robert Lee, 1908-
  The day I owned the sky / Robert Lee Scott, Jr.
    p.    cm.
  Includes index.
  ISBN 0-553-05248-9
  1. Scott, Robert Lee, 1908-    . 2. Air pilots, Military—United
States—Biography.   3. Generals—United States—Biography.
4. United States. Air Force—Biography.   5. Great Wall of China
(China)  6. China—Description and travel.   I. Title.
UG626.2.S36A3  1988
358.4'14'0924—dc19
[B]                                                        87-28988
                                                               CIP

*Published simultaneously in the United States and Canada*

*Bantam Books are published by Bantam Books, a division of Bantam Doubleday*
*Dell Publishing Group, Inc. Its trademark, consisting of the words "Bantam*
*Books" and the portrayal of a rooster, is Registered in U.S. Patent and*
*Trademark Office and in other countries. Marca Registrada. Bantam Books,*
*666 Fifth Avenue, New York, New York 10103.*

PRINTED IN THE UNITED STATES OF AMERICA
RRD      0  9  8  7  6  5  4  3  2  1

Whatsoever thy hand findeth to do, do it with all thy might; for there is no work,
nor device, nor knowledge,
nor wisdom, in the grave, whither thou goest.

—ECCL. 9:10

# CONTENTS

# PROLOGUE:

# THE DAY
# I OWNED THE
# SKY

Long before any of the Japanese bombers saw us, I saw them. We were sitting in the catbird seat, 3,000 feet above them and directly in the fiery ball of the sun. Spread out and ragged after takeoff from the runway at Yunnan-Yi, our eighteen P-40s now flew in tight fingertip elements of two. Before we reached 20,000 feet I saw the glint of their windshields, the discs of their propellers in sunlight. My count reached twenty-four as I breathed deeply in my oxygen mask to slow my pounding heart. Was this what RAF pilots called "getting the wind up"? I tried hard to swallow, to make the lump in my throat go away.

Time after time I remember flicking the toggles of my gun switches to be certain they had been on ever since our struggling takeoff run from that high-altitude runway. All the way, there had been no conversation on the radio. That had been my only order at the hasty briefing: no yakety-yak, and watch me. Now we dove to the attack. Not even the waggle of a wing among the enemy bombers as they grew from vague dots into real Kawasaki Ki-48s. They still had not seen us—we had the advantage.

I kept thinking of an ancient gravestone I had seen when we parked our fighters between grass-covered mounds. An interpreter had slowly translated words of Sun-Su-Wu that had been known for thousands of years. *The only way to win a battle is to make the enemy surrender on the way to the battlefield.* I was still wondering about their subtle meaning as I closed in on the enemy at over four hundred miles an hour.

By now each of my pilots had selected his target. I had learned long ago from my grandfather how to shoot quail bursting from the brush. Never aim at the covey; pick out one target and concentrate on it, never taking your eye from it until it falls. General Claire Chennault had added a great deal in the last six months to what Grandpa had said.

The enemy finally saw us diving out of the sun. We must have appeared much more numerous than we were, because they immediately jettisoned their bombs. It was such a surprise that I yelled over the radio, "We've already won the battle!"

For one brief instant I watched in fascination as those bombs streamed from open bomb bays. I aimed for the leader, who turned away, his gunners already firing arcing lines of tracer at me from far out of range. I now counted twenty-seven bombers, almost overshooting my target as the salvoed bombs began exploding uselessly far below. I was so close that the lead bomber filled my whole windshield as I fired two short bursts before diving beneath the ball of flame it had become. By then I had another target making a tight turn in front of me to get away. I approached at an angle from which not one of his gunners could shoot at me—Chennault had taught me their blind spots—and he went down as shots from six .50-caliber machine guns converged where wing joined fuselage, hitting the fuel tanks, one engine, and the cockpit area.

The bombers scattered like those quail I remembered as a boy, and we followed to take them on individually. The rest was almost an anticlimax, because there were still no enemy fighters. Pure arrogance for the Japanese formation to dare to come naked. I followed two more bombers and shot them down over the Salween River, where Burma begins.

Not from full astern, though, the way I had brought down my first bombers six months earlier. Now, I took them both with quartering deflection shots, and there was not a bullet hole in my plane when the day was done. There used to be before the Old Man schooled me, mad at me sometimes for having enemy oil all over my plane from prop to tail. I had learned much in the months during which I had become fighter commander in his China Air Task Force.

"His good right arm" he called me when I came home with a victory or two and no damage to my P-40. Chennault checked every time.

The night before, Christmas night, 1942, Wang Cook had served us our usual dinner. Nothing special; it seemed we were losing the war all over the world, and we were too busy to celebrate anyway. Doc Gentry, sitting on Chennault's right, passed the Old Man his special peppers for the soup. They were so hot that Tom Gentry and I grinned at each other in mouth-burning memory.

Through the window behind me, I heard Wong Chauffeur talking to his little son out back in the compound where our Chinese servants lived. I wonder now, these more than four decades later and after Chairman Mao's Cultural Revolution, how many of those little boys and girls grew up. They would be something like forty-five years old now.

Just then the field telephone jingled. The radioman asked me to tell the Old Man that the airfield at Yunnan-Yi had been bombed at noon by twenty Japanese planes. It was not too far away, just 165 miles up the Burma Road from our headquarters at Kunming. Not one of our fighter bases, Yunnan-Yi was a terminus used by General Stilwell's American Military Mission to China for Lend Lease supplies flown across the Hump by the Air Transport Command. The AMMISCA unloading had been interrupted, planes had been destroyed, and hundreds of Chinese workers had been killed while transporting freight to the godowns, as the storage caves in the hills were called.

The radio soon became active with terse orders from AMMISCA in Chungking, the gist of which was that General Stilwell wanted Chennault to drop everything and defend the ATC terminus at all costs. The Old Man forgot his peppery soup and turned to me.

"Scotty, fly over there first thing in the morning with every fighter you can find," he ordered. "Make your own operational plans—you've been out here long enough to know what to do. I have only one small suggestion based on my experience with the enemy. The Japanese tend to repeat themselves. They struck at noon today, so watch for them tomorrow at the same time and place. Good hunting."

I was off the Kunming Airfield with twenty-two combat-ready fighters an hour after sunrise, following the Burma Road in its twisting climb from 6,000 to more than 7,500 feet. By the time I landed at Yunnan-Yi, rough engines had reduced our number to eighteen, perhaps twenty. No big deal, I thought; that was normal out here at the end of the very end of the supply lines.

We parked our ships among Douglas C-47 transports being offloaded by rushing trucks. I put my plan for airdrome defense into operation just as I knew Chennault would have in my place, quite confident that Japanese bombers would strike the same time as yesterday. I put up an umbrella of two P-40s—hardly adequate protection but all we could afford in China in 1942—while the rest of us took turns refueling our fighters by hand with wobble pumps in rusty drums of aviation gasoline. With zero hour approaching I dispersed my planes, leaving a couple of pilots standing a "listening watch" as I set about improving our chances.

The fighters had to be dispersed or they would make too easy a target in the event of a surprise attack; having all the planes clustered together was virtually begging for a lone enemy fighter to strafe the entire force and set them ablaze. It was unthinkable to leave those vital fighters grouped together—if I had, I suspect the Old Man would have had me shot—so I separated them and parked them with their tails pulled back into bushes and trees around the rocky field. Now I had to be able to get my pilots to their planes when the *jing-bao* warning went up, signaling that an air raid was just minutes away.

I stopped a couple of trucks and asked the sergeants for a couple of vehicles with which to transport my fighter pilots to their planes. Sergeants are usually the most cooperative people in the world, especially when a bird colonel asks for something. To my utter surprise I received the idiot's treatment, being referred up the ladder to a captain, who referred me to a major. By the time I got to a mud-and-wattle hut and a colonel wearing the quartermaster insignia of the SOS—that vaunted Service of Supply—I was getting madder by the minute. Time was being wasted and the sun was climbing ever higher into a sky as clear as a bell. Damn it, they had been bombed the day before and my orders were to keep that from happening again.

"My name is Scott," I said. "I was sent here by General Chennault to defend this airdrome. I don't need but one jeep and another six-by-six truck, but I need it now."

I explained our vital requirement for transportation to take us to our airplanes with minimal notice, but the SOS officer was going by the book, living in another age. He said his assistants had already relayed my request but he regretted that the answer was no; all vehicles were needed to unload the incoming Lend Lease supplies.

"Your pilots will have to walk to their planes," he told me.

Wreckage of aircraft littered the field, and remains of bodies were still in evidence. Any moment the radio operator would call with a message from the air warning net that more Japanese bombers were airborne, and we would have only minutes to scramble, climb to altitude, and intercept them. And the major wanted us to walk to our planes where they were parked around the perimeter of the field.

This was a war zone about to be thrust into harm's way again. Already I realized that I was the senior combat officer present and the monkey was on my back. I moved to his desk and with his own pencil wrote out an order.

Dec. 26, 1942. Yunnan-Yi, China.

    As senior combat commander this station I do hereby commandeer all surface transportation hereat, and return for regular Lend Lease operations those vehicles surplus to my needs after my own tactical selection has been made.

Leaving that on his primitive desk, I shouted to my men waiting outside to stop the next truck. The SOS colonel was shouting, too, accusing me of interfering with direct orders from the commander-in-chief of the China-Burma-India Theater of Operations (commonly known as the CBI), telling me my actions would be reported immediately by radio and I could expect to be placed under arrest as soon as he had a reply.

One of my men later told me I yelled at the colonel that if I did not do what I was doing, in all probability there would be no operation left. That order I signed is undoubtedly still in the Air Force archives somewhere. My combat report of that day is; I read it in May 1985 at the Chennault Library at Maxwell Air Force Base in Alabama.

I drove away in the SOS officer's jeep, already searching the southwest horizon, where the enemy would most likely appear. Ahead, I stopped another jeep and commandeered it, then another, concluding that I could get my men to their planes more quickly by jeep than with cumbersome six-by-six trucks. Near the radio station and the Japanese air warning net link, which were ours, I went over the plan of action with my three flight commanders, Mooney, Couch, and Harry Pike. I reminded them that radio contact could already have been made with Vinegar Joe Stilwell and word might be out for our arrest. I uncovered my .45 pistol and checked to see if it was loaded, wondering who the hell was the enemy.

At noon—straight up—the radio operator Sasser ran out to announce receipt of a report from the Chinese net: heavy aircraft engine noise in the Paoshan vicinity. The bomber strike force was on its way, all right, and very close—less than a hundred miles to the west. I signaled with the jeep horn, and card games ended instantly. In seconds the three jeeps took off in different directions, covered with fighter pilots. Our mechanics, flown over in a C-47, were already starting the P-40s, other Allison engines springing to life before I strapped in and started mine. We were all shouting to one another from the cockpits and I taxied out, looking behind me to see whirling props as my fighters followed in a curving single file. Then we faced in several directions like a fan and poured on the coal.

Ten short minutes from the time we broke ground, we climbed through 13,000 feet in combat formation. We got them all. Mooney gave his life; Couch was shot down in the crossfire of two bombers but survived. I kept wondering what would have happened there at Yunnan-Yi if those twenty-seven enemy bombers had delivered the loads they had jettisoned sixty miles away.

We formed up over the fires of those crashed Kawasaki bombers. I needed to talk to the Old Man, and Harry Pike made it easy for me. As soon as we reached Yunnan-Yi he called over the radio for me to remain at altitude and head back to Kunming. He would land with the formation to refuel and check on the missing pilots by way of the Chinese warning net; he would also tell the SOS colonel that I was missing in action, presumed dead, in case there was an order for my arrest.

It was nearly dark when I reached the house off Kunming Airfield where I lived with Chennault. As I passed the Chinese sentry at the compound gate, I sensed he already knew of our latest aerial victories over the "barbarian," as they called the Japanese. Two hundred miles meant nothing to the kind of grapevine telegraph the Chinese had, and my four victory rolls over the field before setting my P-40 down on the six-thousand-foot runway probably told him more. He stood rigidly at attention and called out loudly, "A-V-G! *Ding hao!* American very good. Japanese very bad, *bu hao!*"

I was worried about General Chennault. He had not been well, lately seeming always to have that cough deep in his chest. Doc Gentry, the flight surgeon, called it chronic catarrh but as I think back it could have been the early stages of the lung cancer that killed him in later years. I fairly ran to his bedroom, still elated by our success in combat. The twinkle was back in his black eyes but not a muscle moved in his tanned, leathery face. I knew he was laughing inside.

"Well, Scotty, I've been sticking close to the radio and heard all your communications on the successful interception today. What I'd like to know, son; did they come in on schedule?"

"They arrived as you predicted, sir." I tried to sound casual, not to gloat. "We shot down all twenty-seven of their bombers. They didn't even have fighter escort, General."

I told him about the two men we had lost, and that Harry Pike and the flight were still at Yunnan-Yi checking on them. Only then did I get down to filling him in on my commandeering the jeeps. "Harry said he'd tell that SOS colonel over there that I had been shot down," I finished. "It might have been better if I had."

Heck, this time the Old Man laughed out loud. "By God," he

said, "you're learning fast. But you are right—what you did will stir them up over at AMMISCA. Get up early in the morning and we'll fly over to Chungking. I'll have it out with Stilwell. Stubborn as he is, he has never failed to back me up in these matters of airdrome defense."

I did not sleep a wink that night, and all during our four-hundred-mile flight to Peishiyi I worried that I had embarrassed the Old Man. I was a professional soldier as well as a fighter pilot, a West Pointer; had my actions been unprofessional, perhaps personally motivated? It was a long drive in the staff car to Stilwell's headquarters, where Chennault took me in with him to see the commander-in-chief of the CBI.

Vinegar Joe sat there in his campaign hat, seeming almost pleasant although he did not speak to me. He and Chennault discussed the air battle of the day before as if I were not there, the Old Man pointing out that the entire attacking force had been destroyed—four of them by me. He emphasized that not one bomb had hit the airfield to add to the damage done by the twenty bombers on Christmas day. Then he brought up the subject of my having commandeered three vehicles.

Stilwell's attitude changed abruptly. He read a radio report from Yunnan-Yi in which his supply chief cited me for deliberately interfering with the vital Lend Lease operation. Looking up, Stilwell said that I had flagrantly usurped proper authority; he further stated that Chennault had failed to control me, or perhaps had encouraged my actions.

"These are the court-martial charges," he announced. "Specification one, countermanding the orders of the commander-in-chief. Specification two, obstructing the execution of military operations within a war zone."

I tried to say something but the Old Man moved in front of me as Vinegar Joe went on: "I don't care what his war record is or what he did following his irresponsible actions before my representative—which, I might add, are a personal affront to me!"

"General Stilwell," I broke in, "maybe I did go too far under pressure but enemy airplanes were already airborne and I had to make a decision. However, I cannot permit you to blame General Chennault for my actions—"

At which I felt Chennault's powerful grip on my elbow. I looked around and he had me fixed with his flashing eyes, mad as hell with me. For the first time since I had known him he really lost his temper.

"Get out of here, Colonel, now! I have something to say to General Stilwell in privacy."

Hot tears burned my eyes, tears of pure damned anger. It made not the slightest difference that I was out of that office. Through the closed door I heard Chennault's voice and will forever remember every word.

"Now listen to me, Stilwell. Take those trumped-up charges and you know exactly what you can do with them. I am the air commander out here whether you accept the fact or not. This is an active theater of combat and it's all air—there is no ground fighting in China. Colonel Scott works for me and was carrying out my orders; he did what I would have done had I been on the scene. Had he failed to make the decision he made, I would be the one considering charges of dereliction of duty. Furthermore, had he permitted your SOS colonel to delay his action, there might very well be no Lend Lease facilities there today, maybe not even an operational airfield at Yunnan-Yi. I have already recommended Scott for the Distinguished Service Cross for yesterday's combat. Now you withdraw those charges or I will radio my resignation to the President of the United States and make explicit my reasons!"

Chennault had surely stood up for the younger pilot he called his "good right arm," had taken my side when interservice politics reared its ugly head. That was the last I ever heard about the commandeering of those jeeps. The DSC was not awarded, but who cares about a medal? What the Old Man gave me, then and always, is worth a thousand of them. Nothing can ever make me forget his support, the role he played in my life. I can only believe some higher power guided me to meet him.

In the human herd Chennault was a maverick. Some of his individuality must have rubbed off on me because I have also been a nonconformist—a maverick general—in my career. But first I had to meet him, and that took some doing. I had to lie and cheat and surely steal. There's a saying, Never steal anything small. Well, what I stole to meet Claire Lee Chennault was a Boeing B-17E Flying Fortress. Right or wrong under the circumstances, I did it. It is a long story and I have to start at the beginning.

# 1

# THE ROAD

*If you don't care where you are going,*
*Then any road will take you there.*

Well, I cared. There is a photograph dated 1912 that shows me at
age four tugging at the hand of my mother, who is wearing a long
white dress and frilly hat. Small as I am, I am struggling to get closer
to the crumpled wreckage of the first airplane either one of us had
ever seen. Years later she explained the tragedy when we came
across that old snapshot. The famous pilot Eugene Ely, first to fly a
plane from the deck of a naval vessel, had crashed to his death. My
mother said she knew at that moment that I had chosen my profession.

Mama reminded me of it the first time I flew home in an Army
plane to take her into the sky with me. Oh, I knew the road where
my destiny lay very early in life—I would fly! And I was very
selective in choosing my career, because not just any airplane would
suit me. My wings had to be so sophisticated that only the United
States government could afford them.

Nonconformist from the first, I never saw flying as a hobby.
When my brother Boy Scouts constructed three-foot models with
rubber bands and hand-carved propellers, I went after the merit
badge in scouting with the real thing—a machine that would fly with
me in it. It looked something like the Wright brothers' plane at Kitty
Hawk but had no engine or skids; my feet were the landing gear. I
held on to the fuselage (as a boy of twelve, I had already learned

such terms from reading avidly about the Great War) and ran into the wind for flying speed, marveling as I felt the deadweight lessen until I almost flew.

Almost was not enough. One day the idea came that what I needed to launch my glider was altitude. I walked my craft up stone steps and across the wide lawn of a white-columned antebellum home near mine. When Mrs. Viola Napier came to the door, the craft was out of sight with two friends who had agreed to stabilize my wings as I launched myself from the sloping roof of that big house.

"Miss Viola," I asked as politely as I could, "may I fly my glider off the top of your house? I promise to be careful of the flowers."

She was about seventy-five, a widow, and had certainly noticed all the other boys with their toys powered by rubber bands. Then, too, she knew me as the little Scott kid from down the street on East Napier Avenue, and undoubtedly trusted me. She nodded her consent.

My eager assistants, Peter and Ralph Stubbs, helped to raise the glider to the rooftop by pulley and rope, all the way to my runway some sixty feet above the ground. I had my altitude! When all was ready—my friends at each wing tip, and me in my cockpit at the center of gravity—the three of us ran down the gently sloping copper roof into the wind. The brothers let go near the edge and I was flying, already breathlessly imagining myself soaring over an old magnolia tree to the horizon.

Suddenly there came a sharp crack; the wing buckled upward with the sound of doom. My lift had disappeared and I felt the sickening pull of gravity. I already knew the main spar had broken at a knot (I had never heard of aviation-quality spruce) and I crashed in as forlorn a pile of wreckage as had Ely.

Luckily my fall was broken by what I had promised to avoid— Miss Viola's flowers. My center of impact was the middle of a lush stand of thorny Cherokee rose, the Georgia state flower. I can still feel those thorns all these thousands of flying hours later. In the millions of air miles ahead of me it was to be my only crash. The

Lord was simply reminding me of the frailty of life, having already heard my boyish prayer: *"Please God, make me a fighter pilot, and if it be Thy will, when next my country must fight for freedom, make me an ace!"*

The first time I saw a fighter I could not take my eyes off it. Actually there were nine of them, designated PW-9s. I was a paperboy delivering the *Macon Telegraph* so early every morning that my mother had to wake me if I did not hear the alarm and stand by to make certain I did not doze off again. The day that large headlines read BILLY MITCHELL LEADS DAWN-TO-DUSK FLIGHT TO MACON, I jumped out of bed eagerly and had no trouble racing through my rounds.

It must have been in 1920, later in the same year that I flew my glider off Miss Viola's house, that General Mitchell led his flight from Canada to Miami, Florida, with a refueling stop in my hometown. Long before those throbbing engines could be heard, I was waiting for them at Herbert Smart Airport. Among these exalted pilots was the famous Great War ace Monk Hunter—full name Frank O'Driscoll Hunter—from Savannah. I kept a veritable dossier of such heroes in my head because the aces were my idols, my inspiration, from as far back as I could remember.

When the three V's of PW-9s came in and landed I was in heaven, thrilled to stand amid the bustle of pilots and mechanics as the aircraft were checked and refueled. They were the first military airplanes I had ever seen close enough to touch, and I caressed them each in turn as if they were alive, awed by their sleek beauty. When I came to Billy Mitchell's PW-9, my body raced to a thrill as if I had touched a national monument. Then, making my way through the laboring mechanics and ignoring their baleful glances, I did the same with Monk Hunter's.

The cockpit was empty but I saw Hunter plain as day. In my vivid imagination he was there with helmet and goggles and jet-black moustache, the handsomest of all the fighter aces, I thought. Little did I realize that fifteen years later I would be flying Boeing P-12s in formation with him in Panama when he was operations chief of the 19th Wing. We became friends although he was a major and I just a second lieutenant. That's when I learned that his glamorous moustache had been cultivated to hide a scar given him by the rear gunner of a German two-seater he had shot down. I somehow never had the opportunity to tell him how I had grown up on stories of the aces, how he had always been my particular idol because he came from Savannah, so close to Macon. Damn it, I almost felt related to him and never told him so!

While the PW-9 pilots attended a lavish luncheon at the Dempsey Hotel, I did all I could to help push heavy drums of aviation gasoline to those thirsty machines. When the mechanics snarled at me, I moved momentarily out of range before returning to drag a hose or get underfoot some other way. My eyes feasted on gleaming khaki fuselages and yellow wings. They were drab compared with the sleek electronic beauties of today—just linen-covered wooden frames with cracked paint on wrinkled skin—but beauty is in the eye of the beholder, and back then in 1920 they were the most wonderful things I had ever seen.

Walking among those fighter planes, I "lived" the air battles of the World War and reviewed my heroes. There was Billy Bishop, the little Canadian fighter pilot with cold blue eyes. He shot down scores of German aircraft, yet was peeved because the system used in 1917 did not credit observation balloons as victories, even though "balloon busting" was the most dangerous sport of all. So Air Marshal Bishop told me when he visited my command at Cal-Aero Academy in 1940. How I also admired Eddie Rickenbacker, our ace of aces, and Germany's Manfred von Richthofen, who had scored more victories than any other pilot. To a boy in love with aviation, nationality did not matter.

I had the overwhelming desire to smuggle myself aboard one of those nine fighters, slip through the triangular opening of unzipped inspection panels, but the opportunity never came. Billy Mitchell was raring to go when he returned and the very air around him seemed charged. The pilots shook hands and said good-bye to city officials, climbed in and donned leather helmets and goggles, then shouted the magic word *contact*! I leaned into the slipstream behind Hunter's plane, ignoring sticks and stones thrown by the prop blast, and said my own farewell.

Making Eagle Scout meant qualifying for twenty-one merit

badges but I was determined to win all seventy-two. Three—music, interpreting, and sculpture—baffled me but I got all the rest. Going for my sixty-ninth found me in a doctor's office one day in 1923, waiting to be questioned by the doctor on the subject of "safety first." I was browsing through magazines when something slipped to the floor. Retrieving it, I unfolded a long photographic panorama of the Great Wall of China and sat there utterly fascinated, drawn in some way to it. "I am part of your destiny," it seemed to say. "I have been waiting for you."

The magazine was the February 1923 *National Geographic Society Journal,* and its enclosed panorama would be forever etched in my mind. A mile or two of the Great Wall seemed to writhe over the mountains and dip into valleys beyond; I could imagine it stretching on and on, pursuing its desolate way across windswept plateaus and desert sands. The caption identified it as a section near Nankou Pass which had been there for more than two thousand years, part of the most stupendous structure ever raised by the hand of man.

A sentence I could not forget read, "Its myriad cloud-capped towers stand guard in solemn stillness where they were stationed twenty centuries before, waiting for their builders to return." In the photograph there was also a boy about my age leading three two-humped Bactrian camels. After memorizing almost every stone in the Wall, I at last turned to the article, "A Thousand Miles Along the Great Wall," and read it. I know I must have passed my questioning for the merit badge but I have long since forgotten; what I carried away from that office was the resolve that someday I would see the whole of that ancient structure with my own eyes. Surely the only way to accomplish that was by air. Already, at age fourteen, I had helped a pilot from the Great War rebuild an old military airplane with a Liberty engine, then had flown with him to acquire my first full hour of flying. My new fascination with the Great Wall now made flying even more of an obsession, as the two mixed in the most romantic of dreams.

There was only one sure way to absolutely guarantee a career flying military aircraft. That was to earn a commission in the regular Army or Navy, then be transferred to the proper flying school and earn those wings. This special road I had to find led through either West Point or Annapolis. There were many obstacles blocking my path because practically all I had ever applied myself to through high school was aviation, adventure, and scouting, none of which did much to lead me to institutions of higher learning. My summers had been spent in scout camps and as a sailor in the Merchant Marine, where I worked my way across some seas. It was no wonder that, upon graduation from high school, I was woefully lacking in everything vital for college.

I flunked out of two colleges. Then I did something few college failures do: returned to high school for the rudiments of learning I had missed. I had to have been learning a little even to have gone back for what I called my "postgraduate courses," and I think I was spurred on by the tears I saw in my dad's eyes. He was a Clemson graduate, class of 1905. It was a military school and he wanted me to attend it, but we compromised on the Citadel, the so-called "West Point of the South." It could not have heartened him when I showed up home again, having failed for a third time.

"Good God!" he said. "Rob, are you home again?"

"Yes, sir," I answered. "I have decided to attend the real West Point."

Roland, my younger brother, later told me that Dad discussed it with him the next morning, shaking his head in frustration and disappointment.

"How in the world can he succeed at West Point?" our father asked. "That must be the hardest of all."

How indeed? To enter West Point, I had to have a political appointment from a senator or a congressman. That possibility had been investigated, with negative results. The only other avenue was to be so brilliant a student that I might win a presidential appointment at large, but those were surely already cornered by hundreds of eager young men all over the United States who had applied themselves to their studies from the start.

My friend Fate provided one other unexpected opportunity. Almost by chance, I had become a member of the Georgia National

Guard at age sixteen, two years before I was of legal age. The Macon Volunteers needed a wireless operator for their summer camp at Tybee Island near Savannah, and called upon me because I was a ham radio operator.

"Mrs. Scott," I overheard Major Whittaker of the 22nd Infantry tell my mother, "Robert is a tall boy. Just tell him to let my recruiting sergeant think he is eighteen."

Despite my strict upbringing I had been led to tell a lie, and it later qualified me to take my first competitive examination for the United States Military Academy. I failed algebra miserably and felt as though my trusting parents had every reason to give up on me. There was one last hope: enlist in the regular Army after resigning from the National Guard, then somehow win acceptance into a special school I had heard about, the West Point Preparatory School, whose faculty was composed of recent Academy graduates. This time it was final for me; I had to make it and told my parents so. The next year I would be too old to be accepted as a cadet.

I could feel the tension in the air. Mama and Daddy were wondering how their son was going to compete with an entire army of applicants. They must have loved me, though, because I could not help noticing that the light of parental faith returned to their eyes. Dad drove me to Fort McPherson near Atlanta where I enlisted and was sworn in as a buck private in F Company, 22nd Infantry, serial number 6355544. The die was cast.

From the first day I must have changed. I did more than study—I crammed to atone for years of lackadaisical meanderings. There were months of just plain soldiering, from reveille to taps, from KP—kitchen police—to guard duty. Even picking up butts around the barracks when I did not smoke. Only when I had proven my worth was I eligible to request special duty with the West Point Preparatory School Detachment, Fourth Corps Area.

Without realizing it, I had formed the habit of study, one I had never known before, and when the high-pressure preparatory school classes began about the middle of September, I was ready. By Christmas there had been many eliminations but I was still there, and for the first time in my life I was on top.

When that all-important first Tuesday in March arrived with

the annual West Point entrance examination, I was ready and raring to show what I had learned. Then came the day—June 27, 1928—that I was relieved from walking Post Number One around the guardhouse and told to report to the colonel in command of the regiment. He was waiting for me.

"Son," he said, showing me a page from the first General Orders I had ever seen, "I have here your new assignment. The President of the United States is pleased to appoint you a cadet to the United States Military Academy."

Between being a buck private in the rear rank and becoming a West Point cadet, I had a thirty-day furlough which I spent at home, and it was more than a holiday. For the first time I could feel that my parents were truly proud of me. I had always known that they loved me, no matter my faults and failures, but now the light in their eyes repaid me a thousandfold for the long year of work and study. My dad introduced me to his friends as an equal, and I could hear my mother singing as she worked around the house. With the end of the furlough I set out on my new career.

I carried that panorama of the Great Wall of China with me through four years as I progressed from plebe to first classman. While I was still bound and determined to see it, my horizons broadened as my ambition grew to include following the trail of Marco Polo, the Venetian explorer. As a cadet I had been reading translations of works about his travels, and they inspired me to retrace the route he had followed from Venice to Cambaluc, today Peking (or Beijing). The two ambitions tied in, because part of his route followed the Great Wall.

All through second-class year I anticipated writing my engineering course military monograph the next year on the travels of Marco Polo. I would open the treatise with his departing Venice with his father, Niccolò, and his uncle Maffeo. To explain how he covered such a vast distance, I would call upon my new knowledge of logistics. This dream, nurtured for four years, never materialized, because my professor maintained that Marco Polo's travels were of no military interest. The Great Wall, moreover, had not served the military purpose for which it was constructed. I found myself assigned the Battle of Sandepu—one I had never heard of—as the subject of my paper. Disappointment grew as I searched through volumes of military history without finding it. By the time I located a very short paragraph on it in the *Encyclopedia Britannica,* I was mortified.

I learned that the Battle of Sandepu took place during the Russo-Japanese War of 1904–1905. Why could I not write about the first Battle of Manassas—Bull Run, as the northerners called it—which I had heard about all my life? Relatives of mine had fought there and the Glorious South had triumphed. As I considered my situation I resolved not to be deprived of writing about a thrilling battle. However much of a zero in world history my assigned subject represented, I would create an imaginary battle as important as Bull Run. Who would know the difference, if even the *Britannica* had so little information?

Temptation won out. I created a monumental battle in which the Japanese triumphed over a Russian general named Kuropatkin. These bare facts were the only truths in my version of the battle. I made up aerial observation by hot air balloon, and even used photographs of New York City street cleaners in the early 1900s who closely resembled Oriental soldiers. I typed my hallucination on heavy paper that looked yellow with age and bound it like a booklet, wrapping it in vivid red silk ribbon tied in a bow.

It was read through by every instructor in the department. I received a high grade and passed the course but I found my classmates laughing hilariously a few days later as they stood in front of the bulletin board. Standing on tiptoe, I saw that I had been "skinned," which at West Point meant: reported for infraction of discipline. The reason stated on the notice was *"submitting facetious monograph in military art, including imaginative and irrelevant matter in same, and casting demeaning reflections upon the Engineering Department."*

The straw that broke the camel's back was my implicit belittlement of the Engineering Department for assigning me such an insignificant battle. For this infraction I was ordered to report before a tribunal known as the Battalion Board, called the Batt Board in Kaydet slang. It was made up of the three battalion commanders, Army majors who had the power to bestow very real special punishments on erring cadets. Called "slugs," these punishments lasted anywhere from a month to a year, during which you were out of circulation as far as your personal life was concerned. It meant walking the area of the Old South Barracks quadrangle all Wednesday afternoon as soon as classes were out, and again on Saturday instead of going to football games. All with a rifle, at attention in full uniform, rain or shine, sleet or snow. A month was bad; a year made a scar on your soul.

In my spite at losing my ardently desired topic, I had let my imagination run wild and dared to change history. I knew as soon as I faced the Batt Board that I had cut my own throat. There were no smiles on the faces of the Army majors, although I had the feeling they had been laughing before I entered and would laugh again when I left. To my horror my sentence was one year of special punishment.

Now comes the funny part. Almost the day I was slugged, Queen Marie of Romania arrived at West Point for a long-anticipated royal visit. The red carpet was rolled out for Marie and her beautiful daughter, Princess Iliana. The order came for me to report to the commandant, who surprised me by telling me he wanted me to be the cadet escort for Her Highness, Princess Iliana. I was to pay special attention to filling out her "hop card," making certain she danced with the most interesting, handsome, and gentlemanly cadets. Why me? I will never know, especially as I considered myself anything but a "keen file," as ladies' men were called in those days.

The hop card hung on a yellow ribbon from a brass button at the left shoulder of my full-dress jacket. I filled it with the names of the most scintillating lights in the corps of cadets—the football captain, the all-American tackle, the handsome end, the baseball home run king, the Phi Beta Kappa—but by tradition, the last dance of the evening was mine. I was far from a whiz on the dance floor but my classmates said I had the gift of gab, Georgia style, and my usual technique was to keep talking so that my dance partner would not have a chance to realize I had two left feet.

I could honestly tell the commandant that the princess was having a good time. She was constantly in motion on the highly polished floor of Cullum Hall as she danced with her partners and other cadets who waited to cut in, smiling with pleasure to her mother the whole evening. The last dance was always "Army Blue," that soulful waltz whose strains were my cue to lead her across the dance floor.

"Your Royal Highness"—I made my pitch the last evening—"tomorrow, when your mother, Her Majesty Queen Marie, makes her farewell, she will be asked by the superintendent of West Point if she has a royal request. It is most important that she reply yes, that she desires all special punishment be removed."

I could see that the princess understood by the smile on her face. The official good-byes next morning went smooth as silk and the queen exercised her royal prerogative just as I had hoped. Instead of the year, I had served barely a week of my slug when it was revoked. Already in my mind was the thought that Bucharest, the capital of Romania, lay very close to the path Marco Polo trod in 1271 on his way to Cambaluc. As I was now determined to follow in his footsteps very soon, I might even be able to thank Princess Iliana and her mother in person for having rescued me.

# 2

# ON THE
# TRAIL OF
# MARCO POLO

There is an archaic regulation at West Point that says a cadet shall not own a horse, a dog, or a moustache. Had the Powers That Be even suspected that I had a motorcycle that spring of 1932, it, too, would undoubtedly have been outlawed by the book of regulations. I had rented it from a shop in Highland Farms, a red Indian Scout that I practically lived on it during the weekends from the time ice left the Hudson River.

Four years of schooling in tactics and logistics had impressed upon me that no individual, much less an army, can do anything near perfect the first try. Success demands practice, doing things over and over again—what the military calls "dry runs." Thus, as the day drew closer for me to follow in the footsteps of the Venetian, I prepared by becoming completely at home on the vehicle I had chosen for my journey. The Indian was for training; I would buy another motorcycle for the trip when I got to France.

Weekends became training maneuvers conducted in total secrecy—a uniformed cadet could hardly ride a motorcycle openly on the Plain of West Point—to prepare myself for thousands of miles along Marco Polo's route. I soon realized that New York State town roads bore little resemblance to the rough terrain I would probably encounter in Europe and Asia Minor, but in the beautiful wooded hills sloping down past Callum Hall to the Hudson River, I found mountain trails running well past Cranberry Pond that seemed ideal for my purposes. These were bridle paths used occasionally by tactical officers on duty at the Academy—many from the cavalry—or by cadets with special riding privileges.

One Sunday, I was carrying out my training in a reverie, my imagination running wild as I gunned my machine into a tight turn, dipping low to compensate for centrifugal force. Suddenly over the din of the exhaust there came the frantic scream of a frightened horse. I hurriedly braked and watched the terrified animal plunge down the side of the mountain, then across the stream and into the trees on the other side. It was obviously a U.S. Cavalry mount. Between calling soothing words to his animal, the uniformed rider shouted for me to cut my engine. I almost fell off the motorcycle when I realized it was Colonel Robert C. Richardson, the commandant of cadets.

Fumbling to still my raving engine, I leaped from the machine, praying out loud that the "Com" could regain control before both he and his horse were killed. All my plans for a commission as a second lieutenant seemed to hang in the balance, but I dismissed these selfish thoughts and raced down the mountain, determined to reach the Com in time to be of some aid.

Colonel Richardson had everything safely under control long before I caught up with him, drenched to the waist after splashing through the creek. He sat in the saddle, speaking soothingly to the panting animal and rubbing its quivering neck. I stood there at attention, feeling more in a state of shock than the horse. At least, the thought came to me, the Com had not hit me with his riding crop. Finally, having attended to what every cavalryman considers his first duty, he turned his attention to me.

"Don't you know, Mr. Scott," he said calmly, "that the bridle paths are off limits to you, much less motorcycles?"

Only then did he dismount and slowly lead the quieted horse back across the stream and uphill to the path where my motorcycle lay. I tried to explain my fascination with the journeys of Marco Polo, my training for an attempt to retrace his route on motorcycle.

I even discussed with him the enigma that so puzzled me. In all his journeys Marco Polo had never mentioned the Great Wall of China.

The Com listened intently as we walked our mounts down the bridle path. He asked about logistics. Could I make such a journey? Had I considered every angle? I kept waiting for him to revert to being the commandant, to quote some regulation prohibiting my summer plans, but such an announcement never came. When we reached the crossroads near the Cadet Chapel, he remounted to return to the stables. Before he turned away he told me to come see him at some convenient time the following week, saying that he had served as military attaché in Rome before his present duty assignment. Perhaps he might be able to tell me something to help me on my monumental journey.

"Good luck, Mr. Scott," he concluded. "You represent something of an enigma yourself."

Until the Norddeutscher Lloyd liner *Europa* anchored outside Cherbourg harbor, I could not believe I was truly on my way. From the firm of J. Bigard on the Rue de la Paix in Cherbourg, I bought a sparkling new Soyer *motocyclotto* for which I would be in debt to the Bank of Highland Falls, New York, for many years, very proud that my signature as a newly commissioned Army second lieutenant had been all the collateral required. I was well aware that there was little left to cover even Spartan living expenses, and I worried about my written agreement with M. Bigard. If I successfully piloted one single-cylinder Soyer motorcycle across France, over the Alps to Venice, all across Europe into Asia, then to the far end of Turkey where it met Persia and the Soviet Union, then returned all the way to France, *and* if said motorcycle was still serviceable, he would buy it back at half price and I would have enough francs to pay my passage home.

If some catastrophe befell me or the machine during the roughly 24,000-kilometer—15,000-mile—trip, or if he refused to repurchase it after the journey, then I would have to work my way home on a slow freighter. Ordinarily that would be no problem, as I was a rated AB, or able-bodied seaman. This time it would mean that I would be late reporting for flight training at Randolph Field, Texas, so I laboriously translated the complicated agreement into English, with many references to my French dictionary, as M. Bigard watched.

Early afternoon, June 14, 1932, I gave my motorcycle full throttle and was on my way over the Grande Route Nationale toward my long-awaited rendezvous with Marco Polo. The real thing at last, although the Soyer felt the same as the Indian Scout I had straddled during my training. I shrugged my shoulders into my leather jacket, relishing the rush of wind past my lowered goggles. If only the Com could see me now.

Equipment hung everywhere, from a camera over my shoulder to the suitcase on the baggage rack atop the rear mudguard. Below that was a small metal frame holding a gallon can of gasoline on each side of the wheel. On the front mudguard was my international license plate, K-4885, and on either side were two small flags: One was always the Stars and Stripes; the other, the flag of the country through which I was passing. The goggles were the most important item because even a fly could damage an eye at one hundred kilometers per hour, and Lord knows I needed mine for my rendezvous with destiny as a fighter pilot!

I sped out of Normandy those five decades ago, pausing in Paris for a short night and a tank of *essence*. Dawn saw me clearing the Champs Élysées, past the famous junction that was known as l'Étoile, with the Arc de Triomphe, before heading for the Simplon Pass across the Alps into Italy. Then on by Lago Maggiore, Milano, Brescia, and Verona to Mestre, where I left my motorcycle and took a boat to my hotel in Venice. All that night along the Grand Canal I dreamed of Marco Polo; on just such a night in 1271 he had set out for Peking. My departure date along part of the same route was June 27, 1932.

For years I had studied the differing translations of Marco Polo's *Travels*. The consensus was that Marco, his father, Niccolò, and his uncle Maffeo had begun their journey to Cathay by sailing from Venice to Acre in Asia Minor, then traveled northeast through Turkey to Mount Ararat. I had already been that route when I was a sailor in the Merchant Marine, so I was taking the liberty of following a land route the Polos might well have used on one of their later journeys. It would not be easy with the roads as they were then and the difficulties of crossing international boundaries. Bad as the dirt roads turned out to be, it was worse haggling with the red tape of all the customs controllers; at every border I had to prove I owned the motorcycle, write down its horsepower and cubic-centimeter displacement, and certify that I did not intend selling it in that country.

The Dalmatian coast of Yugoslavia was beautiful, especially Ragusa (the ancient name of modern Dubrovnik), the "pearl of the Adriatic," but under my wheels the dust of centuries had hardened into deep ruts that jarred me. Pulverized by heavy wagon wheels, it billowed up and blotted out the scenery as I raced through. Flies lurked in swarms over horse and cattle droppings, sometimes breaking the skin of exposed parts of my face as I drove into them at high speed.

By far the worst recollection I have—one that sets Yugoslavia apart from the rest of the world for me—is of the twenty-eight punctures I had in one day. Every one was from handmade horseshoe nails lurking in the powdery ruts. By the time I had repaired a dozen flats, I did not even bother to take the wheel off the tire; I merely pulled the part of the tube with the hole in it past the rim, cleaned the cut with gasoline, and applied my dry patch. I guess I became an expert after twenty but I cried when I had number twenty-eight. By the time I roared into Belgrade I was praying there would be fewer horses farther east.

To keep my sanity I began setting goals. Each day I would try to break the record of the mileage I had set the day before. Often I would continue to drive after dark to attain my quota of miles before finding lodging, and some nights I never found a place to stay. By the time I reached the Pindus Mountains the roads were so steep and rough I often had to push the motorcycle along. At least the punctures became fewer and after two days without a flat I no longer felt a prisoner of dust and horseshoe nails. Maybe the people here did not use nails as had the Croats, the Slovaks, and the Slovenes; whatever the reason, I breathed a prayer of thanks as I came into Salonika and found the route north through Bulgaria to Sofia.

Northeast on a good highway across the Danube was Bucharest, where I had an invitation to visit Her Royal Highness, Princess Iliana of Romania, but I saw from the map that Bucharest was north of any route Marco Polo would have taken in 1271. I decided to save my visit to the court of Queen Marie for the return trip, and set course due east for the great city I always think of as Constantinople, no matter that my maps said Stamboul or Istanbul.

I crossed the Hellespont into Scutari and realized I had reached Asia on my motorcycle. There I wrote two postcards, one to my parents and the other to Colonel Richardson, the commandant of cadets whose horse I had almost scared to death on the bridle path above West Point. I spent just the single night in Constantinople, as I knew I would be back that way. Right then I set out for Ankara. Of course, all the signs were in Turkish, and it was harder to tell where I was or where I was headed than it had been in Greece or Bulgaria. Before I knew it I had taken the wrong turn and arrived in Eskişehir. My error in navigation should have been evident long before, but the road was so good that I kept hoping until I knew without a doubt that the sun was in the wrong place. After that I navigated by the sun and stars, forgetting the impossible road signs. If I went many miles out of my way, I consoled myself with the knowledge that I was seeing interesting parts of the country, just as Marco Polo had centuries ago.

One very dark night I saw a sign saying ADANA in the beam of my headlight; recalling that Marco Polo had definitely passed there, I revved my motor and took that fork in the road. For a few miles I even tried to sing a happy song but the small road led nowhere, just seemed to ramble. My headlight began to fail.

Then I collided head-on with a flock of sheep, the worst accident of the entire journey. It happened when I began a turn and the headlight flickered off at the crucial moment. I did not see the sheep until I was among them at forty miles per hour and there were bleating, leaping woolly bodies all around me. I could not even fall with my machine until the flock moved off in panic, when I tumbled to the ground and had more of them run over me.

Over the bells on the rams I heard a human voice, high-pitched and sinister in Turkish. It belonged to a shepherd, who quickly realized I was not a predator and coaxed the sheep away so that I could stand. Fortunately, none of his animals appeared hurt by our encounter.

Studying my map by the erratic lamp, I gave up my plan to visit Adana and carefully returned to the fork where I had gone wrong. This time I took the route to Erzurum, indicated as many miles ahead by the map, and followed it to the first town. Daylight had arrived before I reached Sivas, where I located a mechanic by his sign of crossed tools. I slept all day and most of the night while he rewound the magneto. From then on, for thousands of miles, the headlamp never flickered again.

I reached Erzurum two days later, dead center on the trail of Marco Polo and closing in on Mount Ararat. The region turned out to be a military zone extending north and east to the Soviet border, and signs were now in Russian as well as Turkish. The mountain rose more than 16,000 feet and was snow-covered. At its base, I was at the end of Turkey and as far east as I was going to be able to follow Marco Polo that year—or for a good many years to come, as it turned out.

I had covered a thousand miles of Asia since crossing the Hellespont—all the way across Turkey over practically no roads at all. Moreover, I had made good nearly a third of the 7,700-mile trail of the Venetian. It had been forty-three days since I had thundered out of Cherbourg and my graduation leave would be close to finished by the time I could return. To the northeast lay Georgia—the Russian one—and to the southeast, Persia, the way I had to keep going someday. With one longing look I turned and started my return trip.

A visit to the capital of Romania made for an extra three hundred miles on the motorcycle and was the most interesting part of the trip. Though I failed to see the princess, the invitation she had written in Romanian on the back of the hop card proved to be most valid—I was treated like a visiting potentate for the hour I remained at the palace. As I look at the photograph of me astride that motorcycle in the summer of 1932, I know I surely looked too arrogant and unpresentable to have been received by royalty; it was probably for the best that the queen and her daughter were away at the summer palace on the Black Sea. Iliana had told me she hoped I would bring the hop card back to her as a souvenir when I visited, so I left it at the palace and set out again.

From Bucharest to Budapest the route was long and hard and high. I crossed the Transylvanian Alps, so wild in places I caught myself searching for the castle of Dracula. There were over seven hundred miles of twisting switchbacks among the mountains, though the scenery was worth the detour. The rest of my journey passed without incident—only a few flat tires along the Danube to Germany—but nothing could have fazed me after Yugoslavia and Turkey. Fifty-nine days after purchasing my shiny new motorcycle from M. Bigard, I surrendered it to him caked with dust, dented from sheep, its paint sandblasted away—definitely travel-worn but still running. Without a murmur he lived up to his agreement and bought it back for half what I had paid, and I sighed with relief because I now had enough money to buy a ticket on the *Bremen*. I could hardly keep a straight face as he gave me the money; inexperienced in the world of commerce as I might be, surely I had taken advantage of this Frenchman.

After purchasing my ticket I returned to the motorcycle shop to pick up my baggage, and perhaps for a fond last look at my trusty Soyer. When I reached the showroom on the Rue de la Paix, such a crowd of people had gathered that I wondered if there had been an accident or fire. Making my way through the mob, I discovered a motorcycle causing the commotion. It took me a long time to recognize it; I never would have except for the familiar international license number K-4885 on the mudguard. What a metamorphosis! Cleaned, divested of accumulated road film, tar, grease, dust, and bugs mashed into it at a hundred Ks per hour; washed and polished to perfection and sporting new tires, it glistened under a large placard. I translated it with the help of my dictionary:

This thoroughly tested, well broken-in motorcycle presented for special sale, recently piloted across Europe and Asia by an audacious American!

But the asking price was more than I had paid for it new! Now I understood why M. Bigard had smiled as he gave me just enough francs for my passage to the United States. No longer could I go home thinking I had shown Yankee business acumen at its best. From that day I never was going to think I had outmaneuvered a Frenchman.

The *Bremen* had me in New York in four days. After a visit to Georgia, I set out for Randolph Field on the road that truly was mine.

# 3

# FIND THE GIRL

San Antonio, Texas, had a reputation as the mother-in-law of the
Air Corps—such was the number of fliers who had met their wives
there. When I reported to Randolph Field for flight training I learned
why, for there were pretty girls everywhere. They spoke our language too. Born and bred near old Fort Sam Houston, they were
used to military traditions and military men.

The Air Corps was heavily represented around San Antonio,
with our "West Point of the Air" to the east and Kelly Field
to the west. No sooner were hundreds of propellers stilled on a
Friday afternoon than both fields experienced an exodus of officers,
noncoms, and flying cadets bound for the bright lights of San
Antone.

The first two weeks of flight training found me leaving the "Taj
Mahal," as we called the distinctive tower of the headquarters
building at Randolph, to drive into town with my classmates. The
parties were great and I temporarily shed my shyness to regale my
dates with stories of my motorcycle journey across Europe into Asia.
I was flattered by their interest and captivated by their graciousness
and charm, but no matter how I tried to content myself with those
pretty girls, as I drove home to my room in the Randolph Field
BOQ (bachelor officers' quarters) I would always catch myself think-

ing of a different woman. Her name was Kitty Rix and she was far away in Georgia.

I met Catharine Rix Green when I was a West Point cadet during the only summer leave permitted throughout my four years at the U.S. Military Academy. Although I remembered her as poised and sophisticated, she was in fact a high school girl several years younger than I. We did not meet again until my return from Europe on the *Bremen* after my long summer's journey on the trail of Marco Polo. By then she was a student at Shorter College in Rome, Georgia. Knowing that she lived in Fort Valley, just a few miles from my parents in Macon, hurried me home.

Kitty Rix, as her friends called her, was surrounded by young men and did not seem to recognize me. We soldiers had no fraternities at West Point but I recognized a frat pin when I saw one and knew what it implied; each time I saw her after one of her three beaux had visited, she had on a different pin. I was finally able to get a few dates with her, after which I consoled myself with the thought that it was a good thing duty called me to Texas; there, I figured, I would forget.

By the third week of flight training at Randolph Field, it appeared that I had scored a triumph in Bexar County society; my roommate pointed out a piece in the *San Antonio Light* that had me escorting one of the debutantes of 1932 to the biggest social event of the season, the Festival of San Jacinto. The congratulations of my classmates pleased me, but in my elation my subconscious kept nagging, reminding me of that little Georgia girl who kept emerging in what poets call the caverns of the mind. Kitty Rix—my vision of her—kept fading in no matter what Texas beauty I found myself talking to. What made it all the more mysterious was that I had never written to her nor she to me; I had seen her only briefly two years ago, and could scarcely claim that I knew her now—all that I knew was that she seemed already spoken for.

Whatever the reason, I had the unmitigated gall to telephone Joanna, queen of the San Jacinto Ball, and break our date. I knew that she did not believe my excuse of a family emergency forcing my return to Georgia, but I did not let it slow me down as I packed my car that third weekend in Texas. Kitty Rix was a good *fifteen hundred miles* away; my trip across half a continent would have to be nonstop.

I had graduated from motorcycles to a sporty red Chevrolet convertible modified with a fifty-five-gallon drum in the rumble seat. Along with the car's regular twelve-gallon capacity, this fuel load let me cruise from the middle of Texas across Louisiana, Mississippi, Alabama, and perhaps all the way to Georgia. Gasoline was cheap in those days, and to military personnel at the base commissary it was cheaper still. I paid only 5 cents per gallon to top off before turning right, past the sentry at the main gate, headed for U.S. 90, the old Spanish Trail.

There was not much time available to negotiate three thousand miles of vintage 1932 highways; from late Friday afternoon to early Monday morning it was all driving except for a few precious minutes with Kitty Rix. My cruising speed was sixty-five miles per hour because I had to average a mile a minute no matter what. There was no room for tunnel vision, daydreaming, or relaxation, for if I were stopped—even by a friendly sheriff with no ticket to give—I was through. My schedule was honed so fine an angel had to be riding on each of my shoulders if I were to make it.

Before my year of flight training came to an end I made some twenty such dashes in our strange courtship—perhaps my lucky number of twenty-three. I will never forget Miss Mell, dean of women at Shorter College. She had to sit with me while some of the students were searching for Kitty Rix. I must have looked like a visitor from another planet in a rumpled khaki flying suit with U.S. ARMY AIR CORPS emblazoned all over, long bronze zippers from top to bottom, helmet and goggles in my lap. It was even worse in the winter of 1932, when my gear changed to dark-leather winter flying suits with sheepskin collars raised high, making my slender six-foot frame look as bulky as that of a football tackle.

Then I would catch the rapid staccato of her steps and she would sweep into the reception room, all one hundred pounds of her. Beguiling smile, hazel-green eyes laughing at me, honey-blond hair in wavelets swinging from side to side, and a soft voice chiding me with pleasure.

"Scotty, you just don't know the problems you create. Here I thought you were safely across the Brazos River deep in the heart of

Texas, and you turn up like a bad penny to upset my plans. What, oh what, am I going to do with you?"

By that time I was leading her off somewhere to safety for me, beyond the accusing stares of the dean of women. I still had not recovered from that view I'd had of her as she swept through the door, those high heels clicking. To this day I can see her as she was then, and I always will. If the girl of your dreams is rated a ten, then I swear my Kitty Rix was a double ten.

Heading west that weekend I crossed the Mississippi and set as my next goal the Red River, which meant Texas. Suddenly I heard a nerve-racking sound, like a train with a full head of steam blowing a shrill whistle. I looked behind me for a truck but found I was alone on the highway. When I raised my foot the sound abated and I realized I had burned a bearing. My throat constricted at the thought of being found absent without official leave—you are not AWOL until you are caught—and my heart further sank because this was the one and only time I had made the mistake of requesting permission (it had been denied with a resounding "Hell, no!"). Either being AWOL or disobeying a direct order was enough to put an end to the flying career I had planned all my life, so I numbly searched my map as if knowing where I was would make any difference.

The nearest town was Patterson, Louisiana, near Morgan City and the ferry. Then I noticed a dim light off to my left; out there in the boondocks of the bayous any light was friendly, so I turned slowly off the highway and followed it like a beacon. Was it once again that guardian angel of mine arranging destiny? Whatever it was, I arrived at a large wooden hangar with airplanes parked all over and men working late into the evening. At the sound of my troubled car they came my way, one of them guiding me to a parking place and giving me the across-the-throat signal that means "cut your engine."

He was a French mechanic, with only one arm, a veteran of the Great War who worked there for Jimmy Wedell, one of the famous racing pilots of the time. I did not even have to explain the problem before three or four mechanics were underneath the car working on the engine. My being dressed in an Army Air Corps flight suit most likely did the trick. They dropped the oil pan and called me to take a look. The crankshaft was still smoking-hot and bearings one and six—the two at either end that get less lubrication—were bad. The mechanics slipped in thin pieces of bronze, called "shims," as a temporary repair that would get me to Texas.

I thanked them and was on my way, but the hours had passed and I knew I was out of luck. I was still going to be late for flying on Monday morning—this morning. By the time I reached my room in the BOQ, I was ready to prepare for a court-martial. My roommate, Bob Terrill, was studying—he had brains and enough sense to abide by regulations. I nodded but he said nothing as I made my way to the bathroom to clean up. As I was splashing cold water on my face he came in and stood behind me shaking his head.

"You lucky bastard," he said vehemently. "The best part of a whole day late and the commandant doesn't even know you were gone. Know what happened? For the first time in the history of Randolph Field it was too cold to fly, and that Great Boss in the Sky you talk about didn't stop there—he made it so cold the damned pipes froze and they couldn't even have ground school. Hell, Scotty, you and that girl of yours lead charmed lives!"

Those treks, which used up thousands of gallons of gasoline and many tires, also wore out my Chevy, so before the end of the summer I had traded for a streamlined and more powerful Graham-Paige. By the end of the year the aggregate mileage on the two odometers was great enough for me to have circled the earth three and a half times. In a larger sense those tests of my youthful endurance were also part of my training as a fighter pilot. To ward off fatigue—especially when returning to base wondering if those stolen minutes had accomplished anything—I would always take a different route. It was a habit that became my *modus operandi* for aerial combat: I never left a target the same way I had approached it. Do so and the enemy would most likely be waiting with guns trained.

The chief of the Air Corps came all the way from Washington to present our silver wings on graduation day. Rumor had it that the Pursuit Section—mine—was scheduled for overseas assignment in Hawaii or the Philippines. I would have gone anywhere to be a pursuit pilot any other time, and with those shiny silver wings the world never seemed so good. Exotic climes and adventure would have to wait, though, because I knew that if I left I would lose Kitty Rix. It was now October 1933 and she was to graduate from Shorter College the following June; whatever the Army Air Corps had in mind for me, I had to be there.

All during lunch I had my eyes on the general where he sat with other generals and colonels at the head table. Then all at once he was alone, drinking a cup of coffee and reading a newspaper he had taken from his briefcase. I presented myself in the proper military manner.

"Sir, may I ask a question?"

"Certainly, young man," he said. "Sit down and fire away."

I told him the whole story, reinforcing my willingness to comply with whatever the final decision might be. As no order had yet been issued, and as she had almost consented to marry me and was almost convinced that the Army Air Corps was the best life, sir, could I be assigned some other duty temporarily, just until she graduated next June?

He heard me without interruption but I could not help noticing that he seemed more concerned with the taste of his coffee than with my situation. He did take my name and serial number, both of which he wrote down in a small notebook.

"I cannot make any promises," he said, rising from the table, "but I will look into the matter when I return to Washington."

Three days later, telegraphed orders arrived directing me to Mitchel Field, Long Island, New York.

# 4

# AN ARMY PILOT

Of all the mechanical marvels that became mine during my life as a soldier, none stands out as much as my first aircraft. No matter that the Curtiss O-1G Falcon was a two-seat observation plane rather than a fighter; my name was still stenciled on the taut fabric around the invitingly open cockpit. Even with a liquid-cooled Curtiss D-12 engine, the O-1 cruised at only 145 miles per hour. That power plant was virtually a part of the weapon system, it was so loud—its throaty roar could be heard a good ten miles on takeoff or in a power dive.

The trust placed in me by the United States government I accepted as a sacred responsibility, and I fully intended flying that plane until I was so proficient in all its capabilities that I could go up against any emergency. If the greatest golfer in the world practiced ten hours a day, even if his hands became blistered, then I would do the same to be the best pilot, even if it meant flying twenty hours a day. That was my challenge.

I took off from Mitchel Field early my first morning before the paint was even dry on my name, determined to get to know Long Island better than any native who had lived there all his life. There was Hempstead in front of me as I climbed and Garden City off to the north on my right. By then I was turning southeastward toward the Jones Beach lighthouse, and in a flash I was admiring the blue waves of the Atlantic beneath me. Bearing due east I flew toward Montauk Point, the far tip of the island pointing straight at Europe. Beautiful landmarks came over the horizon as I looked down on white sand beaches at Fire Island, Shinnecock Bay, Southampton, and Easthampton. With Montauk Point beneath me I swung back left to Sag Harbor and Riverhead in the notched eastern tip of Long Island, turning east again to Orient Point. It was the "best seat in the house" and I enjoyed it thoroughly until, sated, I set course for lower Manhattan, whose huddled skyscrapers looked unreal in the distance. I returned over the north shore, swinging south from Queens and Brooklyn over Floyd Bennett Airfield for a final dive home into Mitchel Field.

It was no mere orientation flight; that "dawn patrol" and all my flights those first days were simulated combat exercises. I had just landed from number sixteen when the operations officer jumped on my wing and, with his mouth right in my ear, shouted that the commanding officer wanted to see me right away. To my chagrin the squadron CO was a cavalry officer from the Great War, when they had used real horses. Now, with the cavalry being replaced by motorized units, many of the middle-aged officers had been transferred to the Air Corps. They had earned their wings in a quick training course, much of the incentive for which was extra pay for the hazards of flying. The CO was no professional military flier.

"Scott," he began, "the Air Corps is a new branch of the service, relatively young, with no seniority. That is why some of us more mature and experienced people have been brought in to stabilize things. This is the Depression. As squadron commander I must justify every cent expended for gasoline and flying maintenance, and that runs into problems when I receive a report such as this."

He shook a paper at me. His voice rose when he spoke again.

"How many hours have you flown that ship, number sixty-six, since you arrived on this station? How many? Let's see, you've been here one week—one entire week—and all you have done is fly, fly, fly." He stared at me. "How many?"

With great pride, I told him thirty-two and a few minutes. His face turned red. I thought he was going to hit me with his swagger stick but he just waited until he regained control.

"It says here, and you are supposed to have read and signed, that all pilots are directed to curtail their flying to a maximum of four hours per month. This measure is vital in order to conserve fuel and time on aircraft. People like you place themselves above authority and wantonly wear these planes out, boring holes in the sky. You, Lieutenant Scott, have needlessly expended all your allotted flight time for the entire fiscal year. So as of now you are *not to fly at all for the next eight months!*"

He laid down the report and ignored me until I did an about-face and walked out. I soon found out I had additional duties to keep me busy while grounded. Already the squadron supply officer, I now became assistant adjutant and—far worse—officer in charge of the bachelor officers' quarters. My spirits were at lowest ebb when the bugle blowing taps finally relieved me of checking over sheets, pillowcases, and blankets, and counting keys at the BOQ.

The very next morning after my grounding the sun rose with a new lease on life for me. There on the squadron bulletin board was a notice beginning ATTENTION! ALL PILOTS! READ AND INITIAL! Four volunteers were wanted for detail to the Casey Jones School of Instrument Flying at Newark Airport. The space for names was blank, so I signed on the first line, then looked around to see if there was any other interest in the offer. Apparently my squadron mates shared the then popular opinion that instrument flying was a passing fad not necessary to a military pilot in the normal course of affairs.

When the commander sent for me later that afternoon, I was ready to promise anything—manage all my squadron duties at night—provided I could fly at the "blind flying" school during the day. My enthusiasm was soon tempered by his statement that there would be no actual flying in the class; it was something new, instruction in mock-up airplanes known as "flight simulators." I was still grounded, but as I was the only one to volunteer, I could have the temporary duty assignment and drive there every day. Damn! Commute daily all the way across New York, three hours of ground traffic—I could have made it in fifteen minutes in my beloved Falcon.

Casey Jones was a famous Curtiss demonstration and race pilot. I was a prisoner of his claustrophobic little Link Trainer at

Newark Airport for three weeks. That funny short-coupled machine tilted and gyrated on a metal pedestal bolted to the concrete floor until I almost became convinced during a hundred hours that I was actually flying. In the end I had another diploma and new skills—whose value I did not yet fully appreciate—that would put me back in the air. My qualifications amounted to a good start in this completely new profession of instrument flying which would revolutionize aviation and make "seat-of-the-pants" aviation a thing of the past.

I returned to my squadron to note some changes. There were special guests around who looked like "eggheads," as we called scientists and professors. A few questions revealed that they were meteorological experts detailed by the U.S. Department of Commerce to fly with us in inclement weather to gather data. Although I knew other pilots had been through the Casey Jones School before me, I seemed to be the only instrument pilot around, so more flying fell in my lap. The base commander overrode my squadron CO's grounding and I flew more in the next week than I had even in my first week at Mitchel. I caught myself hoping that one of those scientists, whom I frequently flew to Washington, D.C., would want to be flown on the gauges all the way to Georgia in my trusty number sixty-six.

When this windfall flying waned I grew apprehensive that I might be grounded again, but another directive from headquarters in the War Department saved me. This time I was to fly with a special instrument called a barometrograph strapped to the right-hand N-strut of an O-39, the very latest Curtiss Falcon, which, with its 600-horsepower Conqueror engine, was faster and more powerful than my trusty O-1G. I was to fly at precisely the same hour each night at a constant rate of climb, meticulously leveling off at each 300 feet of altitude so that a stylus could mark graph paper on a rotating drum contained in the barometrograph. This procedure was to be followed from ground level to the top of the overcast, up to 18,000 feet. "This mission will be carried out daily," the orders concluded, "regardless of the weather conditions."

Rain, sleet, and snow were bad enough, but gloom of night too. I was once again the only volunteer but I did not hesitate for an instant, as I was still grounded and in the doghouse with my commander; I would have volunteered if the instructions had included doing it all upside down! The 2:00 A.M. takeoff time was perfectly all right with me too. It was necessary because the sun heated the earth during the day, producing vertical air currents, called thermals, that made it impossible for the barometrograph to function accurately.

One night at the Officers Club, when a number of my fellow pilots kept trying to buy me drinks, I realized that I was the butt of a joke for flying so much. Only years later did I learn that their derision—which made me see red for a moment although I did not let it show—masked a similar love of flying. Perhaps they lacked certain skills or confidence, or perhaps their wives took a dim view of their getting up in the middle of the night to fly; whatever the reasons, they hid their envy behind a wall of ridicule. Later in my career, I was often to run into deskbound pilots with a similar attitude.

Because I flew more that month than ever before, it was lucky I was still a bachelor with no wife to be jealous of the "other woman," as pilots in the service sometimes called their airplanes. I next saw Kitty Rix over Christmas 1933, when I drove down to Georgia to see her and my family, and filled her in on all my latest adventures including being instrument-rated and perfectly at home flying "blind." She loved the diploma I proudly showed her which pictured a disreputable-looking duck flying backward wearing sunglasses. She thought that was wonderful and hung on every word I said. When we ran into her special trio of suitors, I noticed with a thrill that every now and then she would leave whichever one she was talking to and run over to me, asking me to tell them all about my squadron commander calling me a "time hog." She would ask that I explain the black box I had to fly every day at 2:00 A.M. By the time I had to return to New York, I felt my case was far from lost!

If I ever wondered if somebody up there was not watching out for me, not "watching every sparrow fall," I had but to review the manner in which fate provided me with the training I needed in my career. Each time it seemed that I had hit an impasse, that other door opened. Now it was to be proved again.

No sooner had the weather-sounding program run its course—leaving me back in the doldrums, living with the fear that I might be grounded again—than That Great Flying Boss looked down and remembered me. I emerged from a movie to hear the gravel voice of a newsdealer at his kiosk chanting over and over, "Army to fly the mails!" Halted in mid-stride, I bought a paper and carried it back under the lights to confirm the startling news. Then I ran off to tell the other pilots.

The date was February 13, 1934—Friday the thirteenth. The Postmaster General, so the press reported, had been advised of gross irregularities in the fulfillment of U.S. government airmail contracts by the commercial airlines. We Air Corps pilots said jokingly that the airplanes must have been sending themselves tons of papers with stamps on them and charging the government by the ton-mile. Whatever the scandal, the President asked our chief, Bennie Foulois, if there was any reason why the Air Corps could not deliver the damn letters. Naturally, being a good soldier, Foulois said: "When do you want us to start?"

The next day resembled mobilization for a military emergency. That meant going with what we had—no preliminaries, no special equipment, no practice flights or training, no modern aircraft resembling airliners. Unmarried volunteers were requested so that bachelors would go before married men. It was a little like a war, I thought. In a way it resembled aerial combat, only our battles would be waged against the elements; nature was the enemy that winter, and she was in a bad mood.

For me personally, it was my salvation and completed my training as a fighter pilot. My instrument rating proved its value and my route could not have been better for me, as it turned out. It stretched from Newark, New Jersey, across the Alleghenies some 370 miles to Cleveland, Ohio, over comparatively low but dangerous mountains we called the Hell Stretch. From there I flew on three hundred miles across the south shores of the Great Lakes to Chicago. I flew day and night—up to a hundred hours a month—and was heartily congratulated for my desire, enthusiasm, and durability. If I was a time hog, as I had been called when grounded for flying more than four hours a month, then this was hog heaven.

The winter of 1934 turned out to be the worst since the turn of the century. From the very beginning, every day seemed to vie with those preceding to see which could breed the coldest and worst front. Ten Army pilots died in crashes. They were far from being all-weather instrument-rated fliers like the airline pilots they replaced, and they also lacked modern aircraft equipped for the task as well as familiarity with the routes.

I completely disagree that it was the fiasco the press termed it, nor was it in vain. It brought home to an unrealistic Congress that the fledgling Air Corps—which someday had to be combat-ready—was still flying antiquated aircraft almost as outdated as those of the Great War. The importance of proper instrumentation was also demonstrated, as was the need for pilot training in their use. Before the six-month airmail operation ended, we already had more modern aircraft being delivered to us. I had no more worries about middle-aged cavalry officers in the Air Corps.

There was one thing still troubling me as I flew my tons of mail between Newark, Cleveland, and Chicago. I found my eyes looking off to the south, where my heart wanted to fly. When the same route day after day grew routine and I began to know boredom, I would catch myself studying the maps and drawing imaginary courses toward Rome, Georgia, down there beside a river named the Coosa.

One day in Cleveland, Master Sergeant Curtiss caught me at my plane as the mail from New York was being unloaded. He was huge, three hundred pounds of muscle, a master mechanic assigned as a line chief during the airmail operation. All enlisted men of flying status had to log a minimum of four hours a month to qualify for hazard pay, and as their lives were on the line, they chose their pilots very carefully. Sergeant Curtiss, who had been my first crew chief at Mitchel, had placed his trust in me from the beginning. I knew from the first flight that we had made together that he approved of my technique, although he never mentioned it.

"Lieutenant," Curtiss said with a guarded smile and a wink, "how would you like to fly south and see your young lady?"

It did not matter that I had just flown most of the night; he had my full attention. We adjourned to the restaurant in the administration building not far from the flight line. It was late March and we sat there having cherry pie and coffee for breakfast while he told me about the two-seater pursuit plane that had been damaged in a hard landing by a staff officer making an inspection—he had leveled off too high above the snow and had stalled in. One wheel was badly bent, both tires had blown, the lower-left wing panel was damaged, and worst of all, the great three-bladed prop was twisted like a pretzel from hitting the ground while turning.

"You know the one," he continued persuasively, "that B/J pursuiter back in the salvage yard behind the Sohio hangar—I've noticed you admiring her. Well, Lieutenant, what I had to tell you is I can make that B/J fly, do it in ten days, working some nights." He passed me a piece of paper. "All you need to do is fly up to Selfridge and bring back those parts—all numbered. Borrow the Bellanca C-27A with cargo space for that big prop. Better yet, rig the use of the aircraft for our flying time this month and we'll have all the help we need with those parts, besides keeping quiet what we aim to do. Heck, Lieutenant, you'll have yourself an airplane!"

I nodded, already feeling good inside. That Berliner-Joyce P-16 was about the fastest and latest fighter. There were only a few of them, two squadrons I thought, one each at Selfridge and Langley fields. Besides, it had auxiliary fuel in the biggest belly tank I'd ever seen. As I looked at Sergeant Curtiss, I knew he had his own reason—those two seats, the second one facing rearward for a gunner to protect the plane's tail. My adventurous crew chief wanted to fly too.

We flew to Selfridge Field the next day. It was at Mt. Clemens, near Detroit, sixty miles straight across Lake Erie. To justify using the Bellanca, every one of the fourteen bucket seats were filled with a mechanic getting his flight time. On the return flight over the frozen lake, we had that big bunglesome metal prop lashed down to the fuselage floor, with enough spare parts piled on top to keep that B/J flying after Sergeant Curtiss rebuilt it.

I worked right along with him between my mail flights, and learned that he really could build an airplane from scratch if need be. What parts we had failed to find at Selfridge, he either "borrowed" in what he called "moonlight requisitions" or he manufactured in the small machine shop Sohio (Standard Oil of Ohio) let us use. In two weeks, right around my birthday in early April, our P-16 was ready for flight test. I flew it alone very early one morning all the way across Cleveland Airport, where there was only one hangar.

My big crew chief reminded me constantly that the world we lived in was a jungle, so be vigilant. Meaning that beautiful, powerful machine could not be parked on the ramp with the normal airmail planes. Some busybody might check the Air Corps serial number and find that Langley Field had written it off as salvage. The snow that terrible winter was our ally; even between work sessions we had always put the Berliner-Joyce back in the salvage yard, shoveling snow on the bright yellow wing and replacing the twisted propeller to fool the casual eye. The final thing we always did was brush over our tracks. It was the perfect camouflage.

The day of our first long flight came. At sunrise we waited until all the airmail planes were being run up, and used the bedlam of competing engines to cover the healthy roar of our Conqueror. We had told the control officer that I had a test flight, which was the gospel truth, and I taxied across the field toward the far hangar. We took off in fairly deep snow; it was not hard to tell my gunner was a heavy man, as the tail stayed down a long time before we cleared the fence, heading due south.

I looked around to see if Sergeant Curtiss was okay. He sat hunched down with his back to me. Those were the days of open cockpits, before we had ever heard of a windchill factor. It was thirteen below zero on the ground and that blasting propeller, turned by six hundred happy horses, produced a slipstream of around two hundred miles per hour. The upper gull wing channeled it straight back and I was *cold,* despite the fact that I was relatively more protected than Sergeant Curtiss, who was getting it right in the back. No wonder he was hunkered down.

We crossed the Ohio River at Portsmouth with the airspeed indicating 200 mph, and stretching out ahead on that crystal clear day was all of Kentucky and Tennessee. Before I had time to do much planning we were hurtling over the Tennessee River at Knoxville, and I could see smoke and a bend in the same great river farther south at Chattanooga. My heart was pumping and no matter what the chill factor was I would not have felt cold. There ahead was the reflection of the sun on the Coosa River. It was little and muddy, but no matter; it was guiding me straight toward Shorter Hill and the Vespers Chapel tower.

We had accidentally chosen the perfect time of arrival over the target. Shorter girls in colorful spring clothes were all over the campus. We waved while circling at three hundred feet and it seemed the entire student body waved back. I wondered if Miss Mell, the dean of women, was down there. Every so often I thought I saw Kitty Rix and I waved frantically. When we turned north to fly home to Cleveland, I waggled the wings in farewell.

Our return to base was uneventful, but as the 545 miles passed I felt the chill factor for the first time. What worried me was Sergeant Curtiss sitting there with that icy two-hundred-mile-per-hour wind burbling off the trailing edge of the top wing straight against the back of his heavy winter flight gear. He seemed to be sitting on his hands, still hunched over as far as he could bend. I twisted around and tried to reach a hand to him but it was too far, so I waggled the wings to get his attention. When he did turn and see me I yelled and asked if he was cold, but all he did was pull one hand out from under to give me a wave and a salute. I knew that meant he had also enjoyed our unofficial training flight and looking down on all the young ladies in the sunshine of a Georgia spring.

With U.S. airmail back in the hands of the chastened airlines and Air Corps pilots back home, things changed dramatically for the better for me. I was no longer a hair shirt to my squadron commander; he went out of his way to be friendly to me although I did not know why. Perhaps it was my having flown every day of airmail duty, accumulating more hours than any other pilot. There was a rumor that an official letter to that effect had come down from Langley Field, but if so I never saw it.

One night at the Officers Club he asked me why I did not fly down to Macon to visit my parents. I almost dropped my drink, and I took him up on his offer that very weekend. Kitty Rix was now home after graduation, and seeing her was far better than that fleeting glimpse from the windy cockpit of the gull-winged Berliner-Joyce.

Back at Mitchel another inspiration struck me one night. I got right out of bed and wrote her a letter but put no stamp on it; I had decided to deliver it personally by airmail to Fort Valley, Georgia. It was, after all, what I had been doing for five months with tons of less important letters. What mobility one had, using such weapons of war for delivery! My ship that day was an O-39 Falcon, the type I had used to fly the barometrograph so many nights.

I slipped her letter into the pouch of an Air Corps message container and wound a yard of bright-yellow cloth around the whole thing before stuffing it in my flying suit. And off I flew from Mitchel Field, across the Narrows to Sandy Hook, then down the Jersey shore and straight to Pope Field, North Carolina, where I refueled. My first leg of five hundred miles had taken three hours; three hundred more miles to go and the jack pines flowed beneath like a soft green rug, with me grinning like a mule eating briars. I kept looking into the rearview mirror and laughing at my reflection. Hedgehopping that way was like driving the fastest automobile in the world—no curves to negotiate, no traffic to dodge. My scurrying shadow crossed the Savannah, the Oconee, and the Ocmulgee exactly where it should have as I met my checkpoints, and there stood my target. No distinctive hill as there had been at Shorter College in Rome, Georgia, but right in the center of Peach County a shiny silver water tank with black letters spelling FORT VALLEY.

I used that tank as a pylon and made a low circle, but high enough to be seen. The engine was cut to a whisper but every so often I nudged the throttle to signal Kitty Rix that I was near the house. After that I pulled the nose up into a climb and swung southward for my target run from the tower to the United States flag waving in front of the post office. My aiming point was the town square, which was more properly a triangle of grass less than two hundred yards from where she lived.

I power-glided down from 500 feet, my yellow message bag held in the slipstream in my right hand. I counted the seconds—one hundred, two hundred—until at the right moment I let go and turned out of the dive to watch it stream like a golden parabola in its trajectory. I waved my wings at the slew of boys running to retrieve the bag and they waved back. With the thrill of hitting the target dead center, I also felt a wave of admiration for the wings that had brought me here. My practice mission complete, I climbed out over the tall elms and turned for home.

As time went by, many of those boys wrote me letters. I have high hopes that some of them joined the Air Force and also became pilots, as they said they wanted.

The pace of courtship intensified. Soon after the first delivery I took off in a sleek new Douglas observation plane called the O-31. You never forgot it once you saw it, a monoplane whose high wing was thin and pointed at the tips. It reminded me of a sphinx moth. I had the pleasure of showing that beauty to Fort Valley, especially those little boys waiting to deliver my second love letter. The next visit was the best yet, made in the latest pursuit ship the Air Corps had. It was a Boeing P-26 "Pea-Shooter" that had been flown down to Mitchel from Selfridge by a friend in the First Pursuit Group whom I had met in airmail duty. He needed a car, so we exchanged vehicles.

The first time you saw a P-26 it looked like a toy. You sat in a very open cockpit with a high "turtle deck" behind your head, so close behind the engine—the latest by Pratt & Whitney, a Hornet with 575 horses—that you felt as though your feet touched the carburetor. (There were actually three P-26 models, with a variation of 500 through 600 horses.) The fuselage had the best streamlining of the day, including elegantly trousered wheels beneath a single yellow wing.

That Sunday I made sure to arrive over my target just as the populace of Fort Valley was coming out of church. I showed the whole town that fast little Boeing, flying in from the north so the sun would not be in their eyes. The shadow of that plane fascinated me; those drag-reducing spats made it resemble a big bumble bee. Kitty Rix thought so, too, and wrote me her impressions in her next letter.

My conscience was clear about these flights because each was a simulated combat mission providing invaluable experience in my training as a fighter pilot. I knew I had to learn to perfection this job I loved best, to be fully proficient when the time came to put my skills to the test. There was a branch of the Army Corps called "attack aviation" down at Fort Crockett near Galveston, Texas. I had met some attack pilots during the airmail operation, and they told me they generally flew so low that they left a wake of prop blast behind them in the treetops. That was the way to hit a target; down at the lowest altitudes the enemy would not see me before I saw him, had delivered my weaponry, and was gone.

So I combined my courtship with low-level navigation. Anybody can navigate from normal altitudes with towns, lakes, and other landmarks to guide him; a military pilot flying a mission that way, though, would be quickly detected and run the risk of being shot down. Far from being a waste of gasoline or a foolhardy exercise, my long flights "on the deck" challenged my concentration and taught me to navigate by dead reckoning for hundreds of miles. There were no checkpoints—such things do not show from zero altitude—but if you learned it you could catch the enemy by surprise and have a better chance of escape. I certainly scared a lot of horses, cows, and people in the process of learning!

With so many of those communications delivered to target, I decided the time had come to press my case. I resorted to less glamorous transportation and drove my car south. When I returned to Mitchel, Kitty Rix came with me for a visit, staying with married friends who felt I had been a bachelor too long. It was the first time she had ever been on a military base, and it showed her a completely different life, one which I could thankfully tell she liked. By the time I chauffeured Kitty Rix home to Peach County she was wearing a miniature of my West Point class ring, which was far more binding than all her collection of fraternity pins.

I talked the base housing officer into assigning me a vacant set of quarters. The house needed an inside paint job so badly that I concluded that was the reason it was not occupied. Such quarters were hard to find, especially for a second lieutenant, but I was determined that Kitty Rix have a house. With these arrangements made I flew down to Georgia to see my folks, using the O-31 with the sphinx-moth wingtips because I needed its extra seat for my brother.

Roland was seven years younger than I, a soldier at Fort Mc-Pherson in the very same infantry company I had once served in.

Neither of us will ever forget his visit, nor will the quartermaster captain who issued me twenty-two gallons of ivory interior paint. Preparing those thirsty walls required our labor for a full week, but we took a break from the drudgery each afternoon. After cleaning up we hurried to the flight line where the Falcon stood, checked out and ready, courtesy of Sergeant Curtiss. Off we would go into what would soon be known in song as the "wild blue yonder."

I could tell my brother Roland lived to fly by the look in his eyes, and he did go on to be a combat pilot during the war. Our daily flying was a vital reconnaissance; we were searching for a resort, a hotel or inn within reasonable range of Mitchel Field, of such character and beauty as to befit a short honeymoon. I settled on a radius of a hundred miles and we began looking. The search went on until, late in the afternoon of our last day, we discovered perfection. It was not up near Cape Cod or along the Connecticut beaches, nor was it south along the Jersey shore toward Atlantic City; what we had found was Montauk Manor, way out on the east end of Long Island.

Roland was a skilled photographer even then and took more than a hundred photographs with an Air Corps K-10 aerial camera. That took some doing: The camera was heavy as a suitcase full of bricks, and that was when I tested its weight on the ground. Back there in the gunner's cockpit, held out by both hands into the slipstream, it must have felt like a ton. I would circle low in the rough air, setting up for an oblique shot and watching my brother out of the corner of my eye as he hung suspended by his safety belt, aiming and shooting. His photograph of Montauk Manor, taken from about 500 feet, looked out across an Atlantic with white sails and whiter clouds. When Dutch windmills showed clearly in the picture, sails turning, our choice was made. All that beauty and remoteness not more than a hundred miles from where we were going to live in our first house.

Kitty Rix married me at West Point on September 1, 1934. She wore a blue suit, superhigh-altitude blue, as the dome of the sky appears above 50,000 feet. Her daddy, Glenmore Green, came up from Fort Valley to give the bride away. The colonel in command of Mitchel Field, a fellow West Pointer, was there with his wife and so was my squadron CO. Sergeant Curtiss had his family there; I remembered putting the wrecked Berliner-Joyce together so that we could see my "young lady," and could not resist saying to him, "Here she is!"

We walked up the long aisle beneath tattered flags that had waved in all the great battles our ancestors fought: Yorktown, Gettysburg and Bull Run, Château Thierry. After the double-ring ceremony we descended the steps of the Cadet Chapel where six of my brother pilots from Mitchel Field faced each other with sabers drawn. Beneath this arch, Kitty Rix and I set out on our life together.

Our house at Mitchel Field was ready for Kitty Rix and she was ready for the Air Corps, even the occasional petty jealousies of a few of the other wives. I returned from a flight to California to learn that they had told her their husbands flew across far less than I, suggesting that she should put her foot down. Some of them, she knew, made just as much as I did flying the minimum required.

"Scotty," she concluded, "you logged over a hundred hours a month during airmail duty last year. You get your four hours in before noon on the first day of every month! Why do you have to fly so much?"

I took both her hands in mine. "Honey, you play the piano. I love the way you play the 'Moonlight Sonata.' Let me ask you this: Who is the greatest concert pianist in the world?"

"Ignace Jan Paderewski," she answered immediately.

"Paderewski practices seventeen hours a day," I said. "You also studied ballet; who is the premiere ballerina?"

"Maria Tallchief."

"She practices eighteen hours a day."

We both laughed but I had made my point. I would continue studying to be the greatest fighter pilot in the world even if it meant flying twenty hours a day.

Sometime afterward, I returned home from a hard day's flying even for me. Way out on a small island off Orient Point is Fort Wright. I had been "spotting" for its great sixteen-inch coastal defense guns as they fired at towed targets thirty miles out in the ocean. It meant circling at 10,000 feet hour after hour, observing the hits and reporting back by radio to the battery commander. Those projectiles weighed over a ton, traveled fast as a rifle bullet, and made a mighty splash when they struck the water. It had been quite a show for me, thrilling at first, but after hours the novelty wore off. I was glad to be home and on the ground.

The cars out front signaled me that Kitty Rix was giving a bridge luncheon. Because my flight suit showed every minute of the hours I had been wearing it, I decided to slip up the back stairs and take a shower. Just as my foot touched the landing I heard my name fairly shouted. The voice belonged to the wife of the base quartermaster and she was raking my wife over the coals about how much I flew. I knew that the criticism she leveled at me in my absence stemmed in part from a resentment of the additional hazard pay I received, an especially sore point with her and her nonflying husband.

"When are you going to come to your senses, dear," the strident voice demanded, "and put a stop to such shenanigans?"

That tense moment will haunt me forever, I was so mad at the heckling Kitty Rix was getting. Part of me wanted to charge but I waited, anxious to hear my wife's reply. There was not a word uttered and the room was so quiet I could hear the cards being shuffled. Then I heard that soft, modulated voice I loved:

"Mrs. Egan," she said sweetly, "I know you play the piano beautifully. But who is the greatest pianist in the world?"

And she went on with the explanation I had passed along to her, chastening the plump woman without raising her voice. Sweaty as I was in my rumpled flying suit, hair in wild disarray from my helmet, I strode into the bridge game with smiled greetings to all four tables of ladies but eyes for only one woman. I bent down and kissed Kitty Rix.

"Thank you, honey," I said, louder than necessary, "for being the best wife a fighter pilot ever had!"

Six months after our wedding, we left Mitchel Field for Panama, where I joined the 78th Pursuit Squadron. I was back in my beloved fighters—or pursuits, as we called them then—this time the glamorous Boeing P-12s. You did not climb into a P-12; you strapped it on and wore it. Some letter must have preceded us saying something like *"Watch out for this one—he has an obsession with flying,"* because my new superiors initially made a concerted effort to load me down with ground duties. When it became evident that I still considered the primary duty of a flying officer to be flying, they relented all the way. The final job was the prize of them all in Panama. I was placed in charge of the auxiliary airfields all over Central America. Some were already built, others were under construction. Why, I even contracted with headhunters to build and maintain my fields. The icing on the cake was that hundred-hour months were again commonplace. I was pleased despite pangs of conscience that reminded me of all those thousands of miles I had driven and then flown to see my Kitty Rix. Now, after less than a year of marriage, why did I seem to be flying the other way?

I loved her more with every day that passed. She understood what the job of a fighter pilot had to be, never hinting that she felt neglected or was taking a backseat to an airplane, and she supported me fully in my obsession with flying. One day I heard her explain to a visitor: "Scotty tells me that someday when he has to fly combat he will be ready."

One of my best friends was another fighter pilot from Georgia, Lieutenant "Corn" Shepherd. We gave him his nickname because he liked anything made from corn, from grits to sour mash whiskey. Corn Shepherd was the best communications man in Panama, a brilliant radio expert who could build one with his bare hands. He converted the radio we had at home so Kitty Rix could listen to us all talking ship-to-ship in our formations above the Canal Zone. She listened in on our fighter frequency of 3105 kilocycles as we tried to shoot one another down in simulated dogfights. Our conversations were terse and to the point, usually something like: *"Break off, wing three"; "I'm going down"; or "You're damn near inside my cockpit with me!"*

But what she really listened for was my transmission in our secret code. I would press my transmit button three times—and she knew that the next message would really be for her—then lean forward until my nose touched the microphone stretched between four short elastic cords before the small windscreen. "Wing nine to wing one," I might radio to the squadron leader, my old hero,

World War I fighter ace Monk Hunter. "Rough engine. Request permission to fall out—dive and clear." She would know that she could start setting the table.

Or she might hear the sound of nine engines chasing each other in a Lufberry circle, what we called the rat race. It was generally known, and a source of amusement on base, that I made dinner for the two of us. I have always enjoyed cooking, so I did not mind having married a woman who majored in drama rather than home economics.

Three years in Panama and we were ordered to Randolph Field, this time for me to teach others to fly. And fly I did, not only with students but on weekend navigational training operations. Sometimes I visited tactical bases to try to keep my hand in on the rare new fighters. The simple trainers I flew day after day bore little resemblance even to the now-antiquated P-12s I had left behind in Panama. There at the headquarters of the Flying Training Command, Kitty Rix returned to her amateur acting at the base dramatic club. I went with her so that we could both take part. She was ever the ingénue and I only the heavy, or sometimes the comic relief. It never mattered to me what part I played; I was only there to watch Kitty Rix.

The years passed and my flying hours multiplied, but I well knew that I was far from aircraft that counted in what I was still certain was my destiny. Europe was already at war and I could only watch in frustration when our latest fighter planes dove in to refuel at Randolph. Their pilots were kids we had recently trained, calling on their former instructors to make us jealous.

Late in 1939 we were ordered to Grand Central Air Terminal in Glendale, California, one of the newest of the new civilian flying schools operated under contract with the U.S. government to train military pilots. It was in this manner that our Air Corps was being greatly expanded. The goal was to train thousands of pilots annually instead of hundreds, as it had been in the past. What I did that first month as assistant to the western district supervisor was to check-ride each one of the scores of civilian instructors in an effort to standardize all the personal flying techniques. About that time I was promoted to captain and we were ordered to Ontario, California, some forty miles east in the Chino Valley south of Pomona. There I was to set up and put into operation what became the largest flying school in the United States. Cal-Aero Academy, with civilian instructors and two hundred each primary and basic training aircraft, turned out more pilots every five weeks than the three hundred trained annually at Randolph with all its facilities.

By the time we were completely up to strength we had more than 1,500 students in training. At times I instructed and flew check rides with twenty men a day. My time-hogging, a stigma no longer, was paying off, but hog heaven it was not, because all my mushrooming hours added up to no experience in anything resembling modern tactical aircraft. And all those kids in new fighters heading through for combat every day, the sounds of their powerful engines high in the sky, made me miss even the biplane P-12, from whose twin machine guns I had expended thousands of rounds of ammunition at gunnery targets, sharks at sea, and even the shadows of clouds on the water.

I would slip off when all the students had been checked and do practice bombing. Mixed in with the fine alfalfa fields of the Chino Valley were lush acres of melons, both the light-green honeydew and the golden victory (the Japanese melon renamed in World War I which we now know as the Cranshaw). The culls, those that were not shipped for one reason or another, became my practice bombs. I would home in on the nearest pyramid of melons, land my trainer, and load up the front cockpit with all the melons that would fit without jamming the controls. Taking off again, I would climb toward an auxiliary field we used for solo students which had a fifty-foot lime circle in the center. Ordinarily an aid in identification from the air, this circle became the target in my after-hours on-the-job training.

My technique was more warlike than those letter deliveries at Fort Valley. I would set up my dive at 1,500 feet and nose steeply, honeydew in my hand extended into the slipstream, toward the inviting center of that white circle. It became a Nazi tank that I had to destroy with a five-hundred-pound armor-piercing bomb on the shackles beneath my wing. I knew I was playing a game but there was great realism as I closed in faster and faster, and the mechanics of trajectory made it a valuable simulation.

Congress would have called it tomfoolery, but that isolationist body had made little provision for realistic training for a war it believed would not involve us. In such a manner did I distribute millions of melon seeds that year. Kitty Rix understood, and she also understood when I spent my spare time on weekends haunting the airplane factories in and around Los Angeles. I visited assembly lines, discussed new fighters with test pilots, and sometimes flew one of the latest types, such as the Vultee Vanguard. Every now and then one of my former students would fly in to show off his Curtiss P-40, sometimes claiming engine trouble to remain overnight and see a local girl. Then, naturally, the "repaired" aircraft would have to be tested and Sergeants Burkett and Peluso would give me a knowing wink before asking in all seriousness if I would mind flying the Tomahawk out on the line?

These extracurricular duties made my morale skyrocket. The P-40 was the fighter written up in the press every day, the plane the American Volunteer Group would be flying to glory—Chennault's Flying Tigers.

That was the situation in my world when our daughter, Robin Lee, was born on old Armistice Day, 1940. Kitty Rix and the baby were fine and now I had two girls to come home to after my student flying was done. Then my boss, General Henry Harms, came to see me. He had heard rumors that I was writing letters to congressmen and senators asking to be transferred from the Training Command to some tactical unit—anywhere they flew fighter planes. I liked him all the more for his friendly investigation; instead of giving me hell for going over his head, he sat me down and explained that I could not be spared from my duty at the most important flying school in the Expansion Program. As I drove him to his plane he painted an inviting picture of my making a great contribution to the war effort while staying home with Kitty Rix and Robin. Moreover, I could expect rapid promotion.

"Bob," General Harms concluded gently, "don't you realize you are ten years older than the RAF pilots flying Spitfires in the Battle of Britain? Hard as it may be to accept, you must realize that being a fighter pilot has passed you by."

*Too old to be a fighter pilot!* And just a year ago I had been too young at Randolph Field to be a squadron commander, and before that too young to be more than a second lieutenant—until the very end—in Panama. When, oh when, had I ever been the right age?

Kitty Rix was happy that I was home and we had a great time with Robin. Happy as we were, though, my wonderful wife understood and was in sympathy with my professional frustrations. She knew I yearned to be where the action was, and that to get there I had to escape the Training Command.

Sunday, December 7, 1941, dawned with the Japanese attack on Pearl Harbor. I was a major then but I certainly was not thinking about rank. If I had struggled trying to be patient all the months before, I was a raving lunatic trying to be patient now. With all my flying experience, somebody at headquarters must already be looking for me. In all that confusion of war I must not let them overlook me; I must go and meet my destiny. The B-4 bag with my war kit had been packed a long time. Every night I wrote more of those treasonable letters over General Harms's head, even after he flew down in person to help Kitty Rix pin silver maple leaves on my shoulders. I was a lieutenant colonel and, or so he hinted to her, I stood a good chance of becoming the youngest brigadier general in the service.

If I disliked myself for going behind the back of such a fine gentleman, I despised myself for trying to leave Kitty Rix. I loved her more than any career, any amount of flying time, more than those soulless airplanes that haunted me. Why did something inside me drive me on?

One night in March 1942, I returned home very late, having been testing one of the latest and most glamorous fighter planes at Lockheed in Burbank. Before I even had the car parked in the garage I heard the telephone. I broke into a run. When I identified myself, the operator told me I had an official call from Washington, D.C.

"Is this Robert Lee Scott, Jr?" a voice asked. "What is your serial number?"

Kitty Rix came into the kitchen as I answered.

"Colonel Scott, this is Colonel Merian Cooper, Military Intelligence, Army Air Corps. How many total flying hours do you have?"

I told him my total of thousands.

"How many do you have in the B-17?" Colonel Cooper went on.

In my surprise I almost botched the great opportunity. *You have the wrong Scott* was on the tip of my tongue. *I am the fighter pilot Scott.* But I caught myself. The Boeing B-17 was the Flying Fortress, surely the finest bomber in the world with its four engines and crew of ten. If this was my ticket to combat, I wanted to go along.

I reached for Kitty Rix's hand. I could feel the beating of her heart and thought of our daughter sleeping safely in the next room. Did I really want to leave all this?

"Colonel, are you there?"

"Yes, sir," I stated. "I am very current in the Flying Fort—over a thousand hours."

My top secret orders would be waiting for me and I was to report to March Field at once to pick them up. Good luck! As I replaced the phone on the hook I felt Kitty Rix in my arms. Then we walked into Robin's bedroom and stood looking down at her. With one barefaced lie I had crossed my Rubicon. The die was cast.

I drove the few miles to March Field. What the message center had for me was a full page extracted from a coded radiogram, apparently dispatched from the Office of the Adjutant General just about the time I put the telephone down. Most of the page was composed of asterisks; these top secret portions would be revealed to me verbally when I delivered a brand-new B-17E to Wright Field near Dayton, Ohio. I breathlessly tried to read between the lines but could gather only that I was to be part of a special task force, code-named Aquila. My departure from my present duty and station was to be immediate.

Kitty Rix helped me to pack. Then I helped her prepare to move back to Georgia to be near both our parents, who could help with Robin. Still a bit dazed, we boarded a train the next day at noon, carrying the bare essentials for the journey. Two days later in Memphis, our ways parted for an unknown amount of time, per-haps forever. I saw Robin and Kitty Rix safely to their Pullman compartment, held them close in my arms once more. Then they were gone. I stood a long time watching their train disappear, my eyes blurry with tears as I realized how fleeting happiness really is—and how final this heart-rending farewell might be. I felt chilled and my throat tightened at the knowledge that this was my own design, brought on by my restless soul. Gone were the only two people who mattered to me in this messed-up world and I had arranged it.

# 5

# BACK DOOR TO CHINA

Task Force Aquila consisted of thirteen heavy bombers—one B-24 and a dozen of the latest B-17Es, the first model Flying Fortress to have a tail gun. The crews seemed mature and well trained, with most of the airplane commanders being, like me, in their early thirties. Colonel Caleb Haynes, the leader, was ten years older than I. He was the dean of the big-ship pilots in the entire Air Corps.

Our mission astounded and thrilled me. We were to be the second wave of an attack on the Japanese mainland in which Jimmy Doolittle would lead B-25 Mitchell medium bombers off the deck of the aircraft carrier *Hornet*. Our force of fewer, but larger, bombers would strike the same day after dark, using fires Doolittle's crews had started as our aiming points.

It was lucky we plane commanders learned the full extent of these orders gradually, because they took some getting used to; the obvious fact was that we were most likely headed on a one-way trip. In the end this mission failed, not through any fault of our own but because the Japanese destroyed the eastern China airfield we needed to reach Mindanao in the Philippines, from where we were to bomb Japan. Doolittle and his Tokyo Raiders, of course, succeeded without our help in their brilliant mission of April 18, 1942.

We did not find out any of this until long after we had taken off at the end of March 1942. It was not possible then to fly west across the Pacific Ocean, so we flew instead southeast to Florida, our jumping-off point for the Southern Ferry Route across the Atlantic.

On the way we passed over Aiken, South Carolina, where generations of my family had lived. Grandparents and great-grandparents, uncles and aunts and cousins by the score, stretching back to the War Between the States, one ancestor even to the American Revolution. There was no way I could fly off to war and not dive that Flying Fortress across the Millbrook Baptist Cemetery, then south along Whiskey Road to my grandfather Llewellyn Burckhalter's white house. Here was the long cornfield where he had once told me when I was a small boy: "You just keep trying, son, and someday you'll fly airplanes." I practically dragged my retracted wheels through the waving tops of new corn at better than two hundred miles per hour, saluting him and the others as only a pilot can, before pulling up—to the great relief of my co-pilot.

Lieutenant Doug Sharp sat to my right. He and the crew chief, Sergeant Aaltonen; my navigator, Jack Horner; gunner Corporal Motley; and all but one of the rest of my nine-man crew were killed during the war. Only Corporal Clifford J. Cobb, the young radio operator, and I survived. Although Cliff had no family there, he ended up living in Aiken years after his too-close look at it from the air, and that is where I visited him recently.

To reach Tokyo the long way around, we flew from Puerto Rico to Trinidad, down the east coast of South America to Natal, Brazil, then over the narrowest stretch of the Atlantic to Liberia. From there we flew down the Ivory and Gold Coasts by Takoradi and Accra to Lagos, where we turned inland to cross Africa at its almost narrowest. Narrow or not, we still had a long flight before reaching Khartoum and Eritrea. Then on to Aden and more than a thousand miles along the coast of Arabia before another long hop across the Gulf of Oman to Karachi, India.

Karachi was the unexpected end of the line for Task Force Aquila; it was there the news reached us that our mission had been aborted. Disappointed as I was at the time, as I look back over the years I can see that the Japanese would have been warned and ready for us, and our second wave would doubtless have all been shot down.

Karachi in April 1942 seemed, if anything, farther from combat than my old job checking students in Ontario, California. It was the end of the line and felt like it, with a hopeless lethargy prevailing. The British and American military personnel acted like refugees, and most of them turned out to be just that: Karachi had become the catch-all of generals and their entire staffs driven from the Philippines, Java, Hong Kong, Rangoon, and Singapore as the Japanese flooded the Pacific. They fought to establish order from crowded hotels, temporary offices on the airfield, even native *basha*s of mud and wattle. It was a mess, and morale was abysmal.

With our mission scrubbed, we found ourselves the prey of all those generals with no commands and no aircraft. I did prevent the first attempt to take over my ship, going to the extent of arming all my crew to threaten anybody who tried to deprive us of our new B-17. But orders, even from as high a source as ours, can be rescinded, and I soon found myself a "refugee" colonel billeted in the over-flowing administration building on Karachi Airdrome. My morale sank about as low as it could go.

There were things about India you learned fast. Like the almost incurable heat rash that people called "Karachi Crud." Or the unpredictable running water that trickled all the time except just when you needed to shave in the morning or take a bath at night. I resorted to bathing with whiskey, an unknown brand called Hunley's that I had bought in Trinidad in anticipation of some auspicious time and place. But this was an emergency.

One especially hot night, unable to sleep, I lay considering my frustrating situation. I must have dozed off because I awakened with a start, remembering all the other times I had encountered seemingly overwhelming setbacks only to have fate smile and provide rescue; that ever-vigilant guardian angel I called my genie had reached out to help me with blind-flight training, those weather sounding flights, and airmail duty. I did not sleep anymore that sticky night but my confidence was reborn.

Colonel Haynes returned from New Delhi with the news that he wanted me to be his deputy for operations at something to be known as the Assam-Burma-China Ferrying Command. We were to surrender our Flying Fortresses gracefully and move all the way across India to an RAF base called Dinjan. His map showed it right on the Brahmaputra River, close beneath the towering Himalayas, where Burma began. Of course I jumped at the job—anything to escape Karachi.

By that time I was a full colonel too, and had been ever since the wheels of my B-17 touched down at Karachi. But for my conscience over my fateful lie, I would have known about my promotion much earlier. All the way around half the world I had wished for letters from Kitty Rix or my parents, but we were on a top secret mission and of course had no APO number. Instead, at almost every stop there was an official letter for me from the Office of the Adjutant General, Department of the Army, Washington, D.C. I was afraid to open them; all I could think was that they had checked and found I had never even been in the cockpit of a B-17 before this mission—let alone had a thousand hours of Flying Fortress time as I had claimed— and they were ordering me back for a court-martial. So with a sigh I opened them out over the Gulf of Oman. The yell I let out, accompanied by my rocking the wings of our great ship, must have convinced our crew that I was crazy until I passed around those messages demanding that I acknowledge the promotion as soon as possible— probably a safeguard against promoting a dead man in times of war.

At Dinjan we set up Assam-Burma-China Ferrying Command, forerunner to the Air Transport Command. Our mission was to become a veritable aerial pipeline moving aviation gasoline, ammunition, and other critical supplies from India to China. It all had to be flown in; there was no other way. All we had were Douglas C-47 transports, military versions of the DC-3 airliner, affectionately known as Gooney Birds. They were great aircraft for that purpose, but— being unarmed and filled with explosive cargoes—they left a fighter pilot feeling naked navigating across enemy-occupied Burma.

Dinjan had just a single runway decked with pierced-steel planking (PSP) to prevent our wheels from bogging down in the mud. Taxiways, also of PSP, wound through the tea bushes of a plantation. We were at a relatively low altitude there, but a few miles east stretched some of the most forbidding terrain in the world. This the pilots christened the Hump, and no other word could have described it better; mere foothills at 10,000 feet, and less than a hundred miles north, Himalayan peaks like Namcha Barwa topping 25,000 feet.

We flew the C-47s at altitudes higher than they had been designed for, unable to divert south because of the danger of enemy fighters supporting the relentless Japanese drive north through Burma. All we could do was play both ends against the middle, as the saying goes, remembering that the lofty peaks were as much our enemy as any Jap fighter. Stay far north hidden by friendly clouds, but remember that those clouds can have very hard centers. One day in clear weather I saw Tali, a peak dead on course from Dinjan to Kunming. My official government map listed it as 15,800 feet high; we were at 17,000 and it was high as we were, or higher.

In those lumbering Gooney Birds at 20,000 feet—with their unreliable oxygen systems—I wondered for the first time just what I had escaped to with my lie. What kept me going was knowing how critical our operations were. Everywhere else we and our allies were losing or on the defensive, however brave. Here in Burma and China, people were carrying the fight to the enemy.

With all my heart I still dreamed of fighter planes, plotting my escape from these "delivery wagons" with no guns. The glint of hope for me was Chennault and his Flying Tigers. From my very first flight over the Hump, I had searched for them in Kunming only to learn they were in Burma. After that I began listening to their transmissions in the clear on the radio, locating and circling on my map the places they named: Paoshan, Lashio, Loiwing. . . .

One day I met a squadron of them at Paoshan. All of these American mercenaries seemed to despise us. We were not allies, it seemed, much less friends.

"You flyboys don't bring in what the Old Man needs," one of them said. "You fly in junk!"

I denied it vehemently, mad as hell and ready to fight him, but he was right. My cargo that day—weighing over six thousand pounds—consisted primarily of bales of Chinese CN paper money printed by the Brooklyn Bank Note Company. I began investigating other cargoes we brought over the Hump and found everything from filing cabinets to GI cans, brooms and mops, typewriters, and tons of typing paper. Valuable supplies back in the United States but useless for fighting the Japanese.

Back at Dinjan, as Operations Deputy of the Ferrying Command, I soon found out why. The supply officer at the headquarters of AMMISCA (American Military Mission to China) was going by the book, officiously ordering supplies in Chungking without any regard to the actual needs of the field commanders. I tried to argue with him but we were from two different services; we might have been from two different worlds for all the good it did me. So rather than beat my head against a stone wall, I let them load my plane with the supplies he requisitioned.

I had been told about a Catholic priest who ran a mission at Sadiya, about twenty miles east where the Hump began, and he needed anything and everything. There, where the Brahmaputra makes a near 180-degree turn after coming down out of the Himalayas, I delivered that useless cargo. Then I returned to Dinjan and had my own people load the plane with what I knew Chennault and his Flying Tigers needed. The second time I took off that day I carried sixteen fifty-five-gallon drums of aviation gasoline and a case of .50-caliber machine-gun ammunition, and several five-hundred-pound bombs. These last went between the drums, where they would not roll around.

We were flying two thousand pounds overweight and the Gooney Bird needed a lot of runway to get off. I set course for Loiwing as we climbed, knowing how lucky I was not to have found Chennault before, when I was loaded with the cargo he despised. This Sunday I was certain he would meet me with open arms. He was a pilot, too, and would appreciate the fact that I was overloaded. I could picture the expression on his face.

Loiwing was a slash cut in a jungle of bamboo, trees, and purple flowers. No hard-surface runway here, just more PSP. To the sides I saw hardstands for fighter planes. I greased that four tons of real war matériel in on the main gear only, by then grinning so wide my face itched. At last I would meet the Old Man; he might even shake my hand.

But he didn't. He raced up in a jeep, splashing muddy water, and waved me off. No doubt about it, his vehement signals were telling me to keep my engines running and take off again as fast as I could. I stuck my head out the window to explain that no takeoff was possible from his short runway until we unloaded, but the idling engines and whistling props were too much competition. Not having a co-pilot, I left the controls in the hands of the radio operator and ran back through the fuselage, dodging rusty drums and bombs as I shouted for Sergeant Aaltonen—still with me from the B-17 crew—to open the double cargo doors.

"Get that transport off this field," Chennault shouted as I dropped to the ground. "There's an air raid on the way. They'll be here any minute! I have one squadron up there waiting but this ship of yours will be their first target!"

"Sir, we're overloaded by a ton," I answered. "Look at the cargo."

The sergeant had both doors wide open to show the drums and ammunition. Somehow he had rolled one of those big orange bombs to the door. He also had a case of Camel cigarettes at his feet. I had eight cases of that scarce supply aboard, my special promise to the Flying Tiger who had set me straight.

"Okay, son, stop your engines," he relented. "Have your crew cut some bamboo and cover those shiny wings. Also the windshield—it can be seen for miles. We'll hope for the best and unload later."

I passed the instructions and raced to catch up with Chennault. No matter what I might look like flying that Gooney Bird, I was a fighter pilot. I had to tell him. The jeep was under a tree and the Old Man was nearby, standing in a hole they call a slit trench. He had a microphone in one hand and a pair of binoculars in the other; while he spoke he panned the sky. I could hear him talking to the squadron leader of the planes aloft. In that dramatic moment I hesitated to interrupt, but I had been waiting so long!

As I knelt to enter the trench, something caught my peripheral vision. I turned and stared at a Curtiss P-40 with an aggressive eye and leering shark teeth painted in bright red, white, and black. It was perfectly silhouetted against the darker green jungle, poised and ready to take off. *Here I am,* it seemed to say. *I have been waiting for you!*

"Sir, that fighter," I said, daring to grab his elbow. "That will be their first target. It will be strafed. Let me get it off the field. I can do it—I am a fighter pilot."

"Colonel," he said witheringly, "have you noticed the insignia on that P-40?"

Of course I had. It was the blue-and-white cockade of the Nationalist Chinese Air Force. I told him I saw it and made no further comment.

"You are in the wrong air force and too high-ranking, too, far too high-ranking to be a fighter pilot!"

I was beginning to understand why he emphasized the word *colonel* when he spoke to me. The AVG hated us regulars. In Chennault's case there was little wonder; as a captain at age forty-seven he had been forced to retire from the Army on the flimsy excuse that he was hard of hearing. It had to be my genie who told me what to say.

"Sir, I have been on my way to meet you an awful long time, and I didn't think it mattered to you what rank a man wore so long as he wanted to fight—in a fighter plane."

The silence after my words was long. He seemed to stand there for ages pondering them. At last he looked me in the eye.

"All right, Colonel," he said, not slurring the rank this time, "let's see how fast you can start that ship and get it off this airfield."

There are six or seven things that have to be done in sequence to start up a P-40: be certain the fuel is on; pump the foot pedal eight times to build up hydraulic pressure; energize the starter flywheel until your ears tell you the exact pitch has been reached; crack the throttle just enough, about an inch; give it six shots of primer; switch on as your right toe engages the inertial starter. Somehow I got that Allison going in record time, the propeller blades blurring and the twelve exhaust stacks shouting happily back at me as I dragged the plane onto the runway and opened the throttle.

The dark-green Burmese jungle was like moss below me as I retracted the wheels and turned into the sun, climbing in a spiral to search for the other P-40s. I could not find them so I sought the enemy instead. As things settled down I realized I was flying behind the roughest engine I had ever heard. Adjusting the prop and mixture controls didn't help much; neither did closing the shutters of the Prestone radiator. The vibration got worse when I pulled up and I realized I could hardly gain any altitude.

With my hands so full I had lost track of where I was. I reached for maps but there were none in the case, so I began looking for the simplest thing of all to identify, the Burma Road. Further checking showed fuel in all tanks, so I did not have to worry about an emergency landing for a while unless the engine quit. I also discovered I was very lucky not to have found that enemy formation, as my guns were empty. Then I saw the Burma Road—so distinctive with its countless hairpin turns between Rangoon and Kunming, and clay as red as that of my native Georgia—and followed it back to Loiwing. I had been in the air more than two hours without ever seeing another airplane and I was now too far into my fifteen-minute fuel reserve. There was my Gooney Bird being unloaded, and close by I counted a dozen P-40s all in line, being serviced. I voiced my thanks to the skies as I landed and taxied in, only then seeing that the man signaling where I was to park was Chennault. This time he looked relieved rather than peeved.

"How did she fly?" he asked as we walked toward the buildings, native *basha*s of mud plastered over sticks.

"Fine, sir, once she smoothed out. The engine seemed rough but maybe I've been flying transports too long. Hard as I tried, I never made contact with the enemy. I just wasted gasoline."

We entered the combination pilot ready room and mess in an embarrassed silence. Once in his office he motioned me to sit down and poured two drinks from a bottle of Haig & Haig scotch. We clinked glasses and sipped.

"I've been worried about you," he said. "The first high-ranking colonel I ever saw who could fly a P-40. Scott, how did you manage to start that engine?"

I laughed and insisted repeatedly that I must have hit the right combination on the controls. No use telling him about that helping genie of mine; he'd have thought I was nuts.

"We've had trouble with that one, Scott," he continued seriously. "That's why none of our pilots flew it today. Every time it comes back from Factory Ten at Lashio something else turns up wrong. Today two mechanics and an engineering officer tried to start it and failed. I didn't know until you got it off the field that armament had unloaded all the guns, preparing to send it back for overhaul."

Sitting there with the Old Man acting friendly, I explained how I had reached the China-Burma-India Theater of Operations, including the lie I had told to escape the Training Command. By the time we had eaten a sandwich and finished that half bottle of Haig & Haig, I had met every man in the AVG squadron. I never admitted what a wreck that P-40 was that he had tested me with—there was no need; they already knew. As he drove me to my Gooney Bird, now unloaded and ready to go, he told me about three new P-40Es being flown in all the way from Accra, where the Navy had offloaded them from an aircraft carrier. Chennault told me he would assign one to me at Dinjan if I promised to use it as it was intended—for combat.

"Go ahead," he said. "Escort those transports. Your boss, C. V. Haynes, will like that. I'll like it, too, now that you know the type supplies we need out here. In between, you can work on your own over Burma or come over here and fly with the AVG. That way you'll learn to use your P-40 against Zeros."

My P-40E arrived the middle of the following week, already decorated with a tiger mouth on the "chin" below the spinner and a baleful eye just forward of the exhaust stacks. Flying Tiger Bob Layher remained with me almost a week, indoctrinating me in the tactics proven over and over by the Old Man. I flew his wing as he taught me never to turn with a Zero or Oscar, which weighed less than half as much as a P-40 and had more horsepower. The essence of such tactics is to deny the enemy the use of his good points against you while concentrating your few advantages on him. They were faster, more maneuverable, and could outclimb us; we in turn had greater diving speed, heavier armament, and armor plate to protect us. I learned to use the sun and altitude to my advantage, to strike fast and keep diving if I missed.

"The Old Man tells you," Layher concluded, "you must use this fighter every day. He says he doesn't have extra aircraft to just sit on the airfield, especially not here in India."

I used it all right, not one mission a day or two or even three; some days I flew up to five. I had a modern fighter plane at my beck and call and all Burma as my hunting ground. After all those years of practice, the opportunity I had dreamed of was here: Burma was teeming with enemy and it was open season. The Japanese had already overrun half of Burma in their drive north to capture RAF airfields at Toungoo, Magwe, and Maymyo—the last a fighter base near Mandalay. On my busiest day I caught four barges loaded with troops on the Chindwin River near Homalin. When I was fired on as I checked them out, I strafed all four until I was out of ammunition, then went back to Dinjan, where a five-hundred-pound bomb was fitted to the shackle that ordinarily held the belly tank. The barges were less than a hundred miles away; I bombed them four more times before nightfall, using the same techniques I had taught myself with those cull honeydew melons near Cal-Aero Academy.

I strafed Japanese truck columns on the switchbacks of the Burma Road; I dove five-hundred-pound bombs at the bridges the enemy used to cross the gorge of the Salween River—in short, I attacked every so-called target of opportunity that presented itself. My armament men, Bonner and Creech, made a major contribution to this process by successfully fitting a thousand-pound bomb under the belly of my P-40; the fighter took off with it just as easily as it had with the five hundreds.

It all sounds as if I were winning the war with that borrowed ship, although these raids hurt the swarming enemy very little. Had Patton's Third Army been charging across Fortress Europe then, or had thousand-plane formations of Flying Fortresses bombed Berlin, all my insignificant P-40 raids would never have attracted the attention of war correspondents hungry for good news. In any event, Kitty Rix began to read in the hometown papers about a wild fighter pilot called the "lone wolf of the Chindwin." I had logged more than a hundred hours of combat in May 1942, and did not know I was making headlines until a letter came from Kitty Rix. It had taken three weeks to arrive and was practically in ribbons from the censor's scissors, but she said I was being called a one-man air force back home and she was frightened by the terrible names the Japanese had for me.

I never dared show the clipping she sent to Chennault, but he had already heard and was evidently pleased I was using his fighter to the maximum. The next time I landed at Kunming he arranged for me to fly combat missions with the Adam and Eve Squadron led by Arvid Olson. Bonner and Creech found more bullet holes in my plane after every "guest appearance" I made with the Tigers, but I relished flying with those seasoned veterans of aerial combat and soaking up more of the Old Man's teachings.

There was a special reason for my seventeen missions with them, and had I known, I would not have been able to sleep. The Flying Tigers were to be inducted into the U.S. Army Forces to form the nucleus of a new unit Chennault would command as a general. He wanted a regular Army colonel to command a new fighter group of his and I was being tested for the job. On June 27, 1942, I landed on Kunming Airfield to refuel after strafing a Japanese truck convoy on the Burma Road near the Salween Bridge. When I headed for the rusty fuel drums and their hand-operated wobble pumps, Chennault's old Studebaker pulled up with Wong Chauffeur driving. The Old Man waved for me. As we crossed that airfield in Yunnan I felt cold apprehension that he was going to tell me my P-40 could no longer be spared. Was he bringing me all the way to his office to soften the blow?

My heart skipped some beats when we entered. What I saw was a summit meeting of the military command in China. Seated in the center was Generalissimo Chiang Kai-shek, and on either side—in descending order of rank—were senior officers of the China-Burma-India Theater. Vinegar Joe Stilwell sat prominently on the Generalissimo's right, Chennault at the end.

They all looked alike in khaki colored by the red mud of the Burma Road. I stood before the line of rough wooden desks wondering what I had done. Chiang Kai-shek spoke very rapidly, apparently without noticing me, to an interpreter who then addressed me.

"Colonel Scott, Generalissimo say how long it take you transfer Assam to Kunming? Your orders now arranged. *You command Flying Tigers!*"

If you are ever going to fulfill your destiny, you have to be at the right place at the right time. I knew that my time had at last come.

"Please tell the Generalissimo," I answered, "I am already here. I do not have to go back to Dinjan."

The Fourth of July 1942 was Independence Day for me in more than one way. On that day the Flying Tigers were inducted into the United States Army Air Forces to become the 23rd Fighter Group of the China Air Task Force, and I was made their combat leader. Kitty Rix's letters told me the war correspondents were still playing up my exploits. About that time a visiting friend of Chennault's brought along a copy of the latest *Life* magazine. When I read the story, I felt like hiding from the Flying Tigers. "Greatest of all the pursuit men is their commander, Colonel Robert Scott," it read, colorfully dwelling on everything from my Georgia accent to the way I fly. "His men are crazy about him." I took some kidding about it, but it was all good-natured. Chennault did not seem to mind and we were all very happy that the forgotten war in China was finally getting some attention.

Had I been in Macon a few days before the Fourth, I would not have known what to think. Suddenly the steam whistles at the cotton mill sounded and the church bells rang. Along with the proud headlines, my hometown had taken to marking my every reported aerial victory in this manner. What more could I want?

Then I received a thin gold locket, very small, with the Air Corps winged propeller on the face. Around this there was engraved a line I will never forget: OUR HEARTS SOAR WITH YOU, OUR LOVE AWAITS YOUR LANDING. Inside, there smiled up at me tiny photographs of Kitty Rix and Robin. That treasured locket went around my neck with my stainless-steel dog tags, the only necklace I ever wore in my life.

# 6

# NINE DRAGON CAVE AND THE TITLE

Nine Dragon Cave is a tourist attraction now. The People's Republic of China transformed that cavern near Guilin, in the Guangxi Zhuang autonomous region, with high-tech illumination whose myriad colors fade in and out among the stalactites and stalagmites. They glow with their own fluorescence after the psychedelic display moves elsewhere, seemingly living deposits of calcium carbonate.

I stood there in the summer of 1980 as the tour guide explained that the entire area had once been the floor of a prehistoric sea. My mind wandered down those paths running for miles into the bowels of the earth, remembering how cool it always was no matter how humid outside. Almost forty years earlier, I had lived in that cave when it had been our combat operations center. One memory in particular, though, now flooded my mind so strongly I could almost feel the scars.

Back in 1942, Chennault had sent me here to carry out an offensive against Japanese airfields at Canton and Hong Kong. Guilin had been Kweilin then; I studied the terrain before landing my formation of P-40s, struck by the strange low mountains that stood like sentinels along both sides of the red clay runway. Fighters with shark teeth sat in revetments but I knew that they were dummies of bamboo and painted fabric designed to lure the enemy into wasting ammunition. Once we were on the ground, the mountains and our new quarters seemed ghostly. The Chinese Warning Net covered the sound of eternally dripping stalactites with a mélange of static and strange tongues. That radio center was a large part of the Old Man's strategy; his "eavesdroppers" could tell him exactly when the enemy was taking off and how many were coming, sometimes even when they opened the hangar doors.

For my first mission as a group commander, General Chennault had dispatched me with seven aircraft—all the planes available to us in the middle of 1942—to escort a dozen of Colonel Haynes's B-25 Mitchell bombers on an attack against a Japanese naval force in Victoria Harbor. Was it arrogance that we took on such a target with such a puny force, or did we just not know any better back then? I felt especially confident because Tex Hill, one of the greatest of the Flying Tigers, was flying my right wing.

We skirted Canton by fifty miles so as not to alert the enemy and turned toward Hong Kong at noon precisely. The B-25s were beginning their bomb run when we closed up, above and astern, weaving back and forth, vigilantly searching the skies. There was no Japanese force in the harbor—if there had been, it had sailed away—so the Mitchells diverted to their secondary target of aircraft and power plants on Kai Tak Island. One after another I saw fighters swarm off the ground below until I had counted twenty-four by the reflections of their windshields. We were outnumbered by far and my throat felt dry, but Tex Hill took the words—if any—out of my mouth.

"Hell's fire, Scotty, we outnumber them today. Let's go get 'em."

And we did. I shouted in exultation as I dove for the lead Zero but Tex beat me to him, teaching me something as he did. I shoved my nose down with war emergency power but he did a "split-S," which was doing a half roll and pulling back on the stick. The best I could do was shoot down number two and pull up, and by that time the highly maneuverable Zeros seemed everywhere. I did not have to search for a target—they filled my windshield everywhere I looked. Suddenly in the diving, jinking, swerving melee there came a lull so unnatural, so quiet, I could hear my own heart beating.

To stay alive a fighter pilot quickly learns to look around unceasingly. I was still doing that but now there were neither Zeros nor P-40s anywhere to be seen. My radio seemed dead when I tried to transmit to my men; then it dawned on me that my helmet was gone. Only as I groped for it on the floor of the cockpit did I realize I had been hit. I could not get my breath, and just as worrying, I could not hear the engine. Everything was silent as a tomb but the prop was still spinning—slowly, though, as if at idle. And no wonder: The throttle had been chopped. I had to have jerked it back to that position when my ship was struck. I moved it slowly forward, afraid to discover worse news, but there came immediately the welcome sound of power. I could have shouted with joy but there was still no air in my lungs; it was as if I had received a knee in the chest.

As the daze wore off I remembered turning as hard as I could to bring my guns to bear on another target. Vaguely I recalled the repeated hits from dead astern that had made my plane vibrate all over, then a hard jolt as though I had flown into something. There was pulverized Plexiglas and blood on the cockpit floor. I explored a numbness in my lower right back and my hand came away a sticky mess. Where was the wound? This was not remotely how I had imagined a bullet to feel; none of the "red-hot poker" sensation I had heard described.

I did a three-sixty looking for my formation and saw nothing. Hong Kong had disappeared. My shadow on the water told me I was very low, but I realized I was flying west up the Pearl River Estuary toward Canton. That was our agreed departure bearing, but since I was alone, that would not do now; I cut north, staying low and barely topping the mountains until I saw the Li River, which I followed home.

Getting the damaged plane in was hindered by the broken windshield but the blast of air felt good and I again had my goggles on. There were too few real P-40s among the dummies; we had suffered losses unless I was not the last straggler. It felt good to be on the ground again. Doc Manget was waiting for me with his big Chinese male nurse, and they insisted on helping me up the hill to the cave even though I had already assessed my wound as minor.

Fred Manget was a medical missionary who had led a life of service to humanity in China for more than twenty years. Since there was no American hospital that early in the war, he set up makeshift clinics where we needed them. He now directed me to a bamboo chair and switched on his gooseneck lamp, one that flickered because of the field's unreliable generator, and began talking as he worked—there was no anesthetic, not even any whiskey. There were shards in my back, particles like birdshot that had exploded from my seat armor when it stopped those Japanese shells. He counted out loud with each small but sharp fragment he found, nineteen in all.

Throughout the process I was questioned by the nurse, a "ten-bowl rice man," to use the Chinese expression, meaning a big person. Perhaps Doc put him up to it but he kept badgering me, always demanding some response until I did something to indicate I was still conscious. It was the same thing each time.

"Colonel, you fly *fieji*," he said, using the Chinese word for fighter, "shoot guns, talk radio to men, all time fight barbarian. Then, very much hurt, fly home! You do all these things alone?"

"Damn it, you know the *fiejis*," I heard myself say finally. "They have just one bloody seat, just one. Where in hell would anybody else sit? No, I don't need any help. I'm a fighter pilot!"

I could hear my angry words echoing, then just water trickling through the mountain, as it had for millions of years. Doc was daubing my hematoma—a swelling of blood beneath the skin—with alcohol; he walked in front of me and my eyes were drawn to his.

"You're wrong there, son. You are never alone out there no matter how many seats your fighter has. If you were, you would not have returned today."

I was trying to say I understood when Doc Manget, grinning, flashed me the thumbs-up and said *"Ding-hao!"* I sat up, free from that flickering lamp I had been staring into, facing the stygian darkness of the cave. Lights, formed into words, danced everywhere on a screen of black velvet. I closed my eyes and reopened them; the lights were still there and they settled down to spell GOD IS MY CO-PILOT. I did not tell Doc about them—the old missionary would surely have called it a hallucination.

That night, still in the cave, I wrote Kitty Rix about the mission, making no mention of the wounds, and added that I would have something to tell her when I got home. There was now a title for the story taking shape in my mind.

# 7

# WE NEEDED THE PARTS

A fringe benefit to leading the 23rd Fighter Group was living in the same house with General Chennault. The small bungalow with its red tile roof had a compound surrounded by a high fence for security, and a Chinese soldier always stood guard at the gate. A typical Yunnan building shaped like an L, it was located near the Kunming Airfield.

The Old Man had the last room on the long side, I was next, and Tom Gentry, flight surgeon of the Flying Tigers, was next to me. The fourth room was reserved for guests until taken over by Colonel Merian Cooper, who arrived to become Chennault's chief of staff. It was Cooper who had made possible my escape from the Training Command when I told him the lie of having a thousand hours of B-17 time.

The short wing of the house held a conference room and, just beyond, a dining room whose table was loaded with jars of hot peppers. Friends sent them to Chennault from everywhere such things grew; he was a connoisseur of peppers so hot they burned the outside of my mouth before I could even bite in. The kitchen completed this wing, and it was Wong Cook's exclusive domain. The families of our Chinese servants lived in the compound.

Living with Chennault was almost like living with my dad—

that close—except that Chennault was a military genius and a natural teacher. It was an education to watch him do the tactical planning for his China Air Task Force; he was a master of aerial and guerrilla warfare, skilled at fighting with what he had, and there was none of the martinet about him. In contrast to other generals I have known, he delegated authority rather than simply issuing orders. He would explain the requirements of a situation and leave the planning and execution of the operation to me, his flight commander. I respected his judgment and idolized him—I would have flown into hell for him.

An equally great privilege was having some of the best squadron commanders I ever met, all friends who went on to higher plateaus in civilian and military life. There was Tex—full name David Lee Hill—leading ace of the Flying Tigers and son of a chaplain of the Texas Rangers. There was Colonel Bruce Holloway, my 76th Squadron commander, who took over for me when I was ordered back to the U.S.A. He did an even better job leading the group into combat, and shot down just as many planes as I did, eventually becoming a four-star general and commander-in-chief of the Strategic Air Command. Or Ed Rector from North Carolina, who became group commander after Tex Hill, who had replaced Bruce Holloway. It was a great circle of men. Then there was Johnny Alison, 75th Fighter Squadron leader, whose actions while on fire one night over Hengyang were worthy of a Medal of Honor.

The Old Man once told me a story about Johnny. Well before Pearl Harbor, when Chennault held the commission of colonel in the Chinese Air Force, he had escorted a group of Chinese generals to Bolling Field at Washington, D.C. They were interested in purchasing P-40s to combat the invading Japanese. One of these latest Curtiss pursuit planes was being flown up from Langley Field for their inspection. The pilot was Army Air Corps Captain John R. Alison of Micanopy, Florida.

Johnny arrived over Bolling precisely on time and put the new plane through its paces with dives, zooms, loops, snap and slow rolls, and high-G pullouts—everything to simulate aerial combat— before coming in for a perfect three-point landing. His demonstration so captured the imagination of the dozen generals that they cheered and there was pandemonium long before he taxied in to shut down. They surrounded the P-40, talking excitedly and congratulating Chennault, even patting the nose of the plane that would someday wear shark's teeth.

"We need a hundred of these," one of them shouted.

"No, gentlemen," Chennault answered, putting his arm around Johnny Alison's shoulder, "what you need is a hundred of these!"

On the night of July 29, 1942, John Alison was a lieutenant colonel and squadron commander stationed at Hengyang in Hunan Province on the Siang Kiang River. For years the Japanese had bombed this city with impunity; when the Americans arrived the attacks continued, although only at night when the moon was full—a "bomber's moon," as it was called. The enemy would follow the river from Hankow.

This night would be different. The 75th Squadron had six P-40s standing by to patrol at altitudes staggered by 500 feet. We would not be able to see one another running without lights, so the vertical separation was to minimize the danger of collision. The Warning Net flashed the signal: "Five bandits taking off from Hankow, course indicates target Hengyang," and we scrambled into the sky. Ajax Baumler was the lowest, then me, then Tex, then Johnny, with the numbers five and six higher still. As we orbited, we watched and waited—each hoping we would be at the right height.

Johnny was the lucky one. Five Ki-48 "Lily" bombers came at his level and he immediately opened fire. The last one on the end went down, then the next, then the third, at which point the fourth saw him illuminated in the flaring light of burning planes and opened fire. His P-40 was hit and on fire but he just kept boring in, firing at number four near the leader. We turned on our navigation lights and closed in to help, shouting over the radio that he was on fire. But he just kept boring in until he had expended his ammunition, the flame by that time a comet tail as long as his aircraft. I kept thinking his fuselage tank must have been hit and any minute he would explode.

Finally he turned away from the last bomber and spiraled down to the river. I watched him belly in near the bridge connecting our airfield to the town of Hengyang, the scene clearly illuminated by the light of the burning bombers. By that time I was almost in formation with him. There was no big splash; he just disappeared. I circled twice, looking aloft for the last bomber, but saw only two P-40s landing. Feeling very useless, I followed them in.

After talking with the other pilots, I went into the operations shack to make out a combat report for General Chennault. I was certain that, come morning, I would have to write another of those "Dear Mrs." letters conveying heartbreaking news. Then I heard the sharp crack of rifles. Could it be an attack? No, fireworks! The Chinese celebrate that way. I heard people laughing and shouting, and raced outside to see more than a hundred Chinese trying to get their hands on a sedan chair. In it sat a very wet and very happy Johnny Alison.

As fast as we could make our way through the throng, Tex, Ajax, and others of us pressed forward to where he sat in all his splendor.

"Johnny, didn't you hear us?" we were all asking. "We were yelling at you to bail out."

"I couldn't, Colonel," he replied. "We needed the parts!"

None of us, not even the English-speaking Chinese who trans-lated for the others, will ever forget those words. Our aircraft were old and obsolete—some all but worn out—and we were at the tail end of supply lines for all critical parts and materials. Wrecked aircraft were never scrapped; they were cannibalized at Factory Ten at Lashio, every piece being used to keep another going. Sometimes one serviceable plane was resurrected from six or seven.

For four days our engineers and salvage crews worked with the best equipment available to raise that sunken Kittyhawk. No sooner would the process begin than the river current, pushing against the 9,400-pound fighter, would capsize the derrick. Time and again the American crews had it almost out of the water only to have it disappear again, barge and derrick trying to follow. The Chinese politely asked us to let them try. At first we laughed, wondering what the backward Chinese could possibly do, but they got their turn. With every American ready to laugh, they swam out towing thick lengths of bamboo, which they sank with baskets of stones. They placed bamboo poles everywhere under the plane, lashing them from fuselage to wingtips with pliable lengths scaled from the surface of that all-purpose commodity. By the third day the P-40 floated to the surface of the Siang Kiang, and the Chinese towed it to the sloping riverbank. One of their mechanics crawled into the cockpit and let the wheels down, and two or three hundred Chinese then dragged it up on the sand with ropes. It looked almost ready to fly as the water streamed out, and fly again it did. Johnny had saved more than just the parts.

We gave the Chinese a party to show our thanks. The mayor of Hengyang—or some high official—said it was no big thing raising five tons fourteen feet. Six hundred years before, in the Ming Dynasty, the people of that part of China had hidden their golden temple bell in the sea to protect it from invading barbarians. Years later, perhaps hundreds, they had raised it in the same manner as our P-40. That bell had weighed thirty tons.

The other day I saw Johnny Alison at the Fighter Aces Reunion at Maxwell Air Force Base, Alabama. All I could think of as we talked again was that night. Instead of the letter to his parents, I had written a citation for a Distinguished Service Cross—the second highest decoration our country can bestow—which he received. I had wanted to make my recommendation for the Medal of Honor but the "Powers That Were" did not understand—they did not fly. Now, after more than four decades, I know that I should have stood firm in my original intent. As General Chennault said so long ago: "Gentlemen, what you need is a hundred of *these*."

# 8

# BISSELL

On Thanksgiving, I shot down my tenth plane to become a double ace. On Christmas, I had three more victories above Yunnan, plus a probable. That night my name was mentioned by Tokyo Rose over Shanghai radio, the only news we heard out there in China. She called me a war criminal and said the Imperial Japanese government had placed a price on my head.

General Chennault congratulated me, adding that he had been on their hit list for years. What worried me was that I knew my boss and friend was on another hit list far more insidious and menacing. We soldiers learn to face our enemies, but how do we do battle with someone wearing the same uniform?

Over the Hump, at the Imperial Hotel in New Delhi sixteen hundred miles from the real war, there was a general named Clayton Bissell who was bent on destroying Claire Chennault. He commanded the Tenth Air Force, a newly activated organization existing mostly on paper, where he used his one-day seniority to the Old Man to full advantage. In six months of hearing and observing, I had come to consider Clayton Bissell that enemy within we have heard whispers about since Roman times.

As I divulge these glossed-over secrets of intrigue within the military service, I hesitate because Bissell is not here to defend himself. He has been gone from us a long time. But then, so has Chennault, and he left us long before Bissell. I was a pallbearer at Chennault's funeral as we bade him farewell in Arlington Cemetery. I can still shut my eyes and see the others who flew for him in China—Tex Hill, Ed Rector, Bruce Holloway, and on and on—but most vividly, through the tears in my eyes, I can see Chennault himself appearing to sit on his own flag-draped coffin on the black caisson.

Shortly before that procession wound its way to the grave, I was a junior member of a board of inquiry into the sordid career of Major General Clayton Bissell. Caught in black market dealings while serving as air attaché to the United Kingdom, he was allowed to request early retirement so as not to embarrass the service. That is why I have to tell this story of the schism between Chennault and Bissell out there in the CBI.

They met in 1931, both captains at Maxwell Field in Montgomery, Alabama. Chennault then headed the pursuit section of the Air Corps Tactical School, while Bissell held sway over bombardment. Surprisingly, for someone who had been a fighter ace in World War I, Bissell accepted as true the then-popular belief that fighter aviation was passé; bombers alone would be needed in future aerial warfare. One of his recommendations of that period was that bombers drag balls and chains behind them to entangle the propellers of enemy planes.

Chennault knew that the long-range bomber would deliver the blow by which an air war would be won, but as his book *The Role of Defensive Pursuit* shows, he also saw the critical role fighters would play in General Billy Mitchell's doctrine of strategic bombardment. History proved Chennault right: The American daylight bombing campaign—eventually so successful in Europe—almost failed until long-range escort fighters could be produced.

Bissell seemed to win out over his rival. In 1937, at the age of forty-seven, Claire Chennault had been forced to retire from the service—booted out is more like it—on the pretext that he was hard of hearing. At that time he was invited to China to organize a modern air force; while there he effectively created a base of operations for the United States to fight an aerial campaign against

Japan, a critical function in the coming war he so clearly foresaw. Then, when Pearl Harbor proved him right, he was recalled to duty by the same service that had belittled him and cast him aside.

Like Billy Mitchell, Claire Chennault worked selflessly and all-consumingly for his country despite its apparent antipathy. The Old Man endured all adversity, refusing to quit or become bitter. His contribution cannot be overstated. The great irony is that, when recalled, he was placed under the one man in the entire service who would do whatever he could to deny him success—and Bissell's promotion to brigadier general, giving him the necessary seniority, had come just one day before Chennault's!

Chennault and his American Volunteer Group—the AVG, or Flying Tigers—had become household words by scoring a fourteen-to-one kill ratio flying far too few obsolescent aircraft against faster and more maneuverable Japanese fighters. What they accomplished against great odds was never equaled by any regular Army or Navy fighter unit.

Thanks to Bissell and his jealous spite, we lacked official support and our supply lines were strangled. Surely General Hap Arnold knew the value of restraining our three experienced squadrons as a nucleus around which to build the 23rd Fighter Group? Yet when the time came to bring the Flying Tigers into the United States Army Air Forces, there was not so much as a compliment for the superb job they had done; instead they were insulted and threatened.

"Any of you who refuse induction into the Army," Bissell told the veteran pilots, "I guarantee to have your draft boards waiting when you walk down the gangplank off the boat that returns you to U.S. soil. And I do mean you return by boat!"

They arose as one man and walked out of the meeting in Kunming. When the induction board toured the three Flying Tiger squadrons, only six agreed to be inducted. And those only because of their personal dedication to the Old Man.

From that rather miserable beginning on July 4, 1942, the 23rd Fighter Group went on to become the backbone of the USAAF in China. It shared with the 49th Fighter Group of the Fifth Air Force, Pacific Theater, the record for longest continuous combat against the Japanese. In three years, the 23rd destroyed over a thousand enemy aircraft while losing less than two hundred. Under Chennault, they did it with antiquated fighters that most other theaters of war refused. Of that nucleus of six experienced Flying Tigers, two gave their lives. I feel honored to have been the first group commander, and despise Bissell for denying it so many other good men; had he been even halfway diplomatic, as General Arnold must have expected him to be, the entire AVG might have remained.

Near the middle of January, I had my greatest day in combat, shooting down four enemy bombers over Yunnan-Yi. Only two were ever confirmed as victories but the other two added to my list of probables. Those kills came in the nick of time; immediately upon landing I was given orders directing me to report to General Henry H. Arnold, Chief of Staff, Army Air Forces, in Washington, D.C. A C-87—a transport version of the long-range and fast B-24 Liberator bomber—was to fly me home to the U.S.A., which made it far from a routine change of station. At our takeoff, the 23rd Fighter Group flew a farewell escort formation in my honor for fifty miles—which brought tears to my eyes.

"Scotty," General Chennault said before I left, "that damned Tenth Air Force Bissell is behind this. First he moves C. V. Haynes as my bomber commander. Now he takes you away. What will he do next?"

The disappointment at being pulled away from my fighter group hurt; what hurt worse was what was being done to Chennault. I dreaded this night in New Delhi, for it was crystal clear to me that my stay in a headquarters where the Old Man was hated was no accident. A redheaded captain was waiting for me when we landed. I knew him to be General Bissell's aide-de-camp, and his presence confirmed my suspicions. He told me to report to the general at my convenience the following morning.

I hated the thought of meeting with Bissell. Could I possibly hold my tongue as I faced the conniving bastard? I did not know and it worried me all night long in the artificial wartime comfort of the Imperial Hotel. "At your convenience" in military parlance falls little short of "immediately, if not sooner," so I arrived early the next morning and was kept waiting an excessively long time.

I recalled Bissell's inspection tours at Kunming during which he acted so pompously. Chennault disliked him so intensely that he refused to meet the aircraft, explaining that he felt ill. I knew in my heart that it was no sham; Bissell made him physically sick. We used to joke to dispel the tension over Bissell's coming. He was flying in to tell us he was giving us the airplanes and supplies we so desperately needed, and which we continued to requisition. Someone would say that perhaps a Japanese fighter had shot down his Gooney Bird and someone else would chime in to say he hoped not, because the pilot, Tex Carlton, was a good guy. One remark I will always remember originated with Doc Gentry, the flight surgeon who loved the Old Man too. He maintained that Carlton was such a fine individual he would gladly sacrifice himself to get rid of that so-and-so.

Our jungle net would track the plane's approach and Chennault would dispatch me to meet it. Bissell would look around as he took my salute, barely returning it as he looked for my boss. When informed that Chennault was not feeling well and would meet him at the house, Bissell would state that the Old Man was not physically fit to be in a combat zone. He always found fault—our pilots did not wear regulation uniforms or ties; we lived in our clothes and they showed it—and after his visits it took Chennault days to recover, as though from a real illness. I knew it was precipitated by Bissell driving away so many of the Flying Tigers. Perhaps it was also the knowledge that Bissell was holding the new fighter planes that had arrived on the pretext that they were needed to defend New Delhi. Defend it from what, so far behind the lines?

Before he left, Bissell would give Chennault a typed letter he had dictated to the personal secretary he had brought with him. It castigated the Old Man, taking him to task for things that were ludicrous in light of the war being fought. As Chennault had no stenographer, it often fell to me to take down his reply to Tenth Air Force HQ in New Delhi. Without rancor, he would dictate something like the following:

Dear Clayton:
Thank you for paying us a visit out here in the boondocks. I appreciate your letter of constructive criticism. You are correct as usual. Our floors are muddy—most of them are mud. Our

airdrome is wet and muddy. It rained and rained here and we had to scramble our twenty-nine old P-40s the day before your inspection.

My pilots do play cards as they stand their 24-hour alerts. They play in between combat missions.

Sometimes they don't have time to shave though I do my best to discourage beards. They interfere with their oxygen masks—practically a part of their uniforms.

Neither are their shoes shined. You see, muddy shoes, wet too, won't take much of a shine.

However, I respectfully call your attention to the fact that our ratio of kills to our own planes lost in combat is over fourteen to one.

Signed,

> C. L. CHENNAULT
> *Brigadier General,*
> *USAAF Commanding*
> *China Air Task Force*

I took stock of myself as I sat there cooling my heels; I looked pretty raunchy in my year-old bush jacket which had been made in India, and my pants were just as worn, although the hotel valet service had pressed them. At last the general asked to see me; I entered to find him counting Indian rupees. He did not bother to look up, so I dropped my salute and stood there.

"Colonel Scott," he said, "I am glad you stopped by, as I wanted to talk to you before you fly to Washington. Though you have an enviable combat record, you have nevertheless been a great disappointment to me."

I managed to hold my tongue.

"You have refused to support me as your commanding general. You are part of the Tenth Air Force but you refer to your headquarters just as the China Air Task Force."

He wanted me to interrupt and argue the point. Again I refused to be baited.

"I am aware of the lewd jokes you are a party to," he accused venomously, "such as teaching a Chinese to insult me and the service we both represent. As you are a West Point graduate, I am particularly ashamed to have you in my command."

I did know about the Chinese gas-truck driver. He knew no word of English but had been carefully schooled to say phonetically: "Piss on Bissell, piss on Bissell!" He met just about every airplane that landed for fuel at Kunming, and would stand proudly by, politely grinning and chanting the phrase as the passengers stepped off. I had never seen him but had heard the story from the Flying Tigers.

As calmly as I could, I admitted I knew what he was referring to but denied being behind it. Realizing it sounded as though I were trying to weasel out, I decided to let him have it.

"However, General," I told him, "I have said something about you several times when disgusted by the way you treat my real boss, General Chennault. Because it could be construed as having been said behind your back, I would like to repeat it here now, out loud, face to face."

He still avoided my eyes, refusing to look up at me.

"Sir, you wear the second-highest decoration our nation can bestow upon its soldiers. The Distinguished Service Cross, for valor. When I saw it I wondered how in hell you earned that medal. And only recently I learned from General Chennault that you shot down five German planes in World War One. When you were on General Billy Mitchell's staff, I also heard. Well, sir, no matter how you earned that award, I came to respect you, even honor you for it. So as one ace to another, I always hoped you would visit China, not just to give Chennault hell and damn well make him ill after each visit. I wanted you there to lead my fighter group with me on your wing, to fly a P-40 in combat with us."

By the gods, I had his attention at last. He was looking at me.

"You did!" he said. "You wanted me to fly a mission with you?"

"Yes, sir," I replied, as softly as I could. "Somewhere over enemy territory I was going to shoot you down."

With that stupid remark, I added that my orders directed me to the chief of staff as soon as possible, did an about-face, and left his office. He just sat there. Much as I despised him for his torture of Chennault, damned if I did not feel sorry for him. Forever and ever that threat to one of my superior officers would remain in my official military history, known as my 201 File. It was far more damning than a police record. Infuriated as I was at the man who hated Chennault, it was foolish of me to have lost control.

Over a year later, when Chennault was on an official visit to Washington, he detoured to visit me in Winter Park, Florida. I was then at Orlando Air Base as operations deputy for a new service known as AAFSAT, the Army Air Forces School of Applied Tactics. Kitty Rix had just gone inside to make sandwiches, leaving us alone on the screened-in breezeway as Chennault was telling me the latest on the upgrading of the China Air Task Force into the Fourteenth Air Force. He was free of Bissell at last.

Right after I left China, General Bissell arrived at Kunming with a planeload of IGs, or inspectors general. There they had conducted a most thorough investigation into all aerial victories claimed in that theater of war, mine in particular, the object being to nullify them and discredit General Chennault.

"Scotty," my old boss concluded, "when the facts were in, the Chinese not only confirmed your claim of thirteen enemy aircraft destroyed in aerial combat, but also the nine you were claiming as probables. Therefore, I am happy to bring you the news that you now have twenty-two confirmed kills to your credit. Congratulations!"

We laughed and drank a toast to the Chinese. Chennault grew more serious.

"Bissell told me something else I have wanted to ask you about. Did you ever threaten to kill him, shoot him down? He swore to me that you did."

"General," I answered, "I am mighty sorry I lost my temper and said anything to embarrass you with Bissell, but I have to tell you the truth. I did get mad and tell him as a brother ace from World War One that I hoped he would come to China and fly a P-40 with us in combat, and that I would shoot him down. That was a while back and perhaps I can blame it on combat fatigue. Anyway, I am sorry if I put any more weight on your shoulders."

Chennault sat there looking at me with a stern face. Then I thought I saw that never-to-be-forgotten twinkle in his eyes.

"That's the way I heard the story from him," he said. "Well, Scotty, do you know what I replied?"

I shook my head.

" 'Clayton,' I told him, 'if I were you I never would fly that combat mission with Scott; I think that son of a bitch *would* shoot you down!' "

The Old Man was laughing. I laughed, too, all the accumulated tension of the incident disappearing, however damning Bissell's vindictive retribution in my file might be.

# 9

# COMBAT—PUBLIC RELATIONS STYLE

Back from China, in January of 1943, I underwent a debriefing by G-2, Army Intelligence, far more thorough than any I had ever been through after my combats. Immediately afterward, General Arnold took me to the ultra-secret War Room of the Pentagon, where I addressed and was questioned by more generals than I had ever seen before. Hap Arnold had introduced me as the first fighter-group commander home from the war, and a blooded ace—stirring words bringing me the first heady taste of fame.

I was then handed over to the public relations people, and it did not take long to realize that I was entering another type of combat, worse in some ways than getting shot at. I was herded around to functions in Washington, I was a guest on all the top radio shows, I answered questions at press luncheons for countless reporters, and so on. Being a pawn in the hands of the publicity seekers left almost no time for my family, one exception being the premiere of the latest Hollywood aviation film, *Air Force,* at Radio City Music Hall in New York which Kitty Rix and I both enjoyed. I tried to do what Chennault had asked—plead for more aircraft in China—but every appearance was prepared for me: canned speeches courtesy of Public Relations. I strayed from the written word one night on NBC, only to have a red light blink out, meaning I was off the air.

I had been around the Pentagon long enough to find out that most of the jokes about the "Puzzle Palace" were true. Was I to remain the prisoner of the biggest headquarters in the world or would they ever finish with me? The answer became only too clear one day when I overheard Hap Arnold talking to his deputy, General Stratemeyer, in another room.

"Keep that fighter pilot stateside, Strat, any way you can," the familiar voice ordered. "No matter how he argues to return to Chennault. He goes back, flies a few more missions, and we lose him—we can't take that chance. There are important things I have for him to do here. He won't like it . . . ."

The words faded out as a door closed or they walked out of hearing. The cold facts sobered me but did not detract from my enjoyment of a Robert Scott day in Macon. Cherry Street, the main drag of my hometown, was decorated with flags and bunting and a colossal picture of me on each lamppost. It was the second such celebration; the first had been six months earlier when a wonderful elderly lady, Miss Dolly Lamar, felt my luck had to run out pretty soon and imposed on the mayor not to wait for my return. The pride my family felt for me made it an unforgettable day.

General Stratemeyer hustled me off to various air bases around the country. I flew the latest P-40K Warhawk, all painted up with grinning shark's teeth and festooned with Japanese flags representing my victories. Luke Field in Arizona was a special one, as Chinese pilots were being trained there in P-40s. About that time I received the first letter from Chennault. "What's happened, Scotty?" it read. "Have they softened you up with a cushy job? Is the food too good over there in the ZI? Have you forgotten China? Things are still the same out here. We're short of airplanes but no shortage of Japs. I need you. . . ."

I realized that this and all Chennault's letters were half in jest, but no matter. I flew back to Washington and got past General Stratemeyer to meet directly with General Arnold. I tried desperately to be released for combat duty, even showing him Chennault's letter, but to no avail. He told me very loudly that I was arguing with him, and the subject was dropped. Instead of China, I was going to Orlando, Florida, to make an "important" talk to the Women's Auxiliary of the American Legion.

"We are in the military profession," General Arnold concluded. "We do not dabble in politics. You go down there and tell those ladies about the Air Forces. If you talk about political matters I will send you to South America where there is no war!"

At that time, a labor leader named John L. Lewis, president of the United Mine Workers, had just declared the second coal strike of World War II. It had slowed production everywhere, precipitating black headlines in the papers every day. Lewis was a pompous terror, a giant of a man with bushy eyebrows, curly gray hair, and a voice like the snarl of a grizzly bear. My opinion of him was as low as or lower than everyone else's but I had no intention of saying so when I began my talk.

For forty-five minutes I held the Florida audience's rapt attention as I talked about General Chennault and his Flying Tigers, flying the Hump and the problems of aerial supply over the highest mountains on earth, and the need for greater production at home. We could not afford any decreases when we were losing the war almost everywhere we were fighting. Then came the question-and-answer period, and almost predictably, the first question was what did I think of John L. Lewis.

"Ma'am," I replied, "I am just a soldier. We do not delve into politics."

"Colonel Scott," she continued, "you have been very forceful and direct in your speech about China and the Flying Tigers. You say you have seen men killed because of shortages of gasoline, airplanes, and other materials. Just this morning, in the same paper where John L. Lewis declared the strike, there were reports of more shortages. Please be frank with me—what should be done with Mr. Lewis?"

I did my best to avoid the question but she was utterly insistent. I had my back pressed to the wall, not just by her but by the entire crowd.

"Ma'am, this is my personal opinion, nothing else," I said. "It is not official and I do not speak for the U.S. Army Air Forces, but if I were to shoot him with the same fifty-caliber machine guns you have commended me for using over China, I would be doing a public service."

I was drowned out and chairs overturned as newspaper reporters raced for telephones. My telephone was already ringing when I got to my hotel room, with reporters from far and wide asking for confirmation of what I had said. I took the phone off the hook. FLYING TIGER OFFERS TO ANNIHILATE LEWIS, the afternoon edition of the Orlando paper said. The next day it was on the radio, and the wire services had picked it up.

At Bury St. Edmunds, an American air base in England, my brother Roland was preparing to take off in a Martin B-26 Marauder. His co-pilot came running to the plane with a copy of *The Times* of London sporting a similarly sensational headline. "Your brother will never be a general now," the co-pilot shouted over the noise of the engines. That newspaper went with them to the target and back.

When I heard nothing from the Pentagon and found I had not been shipped off to South America, I settled into the routine of giving speeches at war production plants. I flew into Buffalo one spring day in 1943 for three appearances, the first being at the Curtiss-Wright plant where they built P-40s. From there I went to the Packard factory where they built the Navy PT boats. Finally, I went to nearby Niagara Falls and Bell Aircraft, where the P-39 Airacobra was born. At all three places, I emphasized the importance of each worker—as great as that of each combat pilot—and spoke out against absenteeism. In my mind was the idea of writing down what I was telling these thousands of war workers for publication by the Army Air Forces; perhaps then they would release me for return to China.

At a party given for me that evening by the city of Buffalo, I was in the midst of a spirited discussion with some test pilots—all of us talking dogfights with our hands—when a minister joined us. He introduced himself as Dean Austin Pardue of the Episcopal Church, saying that he had attended all my speeches that day and hoped I would tell his congregation similar stories the next morning. I did my best to decline—war plant audiences were one thing, but a pulpit? No, sir! When it turned out that Elizabeth Wright, the wife of a Curtiss-Wright vice-president, had suggested it, I had to agree—not only did her husband manufacture my beloved P-40s, but I was their houseguest in Buffalo.

Just that innocently I found myself marching up the aisle of Saint Paul's Cathedral that Sunday morning, flanked by Dean Pardue and with no avenue of escape. My strong impulse was to say very little, express my appreciation for the invitation, and leave, but I felt very clearly my obligation to Chennault to speak out on his behalf at every opportunity. When I looked into all those trusting faces, I realized I had a purpose for being there; before I realized it I heard myself telling the same stories I had told in the factories the day before.

That amateur sermon in Buffalo did not make the papers but it changed my life. Dean Pardue, later the bishop of Pittsburgh, just happened to be a writer. He took me to New York City to meet his publisher. On Monday morning I met Charles Scribner, head of the publishing house; he listened to my stories—with the Dean encouraging me—for four hours. After lunch, Mr. Scribner told me it was a book and asked how long the Army would give me off to write it. I explained that there was no possible way to have time off during a war, but I had three days until I was due to report to Arizona to take command of Luke Field.

All those stories turned into a manuscript regardless, in a way so strange it was noted by Robert Ripley in his *Believe It or Not* the next year. For three days and nights I talked to an inanimate machine, recording close to ninety thousand Georgia-accented words on a hundred wax cylinders. When I signed the contract, Mr. Scribner asked if I had a title. I could never forget the words I had seen emblazoned in the darkness of Nine Dragon Cave—here was the proper use for *God Is My Co-pilot*.

The book was not the military report I had planned to submit to General Arnold, but in its phenomenal success it was destined to reach a far wider audience. I went off to my new assignment, to find that while I had been dictating in New York, a much older colonel had been hurriedly dispatched from Training Command Headquarters in Fort Worth to assume command at Luke. People in the

Command, it seemed, had long memories and still resented my defection.

Strangely enough, it turned out that I was still senior to the elderly colonel at Luke, and thus by regulation was to take over regardless. I was happy as a lark not to be chained to a desk at a training base, though, and the older colonel was only too happy to abet my escape. I flew my painted-up P-40K another four hundred miles west to Chino, California, to visit my old command at Cal-Aero Academy, which by then was in full swing as the largest training base in the country. The civilian operator of the contract school, C. C. Mosely, was a fighter pilot from World War I. He had me make one of my talks to his students, then took me home with him to Beverly Hills. Next day he had me meet Jack L. Warner of Warner Brothers Pictures, and again I found myself telling the stories I had told Charles Scribner. To my surprise and that of General Arnold, whom Jack Warner had to call to make the deal, my book was purchased for a motion picture long before the manuscript had ever been edited.

By the time I returned to Luke, the colonel there had my new orders. I had again escaped Training Command, as I was now deputy commander of a special new group called AAFSAT, the Army Air Forces School of Applied Tactics. At the beautiful town of Winter Park, near my new station, Orlando Air Base, I managed to buy a house with the first money from the motion picture rights to the book. It was a large and rambling estate, somewhat run-down but fully furnished, surrounded by several guest bungalows, flame trees, two giant magnolias, and acres of lawn sloping down to Lake Maitland. All that hidden from the street by a thousand orange trees. Now I knew that should the worst happen, if I never came back to Kitty Rix and Robin, the ten-acre estate could be subdivided and they would have income.

Not long after we moved into The Anchorage, General Arnold called for me. He had new orders for me but they were not to China. I was assigned indefinitely to Warner Brothers as a technical adviser for as long as it took to film *God Is My Co-pilot*. I argued as much against it as a colonel can with a (then) four-star general, which is not much, but Hap Arnold was ready with an answer for every lame excuse I could come up with. He patiently held his temper and told me that he considered such an assignment far more important than flying fighters in combat. What he wanted was a factual motion picture that would be a credit to the Air Corps. Kitty Rix and Robin came right along with me to Hollywood, so I had to count my blessings.

The news of my "cushy" new job traveled fast—as bad news does—because I had hardly reached the sound stages before another letter from Chennault arrived. The newspaper clipping he enclosed shocked me—there on the front page of a Tokyo daily was *Old Exterminator III*, the last of the P-40s I had flown in combat over China. The fuselage and whatever else was left were being paraded down the Ginza, Tokyo's main street. Clearly visible on the plane was my name and the thirteen Japanese flags signifying my victories. An enclosed translation told me that the article stated I had recently been shot down over Nanchang—despite my having been in the ZI (Zone of the Interior—military jargon for Continental U.S.) and out of combat for over a year! It referred to me as the "Hollywood playboy," a name Tokyo Rose had given me that must have derived from my having been technical adviser for a couple of movies before the war.

It seemed that when I departed China in the spring of 1943, Chennault initially left my plane exactly as it was in anticipation of my quick return. When that did not happen, apparently every new lieutenant who flew my fighter preferred to leave the name and victory symbols of the lucky former CO, rather than have them painted out. The one good note in Chennault's letter was that he felt all the publicity for my book and movie might help him get some of the latest fighters, North American P-51 Mustangs. "Don't forget," he concluded, "there's still a place for you here in the Fourteenth Air Force."

All things come to an end, even a Hollywood movie production. With the film finally in the can, there was a party that included a showing at the studio. General Arnold attended with some of his staff. I felt embarrassed as the story flashed across the screen—it was typical "Hollywood" and I could not help wanting to disappear a few times—but nobody got up and walked out. There was a scene that frustrated me; I had very realistically simulated a bellying-in with my P-40K to replace an obvious use of a model sliding down a wire, yet when that scene was reached, the unconvincing model was back in. Jack Warner later told me it was a concession to the unions.

Members of General Arnold's staff voiced their approval at the end of the screening, but the Army Air Forces chief said nothing. No "All right, Scott, your job is done—you can go back to China." After he left I went to the bar to drown my sorrows. While I was sitting there I sensed someone had sat down on the stool next to me. Somehow I knew it was Hap Arnold before I dared glance in that direction. I leaped to attention.

"Scott, I damn well thought I'd find you here," he began instantly. "I've watched you all evening but with all the amenities there hasn't been time to ask you a question that has troubled me for almost a year. It's about that talk you gave to those ladies in Orlando. Before I leave I want the ungarbled truth from you. You weren't really stupid enough to threaten to shoot that labor leader with six fifty-caliber guns, were you?"

"Sir, I said it," I answered, "but I explained both before and afterward that it was just my personal opinion and not that of the War Department."

General Arnold's face turned red. He did not say a word until he was standing and had his face practically in mine.

"Personal opinion, hell!" he said, really letting me have it. "Son, as long as you wear that uniform, remember this—*you don't have a personal opinion!*"

He must have stood there a whole minute letting the words sink in. I could feel how mad he was by the very temperature as we looked at each other eyeball to eyeball. Then he left and I heard his car drive off with the slam of a door. I was the only one there; even the bartender had left. I just kept standing for a long time and never did have my drink.

I received orders to return to Orlando and the School of Applied Tactics, still hoping to be sent back to China. A few weeks later, in February 1944, the movie *God Is My Co-pilot* premiered in Macon and I was required to be there with the principal actors. I kept thinking how tired those wonderful people in my hometown must be of me, but the third Robert Scott day was a great success. They had me ride a water buffalo down Cherry Street in a parade; that animal, part of a circus wintering nearby, was the only thing in Macon that did not seem to like me.

Immediately afterward came word for me to report again to General Arnold. The chewing-out seemed forgotten as he picked up his telephone and pressed a button. "Remember our discussion about releasing Scott back to the CBI?" he asked his deputy for personnel. "Issue orders immediately."

For the second time in my career I wondered if I had been right to persist in my efforts to leave my loved ones. When I received my written orders I wondered all the more; I had been detailed from the Army Air Forces to the General Staff Corps, something I had not even known existed. No longer would I wear the tiny silver propellers on gold wings; my new insignia was a large silver star graced with the Great Seal of the United States, the eagle with arrows clutched in one talon and an olive branch in the other. Kitty Rix thought it beautiful, but my heart sank because the orders stated explicitly that I could never fly over enemy lines again.

# 10

# REUNION
# IN CHINA

I moved back into my old room in the little bungalow. Wong Cook prepared some special dishes he remembered I liked while Gunboat unpacked my luggage and made pointed observations about how long I had been away. I knew he liked me and was happy I was back. My restricting orders stayed in my briefcase; I just did not have the nerve to show them to the Old Man. The last thing he needed in China was a member of the General Staff limited to liaison duties only.

General Chennault told me at dinner about a special job he wanted me to do right away. "Scotty," he said, "we're losing lots more planes and pilots strafing rolling stock than we used to when you were here. I don't know why; that's what I want you to find out."

He asked about a rumored new high-altitude strafing technique and I was able to fill him in, having seen it demonstrated at Eglin Field in Florida. From the cockpit of a P-51, a pilot using lines drawn on the tops of his wings could successfully strafe ground targets from altitudes all the way up to 20,000 feet, differently converging lines giving aiming points for different altitudes above ground level.

Just that innocently I violated my orders, an unhappy alternative to the unthinkable—refusing to do what my conscience told me was my duty. Now here I was, two days later, flying a lethal P-51 with all those high-altitude strafing lines to sight along on the upper camber of my wings. My destination was Sian in the Province of Shensi, nearly a thousand miles northeast of Kunming. My targets were trains; would it be enough of an excuse if I blasted them from a relatively safe height?

In my liaison reports, radioed daily to the Air Force Board, I outlined lectures and other noncombat help I was providing to indoctrinate pilots in high-altitude strafing, but carefully omitted any mention of flying over enemy lines. I sent Chennault, on the other hand, full reports detailing fourteen highly productive combat missions.

For two entire weeks I just forgot my written orders; they did not exist. Every day I had different eager volunteers flying my wings as we covered the rail lines of Eastern China from Sian across the Wei and Yellow rivers, then up past Taiyuan all the way to Tatung. We had success damaging the enemy's critically needed locomotives, and all without receiving a single hit in any of our aircraft.

One day in the second week, we were searching the rails just north of Tatung from 20,000 feet when I suddenly saw the Great Wall. Solid masonry, blue-gray in color, evenly spaced lookout towers—there was no mistaking it. I was seeing in my mind's eye that never-to-be-forgotten photograph in a 1923 *National Geographic* that had so fascinated me as a boy. The Wall below us now ran close by the railroad for miles before curving off eastward to climb the mountains and disappear like a writhing gray serpent.

We followed the Great Wall westward for nearly a hundred miles until, just before the Yellow River at a town called Lao-ying, the ruins ended as abruptly as if they had been washed away in some great flood. I circled Lao-ying on my map and we turned south with the river, heading for Sian.

Long before I cut my engine at the refueling truck I knew trouble had arrived. There was a C-47 parked in front of Operations, a staff plane out of New Delhi. Then I caught sight of an officer, a major wearing General Staff insignia. He must have been waiting quite some time and was obviously impatient, so I decided to get it over with and talk to him before I debriefed my wingmen.

When we had left the refueling crew and found a quiet area, he unlocked his briefcase and passed me a communication classified in a category I had heard of but never seen: EYES ONLY. I had heard that such messages were big trouble, and this one was no exception.

HEADQUARTERS, USAAF
WASHINGTON, D.C.

ARNOLD TO SCOTT: YOU WERE ORDERED CHINA OPERATE LIAISON CAPACITY ONLY STOP REPEAT LIAISON ONLY BETWEEN AIR FORCE BOARD AND FOURTEENTH AIR FORCE STOP YOUR COMPLETE DISRE-GARD MY INSTRUCTIONS MOST EVIDENT ACCOUNT MULTIPLE COM-BAT REPORTS CERTIFIED YOUR SIGNATURE XXXX LIAISON DUTY REVOKED STOP XXXX REPORT THIS HEADQUARTERS IMMEDIATE RE-CEIPT THIS MESSAGE XXXX SIGNED ARNOLD.

I completed my debriefing before packing up and flying back to Kunming, not nearly as worried as I should have been. Surely General Chennault would bail me out with Hap Arnold. I knew I should have shown the Old Man my orders two weeks earlier, but even at that, he had always gone to bat for me.

As I rolled out on landing at Kunming, I saw Chennault's staff car. It followed me and caught up in the parking area. Looking down from the cockpit, I could tell I was not in for a fatherly greeting—the Old Man's granite jaw was too square. He just held the car door open and waited as I shut down, dropped to the ground, and climbed in beside him. We drove to his office with not a word being exchanged. It was easy to tell that the rumor grapevine had already told him about the "eyes only" letter.

Chennault had been a schoolteacher once and could read a page of type faster than anybody I ever saw. He glanced at both Arnold's communication—I suppose I violated the "eyes only" classification but I was caught in the middle and had no choice—and my original orders. His black eyes looked me up and down over the top of his glasses.

"You finally made it back out here but you've turned into a VIP." He let that sink in a moment. "Hell, Scott, we're still fighting a poor man's war out here at the end of the line. I don't need any

General Staff big shots with highfalutin titles, and I always despised the word *liaison*. I needed you back here as you were, just as I needed that strafing technique you brought back and put to use. I still need aircraft and men, gasoline and armaments. What I don't need is one more noncombatant!"

There was much I wanted to say but I knew it was not the time to interrupt.

"Cushy jobs on the home front and publicity change men fast. And that liaison—when a soldier becomes a VIP too important to be spared to fight, then I have no place for him out here. So you go back home to Hap Arnold and keep making speeches and movies for him. Stay on the General Staff. I don't want you in China!"

There was a knot in my stomach as I packed my bag and hurried off to Operations to see about an ATC flight, feeling I had just lost my last friend in the military profession. I would have lost him anyway had I not flown those recent missions, and General Arnold would not now have any reason to court-martial me. When Chennault caught up with me I was really down in the dumps, and I might have tried to avoid another meeting, only I saw a trace of his old smile. He led me over to the shade of the P-51 I had flown, and, assuming the spot he always liked on top of the left tire, he motioned for me to drop down to the ground in front of him. It brought back poignant memories of his schooling in air tactics earlier in the war.

"Scotty, I'm sorry for taking my frustrations out on you," he apologized. "My temper has been getting shorter and shorter these last few months. After you left I read your orders again and I understand. I still have all the VIPs I want, but I remember you telling me your first night back about those new Navy rockets— HVARs, you called them. Then in your combat reports you kept saying that what we really needed out here for those locomotives was those HVARs. Here's what I wish you'd do, since you have to go back anyway and have it out with Hap Arnold: After you've smoothed things over—and I'll help you—bring me back those rockets."

I was beginning to come to life again. "Yes, sir!"

"Get me those rockets, no matter if they are Navy, I don't care how. In the meantime, I will radio Arnold and say you showed me your liaison orders but I thought it imperative you show me that high-altitude strafing in the interests of saving young pilots' lives. I will accept blame for sending you to Sian. You go use that fancy title of yours and get me not only rockets but pilots trained to use them!"

Scrounging that new breed of aerial hardware, the pride of another service, turned out to be a tremendous problem. I butted my head against walls at the Pentagon until I began to feel I was a leper. I was fortunate not to have to face General Arnold, who was out of the country to attend some global meeting about the overall conduct of the war, but I was also denied any possible assistance he might have lent me.

Left to my own resources, I started with the direct approach and put in a requisition for HVARs—high-velocity aircraft rockets—for the China Theater. When the appropriate staff officers discovered that those initials stood for new Navy rockets, I was laughed at, so I tried elsewhere. It turned out there were countless offices for allocating equipment to combat theaters in the Pentagon maelstrom, all known by initials, most of which I have forgotten and never want to hear again. The worst was OPD, the Office of Production and Distribution, headed by a major general who was no friend of Chennault. He took particular delight in turning me down.

After one week and no progress, I had ordered a double something-or-other at a bar when someone tapped me on the shoulder. There stood Commander Joe Clifton of Paducah, Kentucky, fellow ace and well-known commander of Fighting 12 on the aircraft carrier *Lexington*. We sat down and had a couple, which broke the ice for some tall tales. When I admitted my utter failure to obtain HVARs, he jumped to his feet in his excitement. It was easy to see how he had been given the nickname Jumping Joe at Annapolis.

"Come on," he said, "we'll see my boss. If anybody can get you some Navy HVARs, he can!"

"That's mighty good of you, Joe," I said, sadly shaking my head, "but your boss can't help me if the whole Pentagon has already turned me down. I've been laughed at by every general in procurement."

Jumping Joe jammed my service cap on my head. We paid for our drinks and by bodily force he pulled me away from the Statler bar.

"Old son," he said, hurrying me, "my boss is not just an admiral; he's *the* admiral, and more than that he's a fighter pilot first, last, and always."

That was how I came to meet Admiral Marc Mitscher, deputy chief, Operations for Air, U.S. Navy. He was dressing for a party and in a hurry but he heard what I had to say, seeming to know all about what was going on in China, although his questions had nothing to do with Chennault and the rockets. I waited for him to return to the subject as he adjusted his bow tie but we left the room and descended on the elevator to the lobby without his saying another word. We walked to an underground driveway where chauffeurs waited with official cars, and he climbed in, my friend Joe behind him. I was coming to conclude that HVARs were unattainable but felt I had to make one last effort.

"Admiral," I shouted at his closed window, "if I don't get those rockets I can never look General Chennault in the eye again."

He rolled down his window. "How many HVARs are you needing?"

Good lord! I was not ready for that one, had not even thought that far ahead. But I had learned one cardinal rule in the military, way back in Panama: When you ask for anything—airplanes, ammunition, gasoline—always requisition more than you need. Then, when whoever you ask trims that down, you still have enough.

"Five thousand, sir."

"How about a hundred thousand, Colonel? That's a good round number. The war in Europe is winding down and I just happen to know where there are that many five-inch high-velocity aircraft rockets that will soon be surplus. I thought of them as soon as I heard your story. Better they go to Chennault than be given the deep six in the Adriatic. Only one thing. You will have to figure out how to get them from Bari to China."

He shook my hand and wished me luck. I got right on the problem of transportation, utterly determined to keep my promise to my old boss. A single rocket in its wooden box weighed eighty pounds; a hundred thousand weighed eight million. I had a tiger by the tail, especially as space across the Hump into India and China was at a premium. My greatest concern was that "going-by-the-book" general in the Pentagon, already alerted, who would undoubtedly not take kindly to a colonel having a hundred thousand aircraft rockets he obtained outside of regular channels. Delivery of my four thousand tons, therefore, had to be clandestine.

Although I could not bother Admiral Mitscher again, I could call upon my brother ace Joe Clifton. Navy vessels were moving war matériels from Italy to where the war still had to be won against Japan; with Joe's help, each of those ships would take aboard a few thousand pounds of "ballast" at Bari. While "Project Transportation of Munitions" was in progress, I learned that General Chennault's request for a team of fighter pilots trained in rocketry had been approved by Hap Arnold. I was given authority to contact air bases for volunteers, and in one morning I found the twelve I needed—including my friend Major Dallas Clinger—at Richmond, Virginia. Dallas, one of the best of the eager young lieutenants when the 23rd Fighter Group came into being, became my operations officer.

All of us flew our new P-51D-30s to Foster Field, Victoria, Texas, where we qualified in rocketry. That left only the problem of ferrying our tons of rockets over the Hump once the surface vessels delivered them to Calcutta. But again I have to say the Lord provided a way, and he did it through Chennault's friend General Hal George.

My challenge in logistics turned out to be simpler than I had expected. During a lunch near his office at Gravelly Point on the Potomac River, General George—who was head of the Air Transport Command—made me a proposition. If I would take my rocket team to his ATC Transition School at Nashville, Tennessee, where all us fighter pilots would be taught to fly the new Douglas C-54G, he would then allow us to deliver twelve of these big transports— military versions of the four-engined DC-4 airliner—to Calcutta.

This we did, landing at Dum Dum Field on the Hooghly River where we used the C-54Gs to fly our rockets over the Hump before turning them back to the Air Transport Command. General George was undoubtedly pleased that we flew the entire distance without incident.

Chennault's eyes lit up when he watched the crews unloading all those pine boxes of Navy rockets. I had already ordered launching rails mounted under the wings of several P-51s and I conducted a briefing in front of a Mustang loaded with eight HVARs. Whereas both the old Army 4.5-inch rocket we already knew, and the Navy 5-inch HVAR were carried under the wings, the former was launched from an open tube like a trench mortar, and unfortunately it had only about the same trajectory and accuracy as a mortar too. The HVAR, in contrast, required no tube but was suspended by two lugs on a launcher so short it was called a "zero rail." All the pilot had to do was aim his aircraft at the target, select his rocket, set the fuse to explode on contact or with delay, and press the release button on his control stick. The rocket dropped free, and when it was a safe distance from the aircraft, it ignited automatically and was gone with a whoosh! And not with the relatively slow speed of the 4.5; the HVAR had the flat trajectory of a rifle bullet and about the same speed. Its warhead carried more than eight pounds of TNT. Locomotives strafed with .50-caliber machine-gun bullets were quickly fixed, but those hit with an HVAR never ran again.

By the time I had finished my briefing the Old Man had the gleam back in his eyes and I knew I was back in his good graces. I can be proud of myself these more than forty years later for scrounging those Navy rockets and transporting them all the way to China. Dallas Clinger and I led the rocket team to Sian, where a supply of rockets and our armament crews had already been flown in two C-54s. Using it as a base for training Chennault's pilots, we had within a week accounted for so many locomotives that the enemy was forced to run his trains only at night. We then used the great range of the P-51 to catch them ever farther north, on the main line along the shores of the Yellow Sea as far away as Tangshan. Hardly realizing it, I was moving ever closer to where the Great Wall of China met the coastline.

After one mission we returned to Sian to refuel and found orders from Chennault directing us to deploy the rocket team with eight P-51s to escort a flight of Boeing B-29s. They were flying out of Chengtu to attack a steel mill at Antung, almost to the Yalu River in Korea. The operation was a success, though we did not get to try our rockets against enemy aircraft as we had hoped.

No sooner had the Superforts completed their mission than I said good-bye and broke off with the Mustangs in a long, slanting dive over the wide triangular peninsula that jutted into the Yellow Sea below Antung. It was a hundred miles long, followed by two hundred miles of iridescent blue water; I could see to infinity that day.

As we headed toward Sian for fuel, I altered course slightly to Tangshan, hoping to find more locomotives. Tangshan lay dead ahead. Then, as a minute passed I caught myself unconsciously altering course to the right and north, so much so that I became angry at my inability to concentrate. My Mustang seemed to have a mind of its own and it persisted in taking a heading that would lead us directly over Peking.

What was the matter with me? Surely I realized the hazards of flying over that occupied capital in 1944? Japanese antiaircraft would be alerted and waiting. The only thing to do was aim straight for Sian and pass safely south of there. Yet no matter how I tried, each time I checked my compass bearing I caught myself angling farther north.

In that battle with myself we crossed the Yellow Sea to a section designated on my map as the Gulf of Bo Hai. We came downhill flat out from 20,000 feet in a fuel-saving dive, close enough to the sound barrier that our ailerons buzzed and our control sticks quivered in our hands. I sat there as relaxed as possible, enjoying the most satisfying time a fighter pilot has on an escort mission—returning to base with no holes in his airplane.

Just as the more turbulent air of lower altitudes commenced to play with the P-51, I began to distinguish the shoreline ahead. To the south was the big seaport of Chinwangtao; directly before my fighter's nose was a most spectacular piece of geography which stood out above everything. I glanced at my compass for the nth time and sure enough, I had edged still farther north. At six miles a minute that landmark was growing fast. By then we were barely skimming the surface of the Gulf of Bo Hai, closing in with the beach. That was when I recognized it—the promontory of *Old Dragon Head*.

Our course would now take us north of Peking, which would

be just as safe as passing to the south. But the more I tried to figure out how I had drifted that far off course, the more I realized such an error could not have been accidental. Some mystic force—far more than vagrant winds or erratic pilotage—had influenced me in reaching that special point on the east coast of China, because we had made landfall just where the Great Wall finally meets the Yellow Sea.

By that time we were so close I had to pull up to miss Old Dragon Head, and the sound of our engines must have carried all the way to Chinwangtao. Our shadows flashed in echelon off weathered masonry that had been there since before the birth of Christ. I hesitate to say that I was not aware the Great Wall was there; most of my life I had known it terminated in the Yellow Sea and lately I had been studying that coastline like a book. That afternoon, though, I was still surprised at what met my eyes as we topped the promontory. Is there not a possibility that it was some part of the Master Plan?

At first it was just a narrow path of reddish earth between grain fields, bordered by eucalyptus trees and low bushes. Before I could feel disappointment we had closed the two or three miles to the north end of a town—Shanhaikwan, my map said—with a striking masonry tower that had a gate passing through it. At our closing speed it came at me fast, and strange figures beneath the wide Oriental eaves grew rapidly into Chinese characters, five of them. I touched my trigger button and let my gun camera record them for later interpretation.

The Wall became much less ruined as we topped a crest some fifteen hundred feet higher than the beaches, perhaps ten miles west of Shanhaikwan. There stretched before us endless miles of stone Great Wall, its condition improving as we entered rough, desolate terrain. Practically in ecstasy I followed its dips and curves, between saddles and over ridges, topping each crest to find ever more Wall beckoning our eager Mustangs.

I waggled my wings at the abandoned lookout towers and, stalking boyhood dreams, I zigzagged from one to the other as though they were pylons. They were equally spaced, roughly two arrow-shots apart, just as I had read. Somewhere down there would be the spot where that Chinese boy had led his three camels in the photograph that had so thrilled me as a fifteen-year-old Boy Scout; I more than half expected to see caravans making their way alongside the Great Wall now.

My shadow flowed effortlessly beneath me to dive headlong into each new green valley, mesmerizing me as we chased the sun at 350 miles per hour along an endless ribbon of ancient stone. As it explored each undulation in the mountainous terrain, my P-51 silhouette silently shared my jubilation. I must have unconsciously pressed the mike button on the throttle because I heard the words I spoke repeated electronically in my headset.

"Thank you, Lord. Thank you for guiding me here. But please, Lord, grant that I may return someday and walk down there where my shadow walks."

And so, forgetting even the war, I let the Great Wall of China take us five hundred miles on the most fascinating flight in my memory. Had the first emperor of China, Ch'in Shih Huang-ti, directed his engineers to build that structure down the main street of Peking instead of along the Mongolian border, I would still have followed it. My dream, seen from the air, that afternoon became an obsession and I knew I had to come back. My eyes stayed with the Wall as long as possible after I turned south with the Yellow River to refuel at Sian.

It was a few days before I learned the meaning of those five ancient Mandarin characters which had greeted us from the facade of the tower at Shanhaikwan. As soon as my gun-camera film was processed I had a photographic print made of it. General Chennault studied it for a while and then called his interpreter, and even Major Shu had to search through his book of ancient calligraphy to find an answer. The translation, he said, read: THE FIRST GATE IN THE WORLD.

# 11

# Now I Can Go Home Again

I looked down at the crowded deck of the battleship *Missouri* and cranked the canopy of my P-51 open just a slit. Into the slipstream I fed the corner of a Confederate flag that General Chennault had signed a year ago—"just in case you get to Tokyo," he had said. At the cruising speed of the Mustang it soon frayed and the whole corner with his name on it was gone. Almost in tears, I caught myself hoping that some of those threads might settle among the dignitaries gathered for the signing of the surrender documents.

Had I been told to list the ten Americans who did the most to defeat Japan, I would have placed Claire Lee Chennault near the top. Yet on that historic occasion aboard the Mighty Mo, he was not there—had not even been invited. Instead, a whole year before, an era had ended in China when he was relieved and recalled to the ZI. I saluted him in my own way.

He would have laughed; I certainly had a cushy job now. I was named a courier and entrusted with personally delivering the official film footage of the Japanese surrender to the Pentagon. Being assigned to the General Staff Corps had for once worked in my favor, for I was going home the quick way. I traded in my Mustang and became airplane commander of a plush Douglas C-54. Along with an experienced crew, I would carry war correspondents hurrying home to file special stories on the historic scene they had witnessed. We would fly a total of ten thousand miles because we had to land at Wake Island to take aboard some VIPs before proceeding via Hawaii to Travis Field near San Francisco.

No matter how I worked out our schedule, it always came out to our arriving on Saturday. I was not about to spend a weekend in Washington, D.C., waiting for the Pentagon to open up Monday morning, so I worked an alternate course for Orlando, Florida, and found it came out to precisely the same distance. With my GSC insignia and as a member of the Air Force Board, Orlando was headquarters for me, a fact that might help justify my diversion. I had been overseas fourteen months, though, and I could not wait any longer to see Kitty Rix and Robin in Winter Park.

This return had to be the epitome of all my other homecomings. All those cross-country flights and treks by Chevy paled into insignificance compared to flying all the way from Tokyo! It was about time I got to know my daughter, Robin Lee, who was five years old.

It was a wonderful weekend, although the telephone never stopped ringing because photographs of my arrival at San Francisco had made the papers. Monday noon I delivered the cans of film to the Pentagon, where General Auby Strickland let me off the hook for having diverted south; coincidentally, he had been the commandant of student officers at Randolph Field who had never caught me years before when I made my weekend car trips to Georgia.

My first peacetime duty assignment to the Army Air Forces Tactical Air Command lasted less than a year. After a month in cool Bar Harbor, Maine, where we toured the *Missouri* as a family, I took command of Williams Field in Arizona, the first jet fighter school. Even with the most modern fighters to fly, I could not help thinking I was hexed to always wind up in the Training Command. I qualified in the Lockheed P-80 Shooting Star and soon was just as much a time hog as I had been with propeller airplanes.

My one fondest memory of Willie Air Patch was the time I "bombed" the Agricultural Inspection Station at Blythe on the California border. It was a constant frustration to me never to be passed through the station quickly, even when I assured them that I had no fresh fruit, vegetables, corn, or cotton that could spread pests. The straw that broke the camel's back was the time the inspector, after many questions and a superficial examination of my car, suddenly turned to me with a last inspiration.

"Sir," he asked, "do you have any watermelons?"

I sighed as I climbed out of my car to open the still uninspected trunk to prove I had no watermelons, feeling the victim of mindless officialdom. Beyond the fact that hot desert air had now overpowered the rudimentary air-conditoning of my 1948 car, I was irritated that he had not believed the carefully typed statement I had prepared in the forlorn hope of expediting the process.

The sight of a Douglas A-26 Invader on the ramp at Willie gave me the idea. When it came into service at the end of World War II, the Invader had been heavily armed for going in low and fast. Ours, tail number 723, had been stripped of weapons and useless armor-plating so it was feather-light, comparatively speaking; with its two two-thousand-horsepower Pratt & Whitney R-2800 engines, it went like a bat out of hell; with throttles wide open you could sit there and proudly read 375 miles per hour on the deck, even more with the nose slightly depressed.

Major Neil Johnson of Montana, my operations officer in the 3525th Training Wing and one of the greatest pilots I ever met, went with me in search of "munitions." We found what we were looking for at Glendale, Arizona, where we filled two six-by-six trucks with two tons of overripe, oversized, sunburned watermelons. With as much of that load in the bomb bay as would fit, and Captain Carl Hardy from Arkansas enlisted as our bombardier, we were ready.

It is always a thrill, even in the jet age, to start up big radial engines and feel the pull of those thousands of horsepower as you open the throttles. We took off and flew at a proper height over Phoenix and its environs, then descended to hug the ground to our target. The nose was down, airspeed 400 miles per hour, altimeter at zero, the tops of saguaro cacti above our wingtips on both sides as we headed for the impact zone beside the station. I counted out loud as I had when I was dropping honeydews for dive-bombing practice before the war. At the right instant I yelled: "Open the doors!"

From no more than ten feet of altitude, more than a ton of

watermelons dropped in a short parabolic arc to the desert floor fifty yards from the Ag Station, close enough to get the message across but far enough away so as not to risk life or limb of any living thing.

"Right on target," I heard Neil cry. "I never saw such a splash!"

When a solid year had passed, I drove once more through the checkpoint at Blythe. The inspector noticed my uniform as I stepped out to open my trunk.

"Colonel," he said, "one of your boys really worked us over just about this time last year."

He pointed and I gasped, because there before my eyes was the most verdant growth I had ever seen. Watermelon vines vied with one another for space over an acre or two, all the way down to the river. The inspector told me that the biggest melon he had ever seen had bounced through the WELCOME TO CALIFORNIA sign, knocking out the middle word. I stood there shaking my head at his story, my insides fairly quivering, I wanted to laugh so much.

"Did you get the number of that airplane?" I asked, voicing the question that had haunted me for a year.

"Number? Hell's fire, Colonel, that guy was flying so fast and so low, we ain't decided yet what kind of plane it was! In fact, we don't even know if it was one of ours!"


After three years at Williams Air Force Base, I was ordered to take command of the 36th Fighter/Bomber Wing at Fürstenfeldbruck, Germany. There was to be a going-away party at the Officers Club at Willie the last Friday we were there, given primarily in Kitty Rix's honor because of her hard work as president of the Officers' Wives Club. Unfortunately, as time drew close for the event, she was furious with me, madder than I had ever seen her in our fifteen years of marriage.

We had planned to drive to New York together in our new car for the departure to Europe, but a week beforehand I had arbitrarily announced that she and Robin were to take the train and leave me to drive alone. All my attempts to apologize or explain only left her more upset; she was convinced that I was simply getting her and Robin out of the way, that there was finally another woman in my life.

I did not have any ulterior motive. Of course there was no other woman and I did not want to make that long drive alone, but I had recently awakened in a cold sweat from a nightmare about a terrible car accident. We had all three been driving together when I collided with something, some irresistible force, and had been thrown from the car. Bleeding badly, I had crawled around the scene searching in vain for Kitty Rix and Robin. It kept coming back as a premonition but I could not tell her about it because she would either worry or think I was making another excuse.

The night before the party I pulled out my new Air Force uniform. It was 1949 and we had just become a separate service, trading in our old Army khaki for blue. Kitty Rix stood near me in a black sequin dress, beautiful and, rightfully, still angry.

"Scotty, if I were you I wouldn't dress up in that pretty new suit," she said. "You should go to the party as that ape you are always talking about, the one who became a full colonel!"

She was referring to a story I had told for years, one she always managed to laugh at however sick she must have been of hearing it. It was about a lieutenant in a quiet part of Africa during the war who makes friends with an ape, eventually escaping hot and boring alerts by training it to sit in his P-40 wearing a helmet and goggles. The punch line centers on the animal's meteoric success in military life after accidentally being scrambled with the other fighters.

Several times I almost said, "Okay, honey, you win," but something would not let me. So I took another kind of action, flying my T-33 over to Burbank the next afternoon, where I visited Western Costume. They rented me an ape suit and even sewed extra-large colonel's insignia onto the shoulders for me.

Kitty Rix was just apologizing for my having apparently been delayed when I entered. Seeing a gorilla walk in with a parachute draped over his shoulder absolutely broke up the party, with my wife laughing the hardest of all in her contagious way. Glory be, she even ran up and kissed the thick black lips of the ape head I had on. We were still laughing when we got home, and there was no longer any tiny hint that she was irked at me for not driving the three of us to New York.

What had been a premonition became reality. I had been extra vigilant every mile of the three-day drive, when there burst from a side road in the woods to my right a yellow-and-red cement truck. I braced my arms to keep the wheel from slamming with deadly force into my chest, but the side impact flung my left arm behind my back and through the glass of the right door. Blood from the lacerations was the least of my worries; both hips had been twisted out of the seat and my right one had caved in the steel glove compartment, shattering my pelvis as it did so. My first breath told me about my fractured ribs. I got out of the car and gathered up jumbled Christmas presents from the road to lock them in the trunk, knowing I might soon pass out. I almost laughed despite the ribs because I knew my loved ones were all right.

The accident happened on U.S. Highway 80 a few miles northeast of Columbus, Georgia. I was taken to the nearby Army hospital at Fort Benning, where I awoke the next morning to find myself encased from chest to knees in a body cast. The doctor explained that my right pelvis was badly fractured, and since I was over forty, healing would be a very slow process. When he stated matter-of-factly that I would be in the cast for nine months, it slowly penetrated my numbed brain what that meant—flat on my back, cemented in for an eternity.

"Doctor," I finally said, "I've never been sick in bed in my life. I couldn't live like this for nine days, much less nine months!"

"Well, Colonel," he stated sympathetically, "you're here. What can you do about it?"

My brother came to visit first and showed me a copy of the Macon Telegraph. FLYING TIGER FINALLY DOWNED BY CEMENT TRUCK, it said. While he was there, a call came in from New York. It was Kitty Rix. I tried to convince her I was all right and tell her not to come down right away, but she calmly told me she was flying down that day.

When I woke up again Kitty Rix was talking to the doctor. She was seeing me as I had never wanted her to see me—helpless. It was her, all right, but a far different woman from the little girl I had married all those years before. She had taken charge of my recovery and was telling the chief of orthopedics that I had to be freed from the cast no matter what; between the atrophy of muscles and the psychological costs, it would do more harm than good. I lay there listening to my little wife argue with that doctor very politely, rebutting every argument he tried. She knew about osteoblasts and osteoclasts and calcification; better still, she knew her husband and she told him that such restraint would kill me.

I awoke to find myself in traction and free of the cast. Kitty Rix smiled at me from the foot of the bed and I smiled back despite the pain, giving her the thumbs-up. She came around and kissed me, then told me that no matter how it hurt I had to keep moving regularly to bring blood to the healing areas—she had promised the doctor. With her in absolute command, we began a program of chinning a bar over my bed at frequent intervals. Once I laughed so hard my fractured ribs were in agony; the doctor came in and asked my relentless angel-turned-martinet how her patient was. He addressed her as "doctor."

That crash with the cement truck was the start of a new life for us. For the first time I was dependent on Kitty Rix and she was there, the driving force. We worked so hard together that I was sweating up my pajamas and had to have fresh ones sometimes twice a day. We also began exercising my leg at night, possibly because the doctor might not have approved. With each periodic X-ray, he was surprised at the amount of mending he found.

In one month instead of nine, Kitty Rix had me out of traction and into a wheelchair. Then she became my pilot, pushing me down the hall and working with me at physical therapy—all kinds of exercise machines, weights and pulleys, and a whirlpool hot bath for my injured leg. How we worked on the recovery of my muscles! On the thirty-seventh day, the chief of orthopedics arrived with old-fashioned wooden crutches; Kitty Rix again took charge, convincing him that I needed the more modern aluminum ones that braced against the wrists. I was now free of the wheelchair, and before too long of the hospital itself.

About that time the lawyers arrived representing the company that owned the cement truck that had hit me when it ran the stop on Highway 80. They brought me the keys and title to a new car like the one I had totaled, and a check as compensation for the injuries I had received. From them I learned that the truck was bound for LaGrange. If I had traveled by the other route to Macon, through LaGrange and avoiding Columbus, our paths would still have crossed and he would have had another chance at me. Was it all in the cards no matter what?

# 12

# LIFE AT
# THE WORLD'S BEST
# AIR BASE

As commander of the 36th Fighter/Bomber Wing, I had all Europe, Africa, and Asia at my fingertips. Flying a jet fighter was like riding that mythical magic carpet, soothed by the whispering sound of the turbine thrusting you along at six hundred miles per hour. All my life I had dreamed of the far horizons; now they drifted effortlessly beneath. And to think I was paid to do all this!

Quarters at Fürstenfeldbruck were exceptional, all in a heavy Bavarian style of architecture. We lived in a great limestone block-house it was rumored Adolf Hitler had built for Hermann Goering. Next door was the Officers Club, spectacular in size, with *Bier Keller* areas downstairs where fighter pilots assembled to drink beer and sing flying ballads—just as Luftwaffe *Jagdflieger* had done not so very many years before. Impressive too was the *Kaserne* that housed my men, five thousand of them in the single long barracks. Beneath that structure the Germans had excavated an underground firing range in order that weapons training might proceed the whole year. Patton's Third Army had overrun Fürstenfeldbruck before any destruction could be carried out, so my seventy-five Republic F-84E Thunderjets with diagonal blue stripes on their tails made good use of the massive ten-thousand-foot runway.

We were way down south near Munich and everybody seemed

to come to Fursty before traveling elsewhere among the beauties of Bavaria. The base was near the Dolomite Alps and Garmisch-Partenkirchen, and visitors included just about all the NATO high brass right up to General Dwight Eisenhower. He would arrive in his special aircraft, *Columbine,* along with Mamie and her mother, Mrs. Doud. He went fishing as often as possible so I made sure he was guided to the best trout streams in Bavaria, even if I had to pilot him there myself.

"Ike" was a five-star general and I was only a colonel, so I naturally never did get that close. Not so Kitty Rix; she just never met a stranger and was soon close to anyone she met. They were all good friends quite soon, which might have had something to do with how many times they came back.

My F-84, serial number 2299, acquired so many flight hours that two crew chiefs were assigned. Records show that I flew it one thousand hours in 1952, a record that made the *Stars and Stripes* as well as the Paris edition of the *New York Herald Tribune* on May 18, 1953, partly because it was the first time a J65 jet engine—the "bomb with a short fuse"—had run that long without a serious problem. The distance I covered was well over half a million miles.

To keep the crew chiefs on their toes, I also regularly flew any one of the other F-84s. My total for the three years we were at Fürstenfeldbruck certainly climbed over a million miles, providing the basis for my book *Boring a Hole in the Sky.* My very extensive flying also worked to counter a mistrust of the F-84E, a "dog" in the parlance of the pilots who knew its J65 engine would malfunction at the slightest provocation—even explode. The usual cause was an often catastrophic failure in the compressor section known as "corn-cobbing," in which one blade would break off from a wide shaft spinning at 13,500 rpm and wreak havoc with the remaining ninety-five. What remained of the rotor shaft, if you made it back to base, resembled a badly gnawed ear of tungsten-steel corn—you had to see such a thing to appreciate.

The 36th had lost seventeen aircraft and several pilots when I arrived at Fursty, so as a wing commander who loved to fly—and hated desk jobs with a passion—I vowed to log more hours than anyone else. Young pilots with no choice but to fly these troubled jet

Robert Lee Scott, Jr., aged four. Photograph taken in 1912.

Graduation leave from West Point,
summer 1932. Photograph taken below
Mount Ararat in eastern Turkey, halfway through a
14,000-mile motorcycle tour of Europe and
Asia, partway along the trail
of Marco Polo.

Learning to fly at
Randolph Field, San Antonio, 1932.

Lieutenant Scott
at the controls of his first pursuit plane,
a Curtiss P-1 Hawk.

Wedding day,
West Point Chapel, September 1, 1934.

U.S. ARMY AIR CORPS

In front of Curtiss P-40K Warhawk
*Old Exterminator.*

U.S. ARMY AIR CORPS

In *Old Exterminator,*
Kunming Airdrome at Christmastime 1942.

Bob Scott's fifth victory,
making him an ace, was this Kawasaki Ki-48
Lily light bomber.

Colonel Scott helps his
armorer and crew chief load three of his
P-40s six .50-caliber machine guns.

PHOTO COURTESY OF CURTISS-WRIGHT CORPORATION

"The only office I ever liked . . ."

With Chennault during
briefing for a mission all the way to
Hong Kong and back.

PHOTO COURTESY OF CURTISS-WRIGHT CORPORATION

Just back from
combat in China, February 1943.

PHOTO COURTESY OF CURTISS-WRIGHT CORPORATION

A new kind of combat:
speech before Curtiss-Wright workers in Buffalo,
where P-40s were made.

© 1987 WARNER BROS. INC. ALL RIGHTS RESERVED.

Demonstrating to Dennis Morgan
how fighter pilots talk with their hands,
to the amusement of Kitty Rix. Andrea King, who
played her in the movie, stands beside her screen husband,
who wears Bob Scott's leather A-2
jacket for added realism.

With my P-51H at Willie Field,
1949; a fun change of pace from jet training.

VICTOR MILNER, JR.

Bob Scott flies high over Bavaria, 1951.
His Republic F-84E Thunderjet #2299 carries special
Flying Tiger insignia designed for him by
Walt Disney, at the request of film
comedian Joe E. Brown.

U.S. AIR FORCE

The proud commander of
Fürstenfeldbruck Air Force Base, Germany,
prepares to climb aboard *Old 2299*. Scott flew
this F-84 a record 1,000 hours in
a single year.

Catherine Scott,
"Kitty Rix," 1949.

HILLYER C. WARLICK

U.S. AIR FORCE

"Back to my beloved fighters . . ."
In command of Luke Air Force Base, Arizona, 1956.

Abdullah Allazhan
and his grandson Yakub.

From fighter planes to camels:
at Jiayuguan's Tower Fortress, western terminus
of the Great Wall of China.

Running the top
of the rammed-earth Wall.

A lookout tower
along the Great Wall.

A lifelong dream is realized:
Bob Scott, aged seventy-two, stands at the eastern tip of
China's Great Wall in the fall of 1980.

U.S. AIR FORCE

Just before
takeoff in an F-16 Falcon, July 19, 1984.

fighters began to feel better about their job soon after I undertook the contest to fly my 2299 more than any other F-84. I was heartened to hear from the chaplain that they were writing home saying not to worry, telling about how the "Old Man" trusted the "Thud" so much he was the biggest time hog of all. Flying requirements were still four hours per month, which I contend to this day is insufficient to maintain proficiency in any aircraft.

Our primary mission in the occupation of Germany was to show the flag to our adversaries from the Soviet Union. The 36th was one of two fighter wings charged with patroling the area between West Germany and the Iron Curtain. Two of my fighters were shot down west of the Bohemian forest on our side of the lines. Such violations ceased immediately after I gave orders to my pilots to open fire as soon as any Soviet-bloc aircraft pointed its nose at them.

Those hostile lines were a mere seven minutes by jet from the runway Hitler had built us. Fürstenfeldbruck was like the hub of a great wheel whose spokes radiated out to points vital to NATO. Kastrup Field at Copenhagen was 550 miles north, Paris was west, and Rome south—all less than an hour by F-84. The three tactical fighter squadrons in my wing were supposed to be combat-ready. With that in mind, I dispatched each squadron in turn to gunnery training for a week at our target range, Wheelus Field, Tripoli. That meant flying across the Alps, over Rome, past Capri, and on past the island of Malta all the way across the Mediterranean Sea to Africa, a distance of 1,200 miles which the F-84 made in about two hours at 40,000 feet.

One unexpected responsibility took me to the Eternal City. I was to fly Francis Cardinal Spellman from Fursty to Rome—and me just a Baptist. A high honor but what would I have done without all the confidence in flying that my many hours brought? I indoctrinated the smiling, very sharp, slightly plump wearer of the red hat and the archbishop's cross in the use of the ejection seat and oxygen mask for our flight at 40,000 feet. All I could think about was: Oh, Lord, let that engine run and run. I flew him five hundred miles over the Alps into Italy, diving low across the Vatican gardens and carrying on a conversation over the intercom. The landing at Guidonia, the Italian Air Force field, was as careful as if I had a crate of eggs aboard. When I taxied in, there was a traffic jam of the longest black Cadillac limousines I could imagine.

When the procession reached Saint Peter's, we entered through the Holy Door, open only during Jubilee Years, four times per century; I had read that it was supposed to be the way the first Pope, Peter the Rock, had entered. I hesitated behind that procession of monsignors, bishops, and priests, but His Eminence, Cardinal Spellman, looked back and beckoned.

"Come on, Bob, through this door, this way. Part of the ceremony is for you."

That was how I came to meet the Holy Father that day in 1950 and receive my first papal blessing from Pius XII, who signed himself Eugenio Pacelli on a photograph I have framed. All that for being the wing commander of Fürstenfeldbruck and the pilot of a cardinal who wanted to fly to the Vatican.

The USAF jet aerobatic team known as the Skyblazers, part of my 36th F/B Wing, performed all over Europe for the NATO countries. It was a welcome reunion to have them with me because they had been part of my earlier command at Williams Field, Arizona. They had been known as the Acrojets then and would eventually evolve into the Thunderbirds. I flew to their demonstrations with them, usually in their spare plane. After the Skyblazers put on a show for the Italians in Venice, Major Vic Milner and I decided to take a gondola tour. Vic, my wing operations officer, bribed our gondolier with a dollar to let him take over and he propelled us briskly along with long sweeps. He evidently exceeded the speed limit, and as we turned a corner into the Grand Canal we promptly collided with another gondola. The other vessel had black curtains rolled down so that only the gondolier was visible. I saw the very large flowing letters $R_x$ embroidered in gold adorning the curtain, and gasped at the possible consequences—they signified royalty.

As the gondoliers chattered away in Venetian dialect, very much upset, the curtain rolled up and there sat a beautiful lady who I soon discovered was the Queen of Greece. Both Vic and I were doing our best to apologize when to our utmost relief she laughed and said in perfect English that no one was hurt; we were pardoned.

Then she asked if I were not the American officer in charge of the famous jet aerobatic team she had seen perform at the Lido that day. I no sooner said "Yes, ma'am" than she wanted to know if—were her husband to make a request of General Eisenhower—we would bring our wonderful fliers to her country? All because of that collision, I was able to bore another hole in the sky to Athens and fly over the Plain of Marathon.

In NATO war games I worked with the Norwegian Air Force as far north as Hammerfest, surely the most northern city in the world. I represented General Norstad, the USAFE commander, on a visit to the Chief Sultan Haj El Glouii near Marrakech, Morocco; Norstad also sent me to Madrid and other places, the farthest being Erzurum all the way across Turkey almost to Mount Ararat, where I had ridden that motorcycle nearly twenty years before on the trail of Marco Polo. Then there was the flight of two F-84s I led all over Africa, to which General Dean C. Strother had agreed in a weak moment. My premise for the extended tour was the firm belief that when the last great battle of the world was fought—Armageddon—it would be in the air over Africa, where man apparently began. With Vic Milner on my wing, we covered twenty-eight African countries.

Orders came to move the 36th Fighter/Bomber Wing two hundred miles north to a newly constructed air base at Bitburg. We were sorry after three years to leave Fursty, which *Flying* magazine writer and publisher Gill Robb Wilson christened "The World's Best Air Base" in an article by that title. Everybody learned where Fürstenfeldbruck is during the 1972 Olympics, when terrorists assassinated Israeli athletes right next to my old base of operations. Bitburg, a town in the Eifel Mountains near Luxembourg, became topical in more recent years when President Ronald Reagan visited a military cemetery there as part of his itinerary for a meeting of state with Chancellor Helmut Kohl. The irrational hue and cry following the visit centered on the fact that some of the graves were those of Waffen SS troopers; they can be considered good Nazis now, having been dead for over forty years.

Shortly before we moved to our new base, the chaplain mentioned that his church was ready except that it had no bell. Remembering the famous foundry at Erding down near Fursty, I decided to have a bell cast especially for the base, one with the doubly appropriate words GOD IS MY CO-PILOT cast right around the rim. By the time we settled in, a bell eighteen inches wide, weighing 115 pounds, graced the belfry to ring out a greeting. A GIFT FROM COLONEL AND MRS. BOB SCOTT, CHRISTMAS 1952 is cast on one side, and *GUTE LANDUNGEN ZUR 36TH IN BITBURG* ("Happy Landings to the 36th in Bitburg") adorns the bronze on the other. That bell rang true for heads of state Reagan and Kohl recently; it still rings true over the F-15 Eagles of the current "Fightin' 36th."

# 13

# To the National War College

I arrived with mixed feelings in Washington, D.C., to become a student at the National War College. On the one hand I knew that graduation from this highest of the service institutions was virtually a prerequisite for promotion to flag rank; on the other, I realized it would inevitably lead to assignments at the Pentagon. I shuddered at the memory of my earlier encounters with the "Puzzle Palace," recalling what former Vice President Alben Barkley said about it: "The Pentagon reminds me of a log floating down the river with a million ants hanging on, and every damned one thinks he's steering."

This was the route I would have to go if I was ever to become a general. But wearing that star had never seemed all that important. I loved flying fighters, and not many generals flew even the bare minimum required to receive hazard pay. Some of those who did were mere passengers who never actually flew as first pilot. With all that growing doubt about my ability to live in such a dog-eat-dog environment, I almost came to accept having been a wing commander as the pinnacle of my career. "Please," I asked General Rosie O'Donnell, chief of personnel and formerly a famous

B-17 pilot I had known in China, "send me back to my fighters, anywhere."

He was about to grant my request when something in my 201 File caught his attention. He looked up at me in surprise.

"Bob, do you know who recommended you for the National War College?" I shook my head in genuine puzzlement. "Well, he's right over there in the White House. I guess if General Ike wants you in that school, that's where you had better go!"

So Kitty Rix, Robin, and I found a house in McLean, Virginia, and in 1954, I became a student again. To this day I am glad that I attended and flattered that General Eisenhower remembered me from Fürstenfeldbruck. My class at NWC was a select group of about a hundred, made up of representatives from the various military services as well as the State Department and the Foreign Service. I learned a great deal from my classmates, among them armored corps or infantry colonels, submariners, and naval aviators.

The man I became closest to was a faculty member, Admiral Chester Wood, U.S.N. I was president of the class, not by election but by seniority in date of rank, so Admiral Wood passed all instructions to the students through me. He and I gradually became friends. He seemed to know all about me and obviously considered me highly opinionated; his fatherly advice included trying to temper my "oratory escapades" and advising me to follow military orders without question. Go where those orders led and stop trying to change things. My file had told him of my many requests over the years for assignment to operational fighter units, so he had already guessed my dislike of headquarters. He took the liberty of criticizing me, telling me gently but firmly that a time had come in my military career when I had to show greater maturity if I was ever to serve my country in a higher capacity.

"Keep flying as much as you do," he advised, "but stop talking about it. Each time you launch into one of your colorful stories of what planes you shot down, how high you flew to surmount a weather front, how far you flew in a day, or what it was like over the Hump, I notice an interesting reaction in your classmates. Many don't share your enthusiasm but you persist in reminding those who do that such flying has passed them by. There are people over there in the Pentagon, some very high-ranking, who wish they had done even a fraction as much and they are jealous as hell."

I felt lectured-to that afternoon when we parted but I knew it was all in friendship, and I made up my mind to heed his advice. There was just one thing that bothered me: Did the admiral really think the incidents I recounted were tall tales, or even outright lies? He had certainly implied so, particularly when I mentioned trips I had made to the West Coast and back in one day. It continued to bother me, so I called Admiral Wood that night and invited him to fly to Hamilton Air Force Base in California on Saturday. I knew he had friends there at the nearby Navy base and suggested he talk over old times with them, promising I would have him back home that evening.

He was ready and waiting when I arrived at his redbrick quarters near Fort McNair. We were soon at Andrews Air Force Base, where the crew chief and I indoctrinated him on ejection seat procedures, the oxygen system, and use of the intercom. We talked as we flew and I pointed out landmarks and interesting features as they passed below. With one stop for fuel at Grand Prairie Air Force Base, just south of Kansas City, we were soon at Hamilton. His Annapolis classmates took him to lunch while I supervised the refueling of the T-33 and checked the weather and winds aloft. In an hour we were on our way back east, the jet stream at 40,000 feet shoving us along a lot faster than the near-five-hundred miles per hour registered on the airspeed indicator. Fighter pilots love tail winds, I told him. In less than two hours we were at Tinker AFB near Oklahoma City for fuel—I was showing him another route home—and we touched down at Andrews just before dark.

We had covered nearly five thousand miles in less than ten hours. I was happy because I could make the dance at the Army-Navy Club that Kitty Rix had been counting on; Admiral Wood seemed pleased, having talked all the way, even enjoying my zigzagging the ship every so often so he could see the contrail—almost a rainbow in the sunlight. On the way home from Andrews, though, he did not say much except that his throat felt dry; with all the talking we had done breathing hundred-percent oxygen, that was understandable. I was telling him how much I had enjoyed the day when he shook my hand.

"Bob," he said, "I also enjoyed the experience and I assure you I will never again cast the slightest doubt on one of your tall tales. But, my friend—you have damn near killed me today!"

With those words and a grin I could tell was slightly forced, he walked stiff-legged up the steps into his quarters at Fort McNair.

# 14

# STAY THE HELL AWAY FROM HEADQUARTERS!

Just as predicted, my orders took me across the Potomac to the Pentagon after my graduation from the National War College in 1954. I cringed at the realization but remembered the words of Admiral Wood and vowed to make the best of it. Still, I could not help thinking of the story, possibly apocryphal, of Grand Duke Alexis, a field marshal on the battlefields of Russia at the time of Peter the Great. On his deathbed, the grand duke sent for his favorite grandson, who he hoped would continue the family's tradition of illustrious military service. The young lieutenant leaned forward over the bed and asked, "Grandfather, do you have any advice for me?"

The old man squeezed his hand and with his dying breath replied: "Stay the hell away from headquarters!"

Initially I served in PLANS, USAF as deputy of my West Point classmate General Hunter Harris, but I was very quickly transferred to become director of information in the Office of the Secretary of the Air Force. There the Secretary, Harold Talbott, had me promoted to brigadier general over the loud objections—or so I heard—of one faction within the high command. I began my new duties by writing a pamphlet with the title "A Special Study" and having it distributed throughout the Air Force. It had the approval of General Nathan Twining, chief of staff of the United States Air Force.

There were then two factions within the service, and I was part of the dynamic one. A political shake-up after my first year found me chafing under a far less decisive leadership when Secretary of Defense Charlie Wilson, from General Motors, replaced my boss with somebody he could control far more easily, Donald Quarles of the Bell Laboratories. Where Harold Talbott had been an extrovert and all for positive action vis-à-vis the Soviet Union, Air Force Secretary Quarles was a veritable Mr. Milquetoast.

I was to make a speech at the Commanders Conference at Ramey Air Force Base, Puerto Rico, on January 23, 1956. My talk would not be popular with the new guard but I felt it needed to be said; I practiced for weeks on the delivery, resorting to closing the door and going over and over it in front of the bathroom mirror at home. When the time came for me to begin the conference with a morning talk—worst time of the day—I was more than ready to face those generals and admirals without recourse to notes. I spoke of the U.S.S.R. moving ahead in what I called the struggle for supremacy of space, and I advocated global air power with the Strategic Air Command as the vital instrument of that policy.

Secretary Quarles stood and interrupted me, asserting that by giving such a speech I was promoting interservice rivalries which the Department of Defense, and the White House itself, would not tolerate. "Bob Scott," he began unemotionally, "with his flair for Southern oratory has forced me to reiterate my position on a subject I wanted to avoid at this conference. I disagree that SAC is all the answer to peace. I disagree with the program advocated under the name Peace Through Global Air Power. I further disagree that the Soviets have outdistanced us in space. Gentlemen, what we have heard is more of the war words between the services, and DOD is adamant, as am I, that there be no interservice bickering."

I was on the verge of daring to reply to the Secretary when General Curtis LeMay interrupted. "I want to second what Scott has said," he stated decisively. "He is right that something must be done and the American people must be informed; he is also right that

SAC must remain ready to defend them as it has through ten years of global dominance."

Later, LeMay pulled me aside to say he thought the Secretary would fire me on the spot, but added: "Boy, you did good."

By the time I was back at the Pentagon, I could tell I was not long for my job. Then one day Secretary Quarles asked me at lunch how I would like to be relieved of my current burdens and return to flying fighter planes?

My new command was Luke Field near Phoenix. I left for exile in the Arizona desert with rising spirits and no regrets at leaving the Pentagon behind; I was not made for such work, much less the intrigue I saw all around me, and it certainly had been no answer to my deepest childhood prayer: *Oh, God, make me a fighter pilot. And if it be Thy will, make me an ace.*

# 15

# THE APARTMENT

When I landed at Luke AFB there was a telephone call waiting for me from General Thomas White, the vice-chief of staff. I leaped from the cockpit and hurried into Operations to learn that I was now requested to fly down to Florida and make a speech for Congressman Bob Sikes. It was a moment of truth because I had made up my mind not to make any more of those speeches for the Pentagon; they had been my undoing throughout my career. It shocked me now that Tommy White, a man I idolized, was asking me to give another.

The general emphasized how important the talk would be—Bob Sikes was known as "Mr. Air Force" on Capitol Hill—and suggested I give a talk similar to the one he had heard me deliver at Ramey Field in Puerto Rico. "Be sure to emphasize," he added, "that the Soviets already lead in the space race."

Were they all crazy at headquarters? It was precisely that recent talk at Ramey that had led to my being fired. I respectfully refused to make the speech unless I received written orders directing me to do so.

It was General White's turn to be astounded. Did I not know, he demanded, that the Air Force never *ordered* a general officer to make a speech? When I refused to budge he hung up on me. I never

did make that speech and am still glad I had the stubborn, unmitigated gall to do what I did.

Having hurried in to assume command, I then returned to
Washington, D.C., to help Kitty Rix see to the packing of our
household goods. We were forced to sell our new house at a loss
because of a depressed real estate market; worse still, she had to
leave her friends and even the doctors she trusted. I drove us both to
our exile, and all the way wonderful Kitty Rix, whom I loved above
all else, kept her composure except for an occasional expression of
misery.

"Oh, God," she said when she could stand it no longer, "why
did I have to marry a martyr? And, Scotty, why couldn't you keep
your mouth shut and at least pretend to change when that Mr.
Quarles came in?"

On October 4, 1957, the Soviets placed Sputnik into orbit and
the whole world knew who led in the space race. My former
associates at the Pentagon must have wished I were spinning in orbit
right along with it, because, although I would not make speeches for
them anymore, I had made one at the request of Senator Barry
Goldwater, whom I had known for many years. In it I had specu-
lated on the ominous implications of Sputnik, unaware that the high
command in Washington had placed a strict ban on any such talks.
Mine made the local papers with the dire if inaccurate headline AIR
FORCE GENERAL SAYS SPUTNIK AIMED LIKE SWORD AT HEART OF AMERICA.

When I reached my office at Luke, there was a team of investigators from Air Force Headquarters waiting for me. They listened to
a tape I had of my address and found it completely acceptable, and
they also accepted the fact that I had only that morning received a
copy of the directive forbidding talks about Sputnik. The issue did
not fade away, though; it was all too clear that a case was being
built up against me through the Training Command. People there
had long memories regarding my repeated willful escapes from their
ranks. My club officer reported that investigators were auditing my
account to see if I had entertained visiting dignitaries at government
expense. When it was shown that I had paid with my personal
check, they kept on digging in hopes of finding something else.

Such efforts did not worry me, because my conscience was

clear. Then my crew chief came to my office after being questioned by inspectors general hoping to prove my claims of flying time were fabricated, that I actually took credit for other pilots' hours. I flew off to Washington to enlist General LeMay's help in putting an end to the obviously politically motivated harassment, but the new Secretary of the Air Force, Jim Douglas, persuaded me not to do so. General LeMay was under consideration for the position of chief of staff; my asking him to become involved in such potentially ticklish matters might endanger his chances for the position. Douglas also told me that nothing would be gained by my requesting a court-martial; I might win, but in the long run it would hurt both the Air Force and me. In my heart I knew it was not in Kitty Rix or me to put up with such treatment, particularly the possibility of successive transfers; if three moves are equal in trauma to a fire, then we had long since been burned out.

I hated and despised the word *retirement,* but now the proper time had come for me. I was forty-nine and had been in uniform thirty-six years, from the under-age of fourteen when I became a radio operator for the National Guard, to the time I became a civilian again on October 31, 1957. It was a no-win situation that prompted Kitty Rix to say feelingly, "Damn the Air Force! Double-damn the Training Command!"

At my request there was no ceremony or lineup of troops for my retirement; I would mark the event in my own manner. I found out later that my deputy had already complied with orders from Training Command to station guards around my F-84F, tail number 735, but what he did not know was that I had just flown the day before a new North American F-100 Super Sabre; the wing was soon to be equipped with the first supersonic American fighter. The new machine was fueled and ready for my special use.

At precisely nine the next morning I dove in from the north, down runway twenty-one, indicating Mach 1.1 at as near zero altitude as I could make it, thereby breaking the sound barrier on my last official Air Force flight. What better way to end a career that had started with fabric-covered biplanes?

\* \* \*

We were already looking at houses before I made the momentous decision to retire. We would live in Phoenix and I would write more books; I would also rebuild old military airplanes—"antiques," as they are called today—and keep flying. Arizona's perfect flying weather beckoned as I tried to forget that last fighter with my name on it.

When none of the houses we saw were right, Kitty Rix suggested we look at apartments. Condominiums with no yards to worry about were coming into their own then. Phoenix Towers, the first high-rise in the city, was not yet completed but it was the shade of pink Kitty Rix loved for her summer dresses and it had every modern convenience. When the salesman brought us to the tenth floor and into 10D, I knew we were home. As starkly empty as the concrete floor and bare windows were, Kitty Rix had that gleam in her eyes—I could feel the electricity. From the balcony, Phoenix lay spread out as though viewed from the cockpit of a fighter plane; ten miles away due west, sunlight flashed off windshields and canopies as aircraft of my last command came in to land.

I almost gasped when I first heard the price, but I recoverd quickly and resolved never to let Kitty Rix know the details; she trusted me and I had driven her into exile in the desert. I now realize this decision shows another of my failings, that of not being a complete partner with my wife, but I had never been able to resist making every effort to buy everything she really wanted because she asked for so very little. Luxuries that brought joy to those green eyes became necessities.

There was that first dress I had bought her way back after we were married and moved into that freshly painted house at Mitchel Field. Long Island turned out to be expensive and Garden City worse still, but she had made that simple dress look so pretty, I knew it had been made for her and was there waiting. I had ambled off to open a charge account, wondering how I would pay the bill later. People in military service are particularly pressed to settle charges quickly; should they fail and their bases be called, they have to appear before their commanding officers and the delinquency is noted on their records.

That was how I came to write my first story, one about my near crash in an attack plane when a .30-caliber shell lodged in a rudder cable pulley during gunnery training. *Flying* magazine sent me a check, and while a literary career was not quite born, Kitty Rix's party dress was paid for.

By the time I had signed the deed, I had computed how much extra I had to earn each month. When news of my retirement got out I received a contract from a New York lecture agency; this, then, was how I would pay for our new home. I found out later that Phoenix Towers was filled with oil men, bank presidents, board chairmen, and grocery-chain owners. I was out of my league, but fighter pilots are like that when they try to be civilians.

Right then, neither of us could imagine how many months or years I would have to be away making speeches. I sometimes gave eighty talks in ninety days, and I had done hundreds and hundreds by the end of three years. I also wrote life insurance policies and was so successful I was made a vice-president of a company in Atlanta. To meet those notes every ninety days I even turned to writing more books. I traveled to Africa for one and to Vietnam for another. There I learned the tragic truth about that undeclared war, where well-trained men armed with the most sophisticated weapons were virtually handcuffed by our leaders and not allowed to win.

Kitty Rix loved that apartment but hated the years of waiting alone while I caught up with the mortgage. She would help me pack my bag and go with me to the elevator. I can listen now after all these years and hear her saying, "Oh, Scotty, I understood during the war and even when you were director of information in Washington, but now you have retired. Won't this rat race ever end?"

I could only kiss her good-bye with a heavy heart and head off to Fort Worth, Memphis, Chattanooga, or Miami. Once I made a speech in Rome, Georgia, where I had flown that Berliner-Joyce south to catch a glimpse of her at college; never will I forget the letter that awaited me there, or the lonely verse accompanying her sweetness and understanding:

> *Why so hurried, little man?*
> *Come back to me soon—*
> *Me who loves you,*

*Now withering away*
*In this millionaire's apartment.*

Those interminable ninety-day notes were finally met and it could be said that we lived happily ever after—for a time. Robin Lee went off to Stanford and in a few years married a fine man, and Kitty Rix and I soon had four grandchildren. I continued to lecture at a much more agreeable pace and Kitty Rix sometimes accompanied me. I also went on another safari to Africa. It was at a convention of big-game hunters in the Grand Ballroom of the Beverly Hilton Hotel, Beverly Hills, California, that I took Kitty Rix to her last party.

She was extra-beautiful that evening in a flame-colored dress and clear plastic high heels; gloves and accessories meticulously matching. That night in December 1971, I remember thinking back to my long sorties by car all those years before; how her high heels clicked when she came into the waiting room at Shorter College to find me in my wrinkled flying suit. Now we were sitting talking and exchanging greetings with people we rarely saw, looking from the head table to try to find Robin and son-in-law Bruce in the crowd. All at once Kitty Rix clutched my arm, gasping that she had never felt such a sharp pain in her life—like an electric shock in her right side.

At first we just sat there, our small world closing in, my mind numb because I think I had a premonition from the start. Still, I hoped it was a cramp from the car trip, and would disappear; when it did not go away, I led her to the room outside and sat her down in a big easy chair, where I suppose we stayed for ten minutes, praying and making an estimate of the situation. I suggested we leave but it was not long before we were back at our seats for the ceremonies. Afterward we hurried in the car to Robin's house.

There Kitty Rix stretched out on the sofa while our grandchildren did their best to comfort her. We talked in circles, abstractedly, never mentioning the pain, but I could not forget how her face had blanched at our table. Then we said our good-byes and drove to Phoenix and her doctor. She was in the backseat with blankets and pillows.

Every now and then I reached back and held her hand but we did not talk. The doctor met us at the hospital and all the next morning I paced outside the operating room door. One of the surgeons emerged and I could tell by the deliberate way he removed his surgical mask that he had bad news.

"The primary lesion in the liver," he explained, "is too far advanced. It has metastasized. There is nothing we can do. All I can tell you to do is take her home and make her as comfortable as possible."

In the parking lot I walked in as near a daze as I have ever been. When at last I found my car I looked up into the heavens and let out a cry of anguish, not so much for the prognosis as for the final realization of my guilt—all those years either coming or going but so rarely there. For fifty-two days Kitty Rix accepted every insult to her *being* that the rest of her life had to offer. There were tears only twice, and I caused them when my emotions broke before hers. All in the world I could do was care for her and prove that I would never leave her to strangers in a hospital, but what in the world could I really do? Just dole out the drugs called painkillers that I am certain really killed her.

There came a time I could no longer hold back the tears, that late afternoon when she lapsed into a coma, though I did not know enough of that kind of death to recognize the change taking place. The hour had come for her green capsule of chloral hydrate, and I kept trying to wake her, to lift her into a sitting position so she could swallow some water. Moving her evidently caused enough pain to bring her momentarily to consciousness. Her eyes opened briefly, seeing into mine, and she tried to smile.

"Scotty," she said, "you are trying to play God."

# 16

# IN THE FOOTSTEPS OF MARCO POLO, AGAIN

For two years I tried to outrun bitter memories until I finally learned there is no escape. Kitty Rix and I had been happy while I commanded Luke Air Force Base, so I built a small house nearby and settled nostalgically under the traffic pattern of the runway where I had landed my last fighter plane.

I resisted requests to give speeches for years until I gradually realized I was doing it for the wrong reason; guilt feelings at having left Kitty Rix alone while I lectured were keeping me from addressing a new generation eager to hear about my experiences. So one evening late in 1976, I found myself at Luke before an audience of expectant young fighter pilots.

Beginning with a flying tale more than twenty years old, I described an unexpected trip I made while commanding the 36th Fighter/Bomber Wing at Fürstenfeldbruck, Germany. My F-84E Thunderjet had a flame-out above 40,000 feet near Mount Ararat at the far end of Turkey, but I was able to glide to a safe landing—just barely—at Erzurum. While a new engine was being shipped for installation, I covered two thousand more miles along the trail of Marco Polo—one of my dreams—and hunted the rarest big game in the world in some of the highest mountains. Pursuing the greatest of the big sheep, *Ovis poli* of the Pamirs, on foot at nearly 20,000 feet in the high Wakhan Corridor made for a tall tale.

While reliving the experience, I suddenly realized the large map on the wall near the speaker's podium showed the region I was discussing. That was where four great mountain ranges meet, and displayed right in the center was the terrain of the Marco Polo sheep! Surely such a thing as that map's being there was no mere coincidence? No one there, not even I at the beginning, had known what my subject would be. The hand of fate moved again.

Karakoram, Kunlun, and the Hindu Kush; sure the Himalayas were a few feet higher—one of them—but you did not hunt *Ovis poli* there. I described the Wakhan Corridor of northeast Afghanistan, a narrow finger of land barely 150 miles long, running uphill to 17,000 feet all the way to China. Barely ten or twenty miles wide, it is a geographic anomaly originally intended to deny Russia a common boundary with the British Empire; today it separates the U.S.S.R. and Pakistan.

It was all forbidding terrain on that map, much of it in more than one sense. There for instance was Hunza, one of the smallest kingdoms in the world, to which I had been seeking entry for more than twenty years. I saw Taghdumbash, the loftiest pass of all, and Chapchingal, a stopping point which I had almost reached when word came that my F-84 was ready to fly me back to Europe.

The pilots hung on every word as they traveled each foot of those high trails with me. Afterward, many of them came up to share their experiences. The last man waiting to talk with me had flashing eyes and hair as black as a raven.

"Sir," he said in Oxford English, "I am Colonel Singh, Pakistani Air Force, senior officer of the detachment representing my country. I was interested in your talk, General, but you end on a note of disappointment. As the cause concerns my country, I would like to make a suggestion. I believe you should officially request my government to grant access to that highest mountain pass, not as a tourist but as a retired military officer, an ally. In that way it can be arranged."

I told him that I had written many times to the embassy of Pakistan in Washington, D.C., but had always been informed that access to Hunza was denied. I had also written to the Mir of Hunza himself, Mohammed Jamal Khan, but my letter had never been answered. As there was no way to reach Wakhan from the pass of Taghdumbash without passing through that tiny mountainous state, it seemed an insurmountable obstacle. Colonel Singh was a good listener; he interrupted here to remind me politely that Hunza was, after all, part of Pakistan, and Pakistani military troops routinely passed through it.

As simply as that the wheels were set in motion for the realization of a journey denied me for years. Colonel Singh made a direct application on my behalf during a trip to Karachi, and by early December, I had received what amounted to an official invitation from the head of the Pakistani Air Force to be the guest of his country; I was to forward my passport to that country's embassy and let them know when I would like to depart. Winter or not, I decided to leave later that month.

Getting the proper clothes and equipment together took very little time. As I made my last-minute preparations with great excitement, I wondered what had influenced the chief of the Air Force himself to invite me.

"That invitation did not originate with the Air Force, sir," Colonel Singh confirmed. "You must know the Prime Minister or someone high in his office; they certainly know you! After I placed your request in Karachi, I received a telephone call from Government House that showed the caller knew you well. He gave some indication of having served with you during World War Two. He is even aware that you live in retirement near Luke Air Force Base and knows the books you have written."

I racked my brain trying to recall anyone I had met during the war at Karachi, Dinjan, or elsewhere in India with enough political clout to work such wonders.

In mid-December my special travel permit and visa were ready; I picked them up in New York before boarding my Pakistan International flight on Christmas Eve 1976. My Boeing 747 landed in Karachi on Christmas Day, where I was met by another Pakistani Air Force colonel—also named Singh—and given the full VIP treatment; my luggage was whisked away without being examined and my passport was not even requested. I had the warm feeling that someone high up did indeed know me, but whoever it was, he failed to make himself known despite my eagerness to thank him.

My gear was placed in a small military aircraft and we took off in the same direction I remembered landing that B-17E early in 1942. Our course led north toward the Khyber Pass and we landed after eight hundred miles at Islamabad, where we spent the night. The next morning Colonel Singh and I boarded a very small military plane that resembled the German Fieseler Storch of World War II, although my guide called it the "Friendship." However spindly and low-powered, it was an excellent STOL—short takeoff and landing— airplane, ideally suited to our mission.

The flight to Gilgit was thrilling. We threaded narrow valleys 150 miles between snowcapped peaks towering more than 10,000 feet above us, constantly buffeted by updrafts and crosswinds, then downdrafts that tested our ship and its pilot. We invaded this breathtaking realm like some insect and I bowed my head in admiration, half expecting each winding valley to close momentarily into an entrapping cul-de-sac. Final approach brought us low over angrily churning waters where the Gilgit and the Hunza rivers met, and we landed at an airstrip so small, I wondered who had ever had the courage to try it the first time.

I shook the hand of our pilot with all the admiration of an old flight instructor, and after he took off again I stood there feeling very small. Only yesterday I had gazed up at the skyscrapers of New York. Now I found myself among God's infinitely greater skyscrapers, at one of the most remote spots on the face of the earth. Not China yet, but I knew I was on the threshold of my most romantic journey so far.

As the sound of the little *Friendship* faded westward, a Pakistani soldier drove up in a jeep. The first thing that crossed my mind, having seen no roads in the valleys through which we had flown, was how a wheeled vehicle could have made it there? Colonel Singh and I were taken to a small military guard station not far away that seemed to be all there was of Gilgit.

My guide was treated with great deference and was obviously well-known in this remote area. He was thirty-five—half my age—

and robust, a soldier first but also a skilled *shikari,* or hunting guide. We had quickly become friends, and I had admitted my confusion at meeting a second "Colonel Singh." He was no relation to my benefactor at Luke, he told me; every Sikh has *Singh,* which means "lion," in his name. He pronounced his five names for me in perfect British English and I chose the shortest, so it was "Salih" and "Bob" by the time we set out on the narrow road to Baltit, the capital of Hunza.

This hard-surfaced road, running northward sixty or seventy miles, replaced the perilous trail I had long read about, a rocky path scarcely suitable for horses. Camel caravans had followed it along the Hunza River for two thousand years but the common form of transport had long been the yak, a shaggy oxlike beast of burden tamed from the wild. We set out in two jeeps—Salih and myself in the first, two armed soldiers with our baggage in the second—expecting a rapid trip until all road improvements ran out at Baltit; from there on out we would be on foot, depending on yaks to haul our supplies.

The kingdom of Hunza is the real-life inspiration for the Shangri-La of James Hilton's *Lost Horizon.* I had seen the movie years ago but could hardly believe I was at last going to see the home of the Hunzukuts, descendants of Macedonian soldiers who had fought with Alexander the Great hundreds of years before Christ.

Our trek began around the great mountain of Rakaposhi whose 25,550-foot peak dominated the very sky. All around, hundreds of other peaks in the Karakorams rose to more than 20,000 feet and glaciers fed countless rushing streams. We did not make it around the snowy foothills before running into trouble, because winter avalanches had covered or carried away whole sections of the road. We made detours where possible, otherwise waiting while temporary repairs were made. Everywhere people seemed to be expecting us and entire villages turned out to help us make *rafik*s, then cheered us on our way.

I helped make two *rafik*s and was fascinated by this lesson in primitive engineering. Where a break in the mountain road had formed, we jammed entire tree trunks, small end first, into crevasses in the exposed supporting rock. We pushed these makeshift girders flat to bridge the gap and piled branches on them, covering everything with earth and stones which we then packed down. Crossing one *rafik* that hung out over the white water of the Hunza River made for an especially heart-stopping jeep ride.

Hunza *was* Shangri-La for me when I saw it. It was winter, yet the valley through which we traveled was almost temperate. I saw evidence of fields which had recently been green. There were orchards of peach and apricot trees and grape vineyards. Such an isolated valley at the end of the world seemed as strange to me as it must have to Marco Polo, who had in all probability walked this river and climbed those high passes. He definitely gave this region the name *Pamir*. "From here," Polo wrote, "you must walk forty days over mountain peaks, the likes of which I have never seen."

The Hunzukuts are absolutely magnificent, the healthiest and most vigorous people I have ever seen. They live to fantastic ages—125 is common—thanks possibly to pure air, unpolluted streams, and the absence of modern stresses. I had heard that there was only one telephone in Hunza, and that belonged to the Mir. He was more than a king; he was judge and jury, a father to his people. I was afraid I might have to make an official appearance, even though packing for high-altitude travel in the dead of winter had left no room for proper attire in my duffel bag and backpack. Salih put my mind at rest by mentioning that the Mir was away but we were expected at the Royal Guest House. Two yaks led by the Mir's personal servants were available for our use.

After three days we arrived at Baltit and found the yaks and their "pullers" waiting for us. Following a quick rest we set off, climbing, the first day, eighteen miles to Pa-su at the steady two-mile-per-hour pace of the yaks. Next day we passed Langaroar-i-dor. My altimeter read 11,000 feet under a brilliant blue sky and the temperature was far below zero but no wind was stirring. I yielded to pressure and mounted a yak for the first time on the third day out of Baltit. Salih had been encouraging me to ride, out of deference to my almost seventy years; I had resisted until the Hunzukut yak pullers told him that the Mir had insisted.

I soon learned all about yaks the hard way, arriving at two conclusions: first, you cannot hurry a yak; second, even if you have the patience of Job and remember the first rule, the yak will still do you in by stolidly having its way to the nth degree. Mature bulls often stand six feet high at the withers and weigh over 1,200 pounds. Dark-brown hair, almost black, grows short on top and hangs long and wavy underneath almost to the ground.

And what a disposition! The yak looks around to size you up as you sit on his mighty back, far too wide to straddle, then plods along looking for a way to rid himself of you. It might be an outcropping of rock to brush up against, or a branch at just the right height to peel you off; then you sit there trying to outwit the witless yak as his revenge looms inexorably closer in slow motion. If all his gentle efforts fail, he simply folds his legs to plop down on the trail and there you stay. All with no trace of malice—just a sigh and a look of deep sympathy.

At the end of one day I gave up, having been brushed twice to the snow. Salih told me with a grin that I was fortunate it was winter; had I foolishly tried to hurry a yak in summer, the beast would have angled off the trail to lie down in a deep part of the river. There is a Tibetan saying in the part of the world where the *bos*, as it is called, is indispensable: "Offend not a Raja or a yak."

For five days out of Baltit the weather smiled, skies sparkling, not a cloud, no wind to disturb the deep snow. But late on the fifth afternoon things began to change. I had just checked my altimeter— 15,000 feet—and consulted the large-scale map, NJ-43, SU-FU section, to find that we were nearing the Pakistan-China border. There in large letters was the word INDEFINITE with meandering red dots indicating an uncertain frontier. Just then there came a strange feeling in the atmosphere and a drastic change in barometric pressure that made me swallow hard to clear popped ears. I looked out from a shepherd's hut of tumbled stone where we had been making tea.

The yaks and their pullers had sensed the change; the Hunzukuts were pointing at the sky, talking excitedly and shouting at Salih in Burushaski. Seconds later came the first blast of wind which grew into an ever greater gale. One moment the sun hung in a limitless sky; the next, our world became purplish, then black. Shrieking wind hurled old and fresh snow into our faces as a blizzard engulfed us.

The ruined hut was no protection at all but we were already moving anyway—the yaks had instinctively broken trail, heads down, dragging their shaggy hair between treelike legs as they pressed on toward Misgar and Taghdumbash—we thought. The first checkpoint we had, a turnoff to Chapchingal, failed to appear but neither Salih nor I worried; nothing could have been identified in the white-out. There was a rest house there we needed to locate. As time dragged by with no sign of it, I checked my compass and found it had gone crazy—perhaps static electricity from the storm. It seemed to me after estimating the "mean" of its wild fluctuations that we were headed east instead of north, so I pulled out my pocket altimeter to see what it could tell me. I was alarmed to read that we had already descended two thousand feet when we should have been climbing. The yaks had taken over and led us on the path of least resistance, and who could blame them?

Salih considered turning back and we talked it over, our shouted words being ripped from our lips by the wind. In the end the yaks made up our minds for us, because it would be hopeless to try to turn them uphill into the face of a sixty-knot wind. Days passed with no sunrise or sunset, just shades of charcoal and white; I began marking them off on my map when I dared open it in the lee of a rock outcropping or a yak. The storm had struck sometime between Christmas and New Year's, but I was now completely befuddled—we were lost temporally as well as geographically.

On what I thought was January 6, we reached some sort of junction where a broad swath of snow ran north and south between frozen willows. It had the look of a man-made right-of-way. Salih and I took iron-shod poles and walked in widening circles, thrusting them deep into the snow. Five feet below we felt pavement. My map showed only one north-south road, the Karakoram Highway, a thin line well beyond the red dots of the border; we had entered the People's Republic of China!

Though worried, we were too exhausted to think about our predicament. Even the yaks appeared spent, having already bedded down with their pullers. I estimated our position and drew an X on the map in the shelter of my sleeping bag, working by flashlight while outside the endless gale howled on. My last thought as I dropped off to sleep was that I could not possibly have picked a colder, more remote, and less hospitable place than this windy corner of Red China.

Penetrating silence awakened me. I was burrowed deep into my sleeping bag, cold, zipped up like a mummy. The thermometer taped near my head read thirty degrees below zero. Suddenly it dawned on me that the wind was no longer howling and I reached for the zipper. My first glimpse outside took my breath away.

I had placed my bag so that my head pointed uphill, which coincidentally pointed my feet toward the south and a fantastic view. There against the bluest of skies stood a crystal-white mountain so sharp I could almost reach out and touch it, although I knew without having to consult my map that it was a full hundred miles away. This was the King of the Karakoram, Godwin Austen—K-2, the second-highest peak in the world. It shone and sparkled in the flush of daylight as the sun started to rise.

Salih joined me and it was immediately apparent that he was as entranced by the great mountain as I. "Bob, the top of the world up there is eight thousand, six hundred and eleven meters," he said. I bowed my head in gratitude, then looked around. Peaks surrounded us—the Kunluns to the east, Pamirs west and north. Exhaustion had let me sleep deeply last night but now the enormity of our situation hit home. We had violated a forbidden border and Salih had me as an extra burden; Americans were not allowed in China in those less friendly times. But he seemed completely relaxed as he announced breakfast was ready, all the while looking at the shimmering beauty of K-2.

Over chapattis with dried apricots and raisins—my first real meal of 1977—we studied the map and saw we had intersected the Karakoram Highway at K'o-ya-K'o-Pei by a small river listed as Sai-li-Ho. To backtrack would mean a steep climb for thirty or forty miles; our best course lay instead north along the highway some fifty miles to Tashkurghan. There it met the Silk Road that Marco Polo had walked, a realization that held me spellbound.

The AR-15 rifles carried by our soldiers were already hidden among our bags on the back of a yak in anticipation of reaching the border station. It was late on the third afternoon in China when we finally sighted Tashkurghan—in all that time we had been the sole traffic on that road and had not seen so much as an animal or a bird. When we camped I walked ahead to study traffic at that critical junction. Half a mile beyond our camp I sat down beneath some trees covered with snow that provided good camouflage. A thousand yards off I saw another road coming down from the west out of the Pamirs, undoubtedly the trail from Mintaka Pass or Taghdumbash.

With nothing else to be seen I studied my map. Here the Silk Road turned north and ran a mere 250 miles downhill to Kashgar— each time I read that name a shiver ran up my spine! I had dreamed of visiting that point on Marco Polo's route since boyhood; it had taken me so long to get here and I was now so close. Determination rose within me, a wild hope urging me to press on to Kashgar at all costs.

In the gathering darkness I did not see the camel train until it was quite near: men leading two-humped Bactrian camels. Nobody had challenged them at the border and they entered China without breaking stride, the camels walking at more than twice the pace of our plodding yaks. Salih joined me and we returned together to camp to find three trucks parked close by. The newcomers had built a fire and by its light I could see military stenciling on the bumpers of the vehicles. Chinese Army. I was caught, or so I thought when one of the soldiers called out to me.

Salih called a greeting in Urdu or Arabic and explained our situation. I did my best to indicate our friendly intentions. To my surprise they hardly bothered with us as they unloaded to set up their camp. My appetite was not very good that night, despite the cold and the distance we had walked. After dinner Salih and I went over to see if there was an officer present. There was not, we found out, but I passed out some oatmeal and chocolate chip cookies and they broke the ice, hard-frozen as they were. The Chinese in turn prepared to brew some tea for us all, using compressed bricks. I hated that kind of tea where the leaves never seem to settle but get caught in your teeth. That reminded me that I had also brought from the United States nearly a hundred flow-through tea bags; no sooner had I thought of them than I was off to retrieve a handful.

When the water was boiling, as hot as it could be at nearly 12,000 feet, the soldiers gathered in fascination around the pot while I demonstrated those strange-looking bags. They and the cookies had turned strangers into friends. There were eighteen of them, including their sergeant. We learned they were a People's Liberation Army work detail that had been patrolling the Karakoram Highway for ten days, clearing the road of debris from avalanches. They were now en route to their home base in Kashgar.

There was never going to be a better opportunity than this. As we finished off the tea and cookies, I tried to explain by pointing at the map that I was going to Kashgar too. Salih had been looking at me strangely. I caught his eye. As we headed back to our camp I explained my decision and asked for his help, but to my surprise I did not have to argue very much. He felt it would make sense for me to report to the nearest officer of the PLA in any event. We returned to the campsite, where Salih produced my important-looking document with the Pakistani flag at the top and red ribbon at the bottom held in place by a gold seal. I am positive that impressive paper with text in four languages—signed by whoever my friend was in the office of the Prime Minister—swung the deal for me to go to Kashgar.

The next morning found me riding north on the Karakoram Highway—the Silk Road—sitting between the driver and the sergeant in the cab of the lead PLA truck. The great mountain K-2 had disappeared behind, but lofty peaks almost as tall were still all around us. The highest of the Pamirs off to our left in the U.S.S.R. looked no more than twenty miles away; Muztagh Ata, almost 25,000 feet high, soon came into view on our right. Darkness had fallen before we drove into Kashgar.

We drove under an arch with a giant red star and straight into a motor pool. It was so late that I was not surprised there was no official to whom I could show my papers. The sergeant found me something to eat with his men and located a bed for me in the barracks. I realized there were communists all around me; I had been with them all day and they did not seem any different from anybody else.

A security officer awakened me, saying his name was Captain Chou. He was already checking my passport and travel pass before I was dressed. I realized now how to tell enlisted men from officers in the absence of visible rank insignia, as Captain Chou's jacket had four pockets whereas the uniforms of the men I had ridden with had two. I tried to explain my entrance into China traveling with a Pakistani colonel who was waiting for me at the border. Chou left from our breakfast of Chinese noodles to telephone his superior.

To my surprise the man who arrived that afternoon was a civilian, one of the political officials in communist countries called commissars. His big florid face reminded me of Chairman Mao. He spoke very good English but asked me hardly any questions. I made a point of telling him I had been a *fieji*, a fighter pilot, and had lived in his country for three years during World War II. When he and Captain Chou carefully went over my papers, the Pakistani travel permit drew particular attention and respect.

The newcomer was courteous but his judgment was just what I had expected; I had entered an area forbidden to foreigners and was to be returned to Tashkurghan by the next available transport. Three days passed before another road maintenance crew was available to take me back along the Silk Road. As soon as we reached the border, I saw Colonel Singh looking very relieved to have me back again in his charge.

As though to make up for the blizzard, the weather was favorable when we again entered the Pamirs. We climbed and climbed for eleven days at yak pace, up and over the high pass I had dreamed of—Taghdumbash—and at the top my altimeter read 20,800 feet. Up there in that rarefied atmosphere, no matter how tough and well-prepared you think you are, you can do little more than exist. I came to respect the yaks with their great strength and gentle stubbornness. We had almost made it back to Hunza before nature frowned with blackening skies, but by then nothing could have fazed me. At Baltit there were horses waiting to take us back to our jeeps. Our journey to Gilgit presented no obstacles—no need to build more *rafiks*—and Salih and I were soon on the same little plane back to Islamabad. Saying my heartfelt farewell to the yak pullers at Baltit and the two Pakistani soldiers at Gilgit was difficult—I was even sorry to be leaving the yaks. The entire adventure had been something I will remember forever.

One disappointment remained. When I reached Karachi with Salih, there was still no benefactor to meet me. As I had to wait there two days for my 747 to take me home, I had plenty of time to think about how my journey had come about. I went to Government House on my own, hoping against hope to see a face that would jog my memory. I left with no more idea than when I entered of who had remembered me from World War II. Surely it could not be somebody as high as the Prime Minister himself? Still, my passport with the Great Seal of the United States had meant nothing there in China; it was that ribboned page that had saved me time and again. When my two days were up, I thanked Salih from the depth of my soul, knowing I would never forget him. Our special friendship knew bonds forged by shared adventures and dangers. We had been "in harm's way" together.

I had lived a lifetime in five weeks, having been to Shangri-La and traversed it twice. As the jumbo jet climbed on the first leg of my eastward return to the United States, I looked for K-2, remembering that indescribable view the morning after the storm. Lunch was being served when the captain announced that we were now over Burma. I looked down at the Brahmaputra and could see where that big river turned west past Dinjan to flow toward Calcutta. In my imagination I saw my P-40 sitting among all those C-47s at Dinjan, where I had flown the Hump.

Between Dinjan and Chennault's old headquarters at Kunming was Myitkyina on the Irrawaddy River. At that landing ground in 1942 we had struggled to evacuate hundreds of Burmese refugees in our overloaded Douglas transports. I can still see them when I close my eyes, sick and crying children, people carrying their dead. Our C-47s were military versions of the twenty-one-passenger DC-3 airliner, modified with large cargo doors and bare interiors. I flew planes out of Myitkyina with refugees packed like sardines, once bringing out fifty-four people and their pitiful baggage; I had heard of one C-47 that took off with seventy-two people aboard.

British Colonial soldiers controlled the surging crowds and made possible these evacuation flights. They were Sikhs, their leader a major in the Punjab Fusileers who might have stepped out of a poem by Kipling—ramrod straight and fearless; discipline, valor, and loyalty written all over him. He had escaped across the Chindwin River after his unit was decimated fighting the Japanese in the jungle, only to learn his wife had died in the Punjab. Emergency leave had been granted him to rescue his son.

I met them when an RAF operations officer in Calcutta asked me to take on two extra passengers. We were in the air when Sergeant Aaltonen, my crew chief, came forward to report that there was a kid aboard. The boy was a smaller version of his father, twelve or fourteen years old, and I immediately thought of them as "Gunga Din" and "Little Gunga," although I never called them that to their faces. The next thing I knew, the son had been adopted by American and British troops at Dinjan who had heard of the death of his mother. "Little Gunga," whose real name was Ali, pretty soon had a miniature version of his father's uniform complete with beige turban; some Tommy or GI gave him a pair of cut-down khaki shorts and the rest soon followed. Each time I returned from an operational flight, I would check on him. I seldom arrived without some food for them which I would give to the boy—K rations or chocolate from our C rations.

The major brought the boy with him during these evacuations of Burmese refugees. We became close as they supervised the loading of my plane, although there was no time to talk—I would unload one group of frantic refugees and return immediately for another. They kept pouring in, always more, until the day Japanese troops were reported in a village less than twenty miles south of Myitkyina. As operations officer of the Assam-Burma-China Ferrying Command, it was my reluctant decision to suspend operations after this last pickup. I counted as refugees boarded and stopped the flow early, explaining to the major and his son that they were to fly out with me; they would share the cockpit with me where they would not feel guilty about displacing two refugees.

He understood but he made no attempt to come aboard and escape the enemy. I prompted him, telling him the other pilots were making the same offer to the remainder of the Punjab detachment, but he shook his head. "No, sahib. My orders are to remain here and help the refugees."

Time was growing short but I tried to persuade him to let his son fly out with me. He turned to the boy and asked him in their language. The silent shake of that small turbaned head will remain with me forever. The next day I came back in the P-40, gun switches on, and dove across the field. Even before I saw the Japanese flag I was fired upon. For weeks we had been refueling from rusty drums of aviation gasoline under the mango trees at the north end of the airfield; at the first long burst from the six guns in my wings, the entire woods seemed to burst into flames. When I crossed the Chindwin River eighty miles away, I could still see that column of black smoke rising straight up. I wondered if my friends had been caught or killed by the Japanese.

Almost a year after my return from my recent adventures, General Mohammad Zia-ul-Haq overthrew the government of Pakistan, and the Prime Minister was imprisoned to await execution. I could not shake my growing hunch about "Little Gunga," that he had lived through the ordeal of capture by the Japanese to attain high office in the new government. In the year that followed, every time there was a reference to Pakistan on the news I dropped everything so as not to miss a word. Our embassy in Islamabad was burned. Periodically I would hear something about the imprisoned head of government.

Tragically, news came that the former Prime Minister had been unexpectedly and secretly executed. I dug out my Pakistani travel permit and was sadly examining that indecipherable signature as Walter Cronkite gave details of the man he called the most popular politician to have come to power in Pakistan's thirty-two-year independence. He had been born, Cronkite reported, near Karachi in 1928—just the right age to have been Ali, that boy I knew in 1942. I remembered asking him once in the Operations *basha* at Dinjan to point out on a large wall map of India where he and his father lived. Without hesitation he put his finger on a town in the Sind Desert, two hundred miles from Karachi.

Behind Walter Cronkite, who was still talking, there flashed the image of a letter reportedly smuggled out of prison before the execution. "If I am assassinated on the gallows," the translation was given, "there will be turmoil and violence, conflict and conflagration. . . ." What shocked me into attention was the scrawl with curlicues at the bottom in a language I did not know—exactly the same signature as that on the travel permit in my hand, that of *Zulfikar Ali Bhutto*. "Shortly after two A.M.," intoned Walter Cronkite, "the prisoner, gaunt and ailing, was led from his dungeon cell to the scaffolding and hanged. The last thing he said was to once more protest his innocence of any crime. His body was cut down and flown in a waiting police plane to the town of Larkana, two hundred miles northeast of Karachi in the Sind Desert. There, in a family burial ground, Zulfikar Ali Bhutto was hastily interred before news of his death was released in Pakistan."

# 17

# JOURNEY TO THE
# GREAT WALL

Dr. DeLoach always joked about how healthy I was. He would smile wryly and comment: "There you go again, flaunting your teen-age blood pressure and your heart strong as an ox. Put your clothes back on and we'll go to lunch. Then you can fly back home to the desert and come back to see me next year."

That had continued for nineteen years, up until 1978. This visit I knew something was wrong by the length of time he studied the large chest X ray. Finally he directed my attention to a shadow above my right kidney that had him concerned. He sent me to another doctor for a second opinion, and that led to other examinations by more doctors. Although I have always been an optimist, way down deep inside I suspected that my routine of carefree decades had come to a screeching halt.

My world shrank from a boundless sky to claustrophobic hospital walls, a prison sentence of blood workups, angiograms, nephrotomograms, ultrasonics, bone scans, CAT scans, and other tests leading finally to a "last mile" on a hospital gurney. All the way to the operating room a cheerful nurse held me from despair with her boundless optimism, but I was seventy and part of me said this had to happen sooner or later. Yet the rest of me never believed it—poke or prod as I might, I never felt a pain nor found a sign of the malignant mass that tests said was there.

Count back from my favorite number, the doctor told me as the anesthetic began to take hold. I started at twenty-three, my lucky number from my earliest days—my Boy Scout troop in Macon, the day of a summer month in 1930 when I met Kitty Rix, the combat outfit I led in China, the Psalm of David . . . Instead of counting back, I kept repeating "twenty-three" for luck.

Swimming up from the depths of unconsciousness seemed to take ages. Flashes of awareness, then back under, lulls and lurid dreams, until at last I was awake. I was back on the gurney in Recovery. That was a misnomer for sure, I thought; how in the world did a seventy-year-old patient recover from having a cancerous kidney removed? Had voracious diseased cells already spread through my bloodstream? For the first time since it all began I felt like giving up.

"Bob, are you awake?"

One of the surgeons grinned down at me, his face close to mine. He actually laughed as he pressed something into my hand.

"Feel that, General? Now there's a real souvenir for you. Your 'cancer.'"

I felt and saw a bit of steel something like a broken knife blade but it did not register right away. He realized it and explained.

"That bit of foreign matter caused the mass the X ray showed as a shadow. Nature had grown a cyst around those sharp edges; then what we call a 'shroud' had formed and filled with fluid. Anyway, all that counts is that pathology shows everything benign. No malignancy. There was no need to remove the kidney."

Doc Manget had missed one. I looked at the chunk of metal that had been blasted from the seat armor of my P-40 thirty-six years earlier and felt what I can only describe as the commutation of a death sentence. I remembered that day in Kweilin when Doc had removed nineteen other bits of metal like the one in my hand; I did not even have to concentrate to feel again how every scar had burned after that primitive operation, performed without anesthetic in Nine Dragon Cave.

"Thank you, Lord!" I said.

My little nurse stopped the gurney and asked if I were in pain. I shook my head and held up that bit of blackened metal. "No, ma'am, I'm fine and getting finer by the minute."

The next morning I woke up to see tall long-leaf pines wave their branches in sunlight. I realized a new world was opening up for me and I knew my fear had not been of dying, but of not really being able to live any longer when there was so much I wanted to do. A most efficient nurse entered my cubicle, flashed a smile, and asked how I was. I told her fine. By that time she had removed the wide bandages that had covered my right side. There were forty gleaming metal staples around the angry wound, looking a bit like a zipper, instead of the stitches I had expected.

She said it was time for my *first great step,* necessary to ensure that there were no post-surgery adhesions. I did a sit-up like those I had done for years and years—keeping fit to walk the Great Wall—but before I could swing my legs to the floor, a searing pain stabbed me from my stomach to my backbone. I had felt that red-hot poker at last and there had to be cold sweat on my brow. As the pain gradually subsided she told me that she had intended to help me rise, and we both laughed—which was better than crying.

Within days I was out of Intensive Care, the IV needles out of my arms and the precautionary pacemaker removed. I shouted for joy, first being careful to lock myself in the bathroom so they would not think I was ready for the mental ward. When I was back on my bed I contemplated the future—a future I did not think I had a few days before—and I vowed to complete the trail of Marco Polo. A greater dream still lived within me, and that was to follow the Great Wall of China from end to end.

The longest journey begins with but a single step. I estimated the distance from my bed to the bathroom door, from there around the far wall and past the two empty beds back to my own. Pacing my "closed course" out to thirty yards, I computed that fifty-nine revolutions would equal a mile run. I started by walking, then gradually increased my pace to a full run. The very next morning, as I was stepping up the pace and counting out loud, the hall door opened and there stood both surgeons. They stopped, possibly aghast, and so did I. Then everybody laughed. "How many laps to the mile, General?" one of them asked.

It did not take long for news to spread through the hospital that there was an old fighter pilot who ran laps in his room just for the hell of it. By the end of the week I had every nurse and several of the doctors indoctrinated and pulling for me to tackle my final trek from Kashgar along the Silk Road to the Marco Polo Bridge near Peking. Interestingly, I found a book there in the hospital library written in 1909 by a famous archeologist named Giel, who had tried to follow the Great Wall of China and failed.

"Nobody but nobody, not even a Chinese," he wrote, "has ever seen all the Great Wall!"

There was my obsession in black-and-white. I was extremely eager for my release—any patient who runs a mile in his room twice a day is more than ready—and my request was granted on the condition that I remain an outpatient, meaning I had to stay in Aiken and report back each week until my doctor pronounced me fully recovered. It was May and the dogwood and azaleas were in bloom, and it was all I could do not to break into a sprint as I thanked all those wonderful nurses, and the Lord, too, before driving away with my cousin Walter Burckhalter.

I stayed with my Aunt Lillian, known to all the family—and to much of the town that had once elected her Woman of the Year—as "Big Sister." She was over eighty then and lived a life—as she still does—devoted entirely to others. The day after my surgery she had appeared in the ICU dressed in a nurse's uniform, access granted where it was denied everyone else because she was a "candy striper," one of those Good Samaritan ladies who do so much in a community. With her I got the finest care and therapy possible. Sometimes she must have stayed up all night cooking special delicacies. I never heard a sound, hardly ever saw her except when she called me to a meal or brought one into my room. Breakfasts were always something nourishing and tasty; dinners often smothered chicken and rice, as only Big Sister could cook it. I rested and read, wrote letters, and slipped out the back door to continue my exercise, walks that soon became runs along a training route.

Before my short recuperation ended, I had already run a seven-minute mile and was closing in on the six-minute ones I had done before surgery. I said good-bye to all my relatives and headed for Arizona, curbing my impatience and driving just four hundred miles a day instead of making it a flat-out race against time. Did they really think my temperament had changed with the operation, that I could actually limit myself to a hundred miles a day?

My heart sang to hear the afterburners of jet fighters scrambling into the sky from the runway at Luke Air Force Base. Home again under the traffic pattern, I dedicated myself to the seemingly impossible task of crashing the political barriers blocking my entry into the People's Republic of China. For years I had written letters to the Chinese embassy in Washington, D.C., with no success; now I began a veritable barrage, dispensing with modesty to itemize my military record and emphasize that I had flown side by side with Chinese fighter pilots during World War II. I went all-out, little realizing the hundreds of such letters I would eventually write.

I would need to travel in remote areas closed to foreigners, with freedoms far beyond those provided by package tours. A passport alone meant nothing without a visa, but individual visas were not issued to tourist groups—the tour leader held a collective visa for the entire party. I therefore did not even consider the few travel packages then available. Going on my own would require a special travel permit, but all my letters requesting that crucial document were ignored.

To distract myself from these hard realities and to make sure I was in the necessary physical condition, I increased my fitness program. I did not jog; I ran ten thousand meters every other day. I attended a class in bodybuilding with younger people, working with weights and doing countless push-ups and sit-ups. Never forgetting that "last mile" on the gurney, I also had exercise equipment at home, where I continued my training in front of the television.

When the months added up to a year, I changed tactics and circumvented the embassy to write directly to Chinese government officials in Peking—now definitively Beijing. On the home front I launched a campaign the likes of which had never been seen, writing every congressman and senator I knew and many I did not—the same approach I had used to escape my Training Command desk and fly off to combat in 1942. When 1980 arrived with no success, I modified my plan yet again to concentrate on those highly placed individuals who could or would help me the most. American Ambassador Leonard Woodcock in Beijing was courteous and genuine in his efforts to assist me. Senator Strom Thurmond of South Carolina, a cousin of mine, replied instantly to say that he had assigned an assistant to press my case with the U.S. Department of State. Senator Thurmond himself visited the Chinese embassy and met with the ambassador, finding out that the latter individual believed I wanted to ride a camel on top of the Great Wall! I can only blame the language barrier for his mistaken belief that I was interested in such a dangerous and senseless stunt. The Chinese first secretary told Senator Thurmond a more serious obstacle, the fact that I had flown during the war for Nationalist China, "Chennault and Chiang Kai-shek."

It was of course former President Richard Nixon who had first opened the Bamboo Curtain a crack. Busy as he was moving from California to New York City, Mr. Nixon replied by return mail to say that he had written the embassy of the People's Republic of China on my behalf; moreover, he had personally telephoned the Chinese ambassador to request that a visa be granted.

In two years I typed almost three hundred letters, each five to seven pages long, double-spaced. I also joined organizations promoting contact with China, sponsored the exchange of scholars between our two countries, and otherwise left no stone unturned to realize my dream. A letter from Luxinshe in Beijing—the China International Travel Service I later came to know as CITS—finally arrived to say that the itinerary I requested was impossible because of the shortage of tourist facilities and interpreters. There was the problem right out in the open—what I call the "Holiday Inn Syndrome." No matter that I required no hotels, since I would be carrying my own equipment for "board and room"—it was inconceivable that an American should rough it. As for the shortage of interpreters, I told them of my three years in China and my two years studying Mandarin, which I continued to study as I waited for permission to make the trip. I needed neither plush hotels nor interpreters.

By early 1980 my baggage was assembled and ready, changing only with the seasons. It had been packed and unpacked, culled of any extra weight to make certain I could carry it on my back for hundreds, even thousands of miles. The overall weight I had settled on was seventy pounds in "soft" luggage—not an Air Force B-4 bag but a strong polyester case resembling a Navy duffel bag with straps for my shoulders.

One important criterion was that it resemble something a Chinese might carry. My clothing was selected to allow me to blend in as much as possible: denim jacket and jeans and polyester trousers, all blue. Even then the possibility of having to pass for Chinese was on my mind.

To be certain I was ready to depart the moment permission came, I ran the ultimate test one night. I baked and packed 1,200 oatmeal and tollhouse cookies, then turned my back on the luxuries of home and spent the night in my walled backyard. Out there on the Astroturf beneath the orange trees, I set up my camp as though on the Great Wall half a world away. Did I have everything I would need? I checked my sleeping gear, my camera and its supplies, my toilet articles. Did I have seven pairs of socks and three pairs of Adidas running shoes?

So many years had passed since the day I had flown my P-51 over the Great Wall and prayed that someday I might walk where my shadow raced. Was that prayer ever to be answered? It seemed I was failing everywhere—running up, to use a pun, against a stone wall. Then came a ray of hope from a totally unexpected quarter: a framed color photograph of Pope John Paul II. With it, stamped with the Vatican seal and signed, there came a blessing. "The Holy Father," it read, "paternally imparts his Apostolic Blessing to Robert Lee Scott, Jr., as a pledge of Heavenly Favors, and upon the journey he seeks."

How a fighter pilot baptized at the Tatnall Square Baptist Church in Macon, Georgia, came to receive a papal blessing is too long a story to tell in detail. Suffice it to say that it was the work of a wonderful and unique friend named Charlie Russhon, a huge bear of a man who served as a combat cameraman during World War II and went on to a fascinating career in film and television production. Rush, a seventh-generation New Yorker who never lost touch with his Irish roots, did not drink or smoke or cuss. His favorite breakfast was four scoops of ice cream, all different flavors; his favorite drink, a root beer float with two scoops of vanilla, which might have influenced Milton Caniff to choose the name Charlie Vanilla for the expediting character he patterned after Rush in the "Steve Canyon" comic strip. Irrepressible and charismatic, Charlie Russhon's great gift was achieving the impossible. His passing a few years ago left the world a far less interesting place—less happy, too, for those of us who knew and loved him.

Receiving that papal blessing in July 1980 was somehow a turning point for me. I hung it above my typewriter to inspire me as I wrote my letters. Shortly afterward I was dreaming about following Marco Polo's trail along a Silk Road crowded with camels when I woke with a start. As I reviewed the dream—which had also brought me back to where I had flown my Mustang over the Great Wall—I suddenly realized the answer was within me. All I had to do was get inside China any way I could and the rest would take care of itself.

This conviction was based on some subtle shift of inner awareness. It was absolute, and by morning I had made my decisions. If I had to be a tourist to get inside China, then by the gods I would be a tourist. Like the camel who got his head under the tent flap, I would breach the Bamboo Curtain. By nine o'clock I was on my way to the nearest travel agency.

Within the hour I had found a package tour so far different from the others that I could not help thinking it tied into the dream and Charlie Russhon's papal blessing. The Explorer's Tour did not confine itself to the highly advertised coastal cities from Guangzhou to Shanghai; in thirty days it went virtually all over China—including Xinjiang in the far west—before terminating in Beijing. The travel agent told me it was the first time this tour had been offered, and all twenty-six places in it had been booked solid for months but an illness had forced a cancellation just the day before. I handed over my passport and paid on the spot, impressed that providence had sent me there just at the right time.

Would the Chinese embassy recognize my name, perhaps have it on a list, and refuse my addition to the group visa? But there was only a pleasant surprise when my passport came back; there in all its glory the number 23 had been taped to the front, my lucky number that had recurred all my life long.

# 18

# ACROSS THE
# SHUM-CHUN
# RIVER

On the 747 flying from San Francisco to Hong Kong, I made what few plans I could. Excitement deep within me told me the realization of my dreams was at hand, but my rational mind could find little to justify such optimism. If security was so tight in the next thirty days that I never managed to break off on my own, I would at least cover a large part of China I had been wanting to see. I found I was somehow counting on the American embassy in Beijing, where I felt I had a friend in Ambassador Leonard Woodcock.

At Hong Kong's Kai Tak Airport, I stood under the wing of the Boeing and looked high above Victoria Harbor. Right there in those same blue skies I had led seven P-40s in a screaming dive from 18,000 feet to strafe Japanese generals in their penthouse atop the Peninsula Hotel. Then in an instant all that had changed; my eyes followed the path my plane must have flown when I saw Japanese fighters taking off from the very spot where I now stood. Right there, too, was where I had been hit almost thirty-eight years ago. Twenty chunks of metal; the scar from the one old Doc Manget had missed was already two years old.

We were an interesting if motley tour group ranging from children to adults as old as I, among us two doctors of medicine and three of psychology, an interior decorator, a college professor, several middle-aged teachers, a retired Army colonel and another from the Air Force—the last being my old wingman and fellow ace, Dallas Clinger. The morning after arrival we caught a train at Kowloon Station for the three-hour ride to Guangzhou. The first half hour took us through tall buildings and I saw how apt the term *Bamboo Curtain* was: Construction sites were latticed with countless lengths of bamboo, some enveloping twenty-story buildings all the way to the top. All that would have been steel at home. Then we crossed the Shum-Chun River into the People's Republic of China and the development of Hong Kong disappeared.

The Union Jack now gave way to the dramatic red banner of mainland China, with a single large gold star in the upper corner and smaller ones in an arc. I had made it back to China. We spent the night in the Baiyun Hotel and boarded a Soviet-made Ilyushin airliner at noon the next day for the thousand-mile flight to Xi'an (which I had known as Sian). It was July and *da shu*, which means "great heat," and the fuselage was already stifling even before two hundred passengers filled every seat. Sweat, not perspiration, poured as we sat dehydrating, clothing soaked. Finally the turboprop engines turned over and we were taxiing, but still no air-conditioning. That came after we were airborne, the manual kind: We were issued souvenir fans which obviously meant we were to cool ourselves. I did not blame the Chinese so much as the Soviets who had sold them this cramped dog of an airliner, but I forgot my own discomfort as soon as I saw that my fan bore a hand-painted scene of the Great Wall. It was a good omen.

Xi'an was famous when it was the oldest city in the world eleven centuries before Christ. Then known as Chang'an, it had also been the only city with over a million people. Coincidentally the place in Shensi Province (now spelled Shaanxi) where I had landed with those HVAR rockets for General Chennault in 1944, Xi'an had recently become famous all over again when well diggers drilling for water made an extraordinary discovery in 1974. An obstruction sixty feet down brought to light at least eight thousand life-size ceramic figures: armed warriors with their bearers, horses drawing war chariots—all seemingly ready for battle. The statues were similar except for the faces, which are living images as different as fingerprints of the men and horses who made up the bodyguard of China's first emperor, Ch'in Shih Huang-ti.

An archeological treasure equal to the tombs of the pharaohs, this is the royal grave complex of the first emperor himself, whose name—Ch'in—gave rise to the Middle Kingdom's modern name of China. His ceramic squadrons and phalanxes had stood guard undisturbed for 2,200 years at the four entrances to his fifteen-story earthen pyramid, a tumulus known as Mount Li. The surprise to archeologists was finding statues instead of the remains of real soldiers such as had been unearthed from later periods. Going back to the Shang Dynasty, 1700 to 1100 B.C., warriors, women, servants, and horses were commonly entombed to serve their rulers in death as they had in life.

Although I have little feeling for works of art that thrill the average tourist, it was a memorable moment for me standing there at the edge of an excavation as large as two football fields, thirty to fifty feet deep, now protected inside a new building as large as a giant aircraft hangar. I marveled at row upon row of statues standing as they had for more than two thousand years, those tumbled by forgotten earthquakes being carefully repaired. Their faces haunted me, expressions of happiness and satisfaction, even joy—perhaps the artists had caught the relief of subjects permitted to live out their lives while their effigies stood guard. I wanted above all else to climb down and stand among those ancient soldiers, posing for a picture with my arms around their shoulders, but there were guards and NO PHOTOGRAPHY signs abounding.

There followed two dreary days in Xi'an geared to the hardened tourist. First a visit to the bell tower in the old city, then the drum tower, then the great mosque, followed by meticulous inspections of the Big and Little Wild Goose Pagodas. One temple I could have endured, however it tried my patience, but by the end of the third day I had exceeded my limit. Where was the Great Wall, surely the most dramatic structure ever built by man? Why did my fellow travelers not want to see it as much as I?

We boarded a plane for Lanzhou, three hundred miles westward. There we had dinner while the Soviet airliner was refueled. I watched the daylight hours slip away and I did not even bother looking out the window when we took off again, because it was pitch-dark; no chance of seeing the Great Wall, whose course we paralleled for three hundred miles as we flew to Urumqi, the capital of Xinjiang, twelve hundred miles away. Add to all that, the discordant and nerve-racking beat of the four engines, whose propellers were never synchronized in four solid hours. Two in each ear they kept shouting at me: "Out of sync, out of sync." Everyone seemed fast asleep; as I looked around only one man seemed alive, Dallas Clinger, my wingman from combat here in China many years ago.

Long after we landed and I was in bed at the Kunlun Hotel, I still heard the beat of those miserable engines. I lay there thinking about tomorrow, my mind racing; this was the far West, where I would begin my escape. The next morning I felt I had a new lease on life. No more pagodas, zoos, museums, or temples; I had five days in Urumqi, ample time to experiment, and we were far enough removed from the big cities that I felt the security forces of the People's Republic of China might be quite slack.

The railroad ran southeastward just over seven hundred miles to Jiayuguan, the end of the Silk Road and the western terminus of the Great Wall of China. I put my plan into effect by telling Rowena, the tour leader, that I had come down with an upper respiratory infection—a plausible story, as several people in our group already had colds or the flu. When they drove off to see rug factories, pagodas, and a temple or two, I dressed like a Chinese, put on dark glasses to hide my round eyes, stooped to hide my height, and imitated the typically Chinese half-trot I had so often observed. I almost fooled myself and attracted no attention as I made my way to the railroad station to buy a ticket to Jiayuguan and the Great Wall, but all my efforts that day were for naught.

There was the railroad station, all right, but no ticket windows or ticket sellers as we know them. Even if there had been, I soon realized I could not take a train anywhere, even if I were a citizen and looked as Chinese as Chairman Mao. Travel is very much restricted in the PRC, where the average Chinese is expected to stay within a few miles of his home. To do what I had planned, I would need a very important document known as a travel permit.

The next day I begged off with the excuse that my cold was

worse. Being the oldest in the group and having gray hair that was almost white, it was not too difficult to convince the sympathetic tour director. This time I scouted out the buses, but travel by that mode was even more restricted than by train. Then I discovered that there were no private cars in China; the only way to obtain one was to hire one from China International Travel Service. All the doors to travel seemed closed to me.

Just the same, my five days of frustration were not wasted. I had experimented in Urumqi, there in the shadow of the lofty Tien Shan, learning the vital elements of escape for the weeks to come in a sort of on-the-job training. If security was tight, I at least had a *modus operandi* by which I might escape at a later date. The last evening I reported myself cured of my illness and flew off the next day with the group to Lanzhou. I had my camera ready to photograph the Great Wall as we again passed over the West Tower at Jiayuguan, but once more I was denied sight of what I was beginning to think of as a sort of great white whale in my life; droves of cloud assembled on all sides to blot out all sight of the valley of the Qilian Shan where the Wall ran.

Lanzhou is the Houston, Texas, of China, a smoky and smelly city with oil refineries and other industries. No sooner had we arrived than Rowena, the tour leader, called a special meeting to ask if there were any side trips we wanted to make. As she asked, I had the feeling that she was looking pointedly at me because of all the excuses I had made to beg off pagoda and temple visits. I had become a thorn in her side but hated to be considered a chronic complainer, because all tours already have enough of those. I did not answer as other people offered other opinions, but she came back to me and asked again.

"Here we are within a mere seventy-five miles of the Great Wall," I said off the top of my head. "It is just north of us along the Yellow River. What I would like to do is make a special trip all by myself and at my expense, right here." By this time I was up in front of everyone, pointing to the Great Wall on my map. "What I want to do while you all visit the damned pagodas and temples, even the zoo, is hire me a car through CITS, even take a taxi if I can't get a car, and drive north along the river to see it. I wouldn't subject any of my pagoda-oriented companions to such hardships with me."

Well, of course my tour mates laughed, all except Dallas Clinger. Nevertheless, we were to be in Lanzhou several more days and it was an opportunity I was determined not to lose. Rowena arranged another meeting for noon the following day, this time with the mayor and one of the highest political officials in the Province of Gansu. She had already broached the subject of a visit to the Great Wall on my behalf and I was feeling hopeful for the first time.

As the meeting began I placed one of my maps on a table and pointed out with a red pencil where I wanted to go while the interpreter translated. I made a matter-of-fact presentation, calling the Wall by its proper name in Chinese to help establish my credibility as a serious researcher: Wan Li Chang Cheng—the long rampart of ten thousand *li*. I stressed what a wonderful country China was, and what a wonder of the world its Great Wall.

The mayor arose and held a lengthy conference with the political commissar of Gansu. Then he came over and dramatically shook my hand, looking so pleased that I just knew the curse had been lifted and I was about to visit the Great Wall, touch it with my hands, after all those years of wishing. When he finished speaking, the interpreter translated.

"Comrade mayor say he understand all you tell him. But Great Wall all broken down, finished. Nobody want to see broken-down Wall. Also, Wan Li Chang Cheng very far from Lanzhou, very rough road go there. Too rough. Much danger."

I refused to give up and tried repeatedly to explain the difference between foreign tourists who want to see pagodas, and soldiers who could walk that mere seventy-five miles, given enough time. I admit I played heavily on the soldier part, that I had fought for China during World War II. He invariably came back to the phrase "Nobody want to see broken-down Great Wall."

Slowly something came back to me about the Chinese that General Chennault had tried to teach me years ago. There is an intangible called "face," which Americans never fully understand because our culture lacks the Oriental concept. The Great Wall is a national treasure in ruins; to have foreigners see it as eons of neglect had left it caused them to lose face. It was unworthy of display. I realized that I was beaten.

I thanked them all and went with the tour group to the zoo. As I looked at the giant panda sleeping in the hot summer afternoon, I had the feeling that he and I were resigned to our fates and no longer fighting back. I would wait my turn and learn more, I resolved, and sooner or later, damn it, I would escape.

Rowena was increasingly sympathetic to my desires and suggested that we two attend a play. I was not in the mood for it and was going to refuse until she mentioned it was about the Silk Road—*Yipek Yoli* in Uigur—and had been famous in China for hundreds of years. I was thankful now, and fortunate that I did go, as I consider it one of the most fascinating plays I ever saw. It made no difference that I did not understand a word of it; right before my eyes was portrayed the very history I had been studying all the years of my growing obsession with the travels of Marco Polo. Providence had so far denied me all but the smallest glimpse along the thousands of miles of this journey, but that night I had been led along the Silk Road by actors in full costume against elaborately painted scenery.

Huang He, the Yellow River, flows from the mountains of Qinghai Province near Tibet right through Lanzhou before turning slightly northward for four hundred miles to Inner Mongolia. There it turns east and finally south, forming a thousand-mile horseshoe called the Great Bend. Our itinerary out of Lanzhou called for us to follow the river north on our way to a place in Inner Mongolia called Hu-Ho-Hao-T'e, where we would visit the Mongols. I knew that some seventy miles out of Lanzhou we would pass through a gap in the Great Wall at the exact place I had wanted to visit by hired car. Our train would then follow the river east for another hundred miles before turning north again and passing once more through the Wall at a place called Yinchuan. Somewhere on this trip I had to see something!

But no. As we neared the first gap I had my camera ready in anticipation, and as we turned eastward I ran from one side of the train to the other but saw nothing that resembled the Great Wall. Two hundred miles north of Lanzhou, our train puffed into Yinchuan and stopped. I ran off with my camera, found a signal ladder, and climbed the metal rungs as the train crew watched in alarm. It had to be out there but I never saw it, and would not from here on out because it continued eastward across the Ordos, as the region within the Great Bend is known. I dejectedly put my camera away as we journeyed farther into inner Mongolia to spend three nights sleeping in a yurt, the igloo-shaped local habitation of thick felt. Then to Datong (formerly spelled Tatung) for a few days and on by train to Taiyuan, from where we would fly to Beijing. I hoped my travels with the tour group would end there. That day in 1944 when I had flown my P-51 fighter along the Great Wall, praying to return someday on the ground, it had been at Datong that I had turned back toward Xi'an to refuel. I knew the masonry Wall continued that far and a little beyond the Yellow River before giving way to the rammed-earth Great Wall of the West, so as we prepared to depart Datong, I had my camera ready again.

We made the trip at night. Was I ever going to see it? Was there some kind of a hex on this trip, or some reason why I was being tested to the extreme? Then I remembered the papal blessing, those prayers from a very high place, and I took heart.

From a post office in Inner Mongolia, I had dispatched a telegram to U.S. Ambassador Woodcock in Beijing, informing him that I would be arriving there on August 21 and respectfully requesting that arrangements be made with officials of the PRC for me to leave my tour group at that point. I also asked specifically for a personal visa and a travel permit to allow me to enter the military zone of Kashgar, so that I could follow the Silk Road from there to Jiayuguan, with the eventual goal of following the Great Wall all the way to Shanhaikwan and Old Dragon Head at the Yellow Sea. As we boarded the train to Taiyuan, I kept saying to myself: "By now the ambassador has my message." When we boarded a small British airliner for Beijing, I just knew he was working to aid my escape from the tourists.

No sooner had we landed than it was evident that security was tighter in the capital than anywhere else I had been in the PRC. It was lunchtime but I did not even want to think about food in my excitement, knowing the American embassy was nearby, relatively speaking in a mega-city of seven thousand square miles. My request to go there fell on deaf ears, but I realized that the Friendship Store—an official Chinese store for foreign visitors—that many of my fellow tourists would visit was on the Chang'an, the main street of Beijing, and from there it was only a block to Guang Hua Lu and the Chinese "Embassy Row."

I was off the bus and almost running to the destiny I felt in my heart. It was hot and humid that twenty-first day of August as I ran from flag to flag, looking for the U.S. embassy. When I saw the Stars and Stripes waving high above number 17, I hesitated just for a moment, wondering if I looked presentable after all the traveling. I need not have worried. My telegram from Inner Mongolia had arrived and everyone was alerted. All the personnel, moreover, seemed to have either read or heard about my numerous letters. Hardly had I entered and presented my passport than I was greeted by the assistant Army attaché, Chief Warrant Officer George Williams. Although I did not know it then, George would be my host for the rest of my stay in China and we would become good friends. He shook my hand as though he had anticipated my arrival with genuine pleasure, then took me into his office, where I met Captain Samuel Monk, the U.S. naval attaché, who broke the news to me that the embassy was honoring vice-presidential candidate George Bush with a cocktail party and the ambassador was expecting me to attend.

With my sad state of dress in mind, I almost declined, but my new friends had already considered my problem. All I had to do was go back to the Friendship Store and buy what I needed. They even provided an embassy car with a Chinese driver, and after I had outfitted myself, it took me across the city to my hotel—also called Friendship—so that I could ready myself for the reception at the ambassador's residence at six.

What a change had taken place since I had reached the safe haven of the U.S. embassy. I had been treated like a five-star general on some vital mission rather than a retired fighter pilot. Feeling very grateful to Ambassador Woodcock and his staff, I washed my dark-blue shirt, which was fast-dry, and used a Chinese cleaning fluid I had bought to make my pants navy-blue again. Had Gucci had an outlet in the Friendship Store, I would have bought the best shoes, but I had to settle for black silk slippers costing three yuan—almost $1.75—to replace my running shoes. My evening attire was completed by a new dark-blue denim Mao jacket with four pockets. So dressed, I met Ambassador and Mrs. Woodcock, and stood in the receiving line to meet George Bush.

The reception changed my status. There I met the air attaché, Colonel William Webb, USAF, to whom I had written months before. He startled me by telling me that at the end of the reception I was to turn my passport over to Lois Williams, wife of CWO George Williams. As a member of the embassy staff, she would then arrange to have my name removed from the group visa of my tour. After that I could expect soon to have my own special visa for travel within the People's Republic of China.

I stood there in my less-than-two-dollar Mandarin slippers, waiting like Cinderella for midnight to strike, when I would find out it was all a dream. But it was all true, as though somehow I had become a member without portfolio of the U.S. embassy. After dinner at the home of Captain and Mrs. Monk, I was driven home in an embassy car, feeling ten feet tall all the way. When I closed my eyes and sought sleep, I saw the face of Pope John Paul II, who had blessed this journey and written above his signature, "This Pledge of Heavenly Favors I do impart." The last thought I had that night was to thank the Lord for such a friend as Charlie Russhon, who had interceded for me with the Holy Father—even if I was a Baptist.

# 19

# AT LAST, THE VISA

Because of rigid housing restrictions in overcrowded Beijing, it was necessary for me to have a place to stay before my name could be taken off the Lindblad Tour visa. Lois and George Williams took me into their apartment on the top floor of a high-rise overlooking the Chang'an, giving me their son Tom's room while he was at school in Japan. I stayed with them on my periodic returns to Beijing for the next travel permit, and I will be forever grateful to them for their unflagging hospitality and boundless kindness to me.

When Mr. Wu, the Chinese in charge of liaison between the American embassy and the government of the People's Republic of China, gave me my visa, I am certain he little realized what it meant to me or how long I had been waiting. Obtaining a travel permit to begin my journey would take a bit longer, and as I had not even said good-bye to my former companions, I decided to re-join the tour group on their visit to the Great Wall at Badaling. As usual, though, something again went wrong; at the last moment someone talked the tour leader into visiting the Ming Tombs, which relegated the Wall trip to a hurried afterthought late in the afternoon. That was the last straw—I had been waiting far too many years to postpone our meeting now.

I hired a taxi just as the sun was rising and Beijing was already teeming with traffic. It seemed as if all three million bicycles and twice that number of pedestrians were going our way on the narrow asphalt highway north. Every imaginable conveyance filled the road, including tour buses, tractors pulling riders on trailers, carts with great mounds of colorful vegetables, and people on foot carrying cabbages, carrots, beans, and eggplants on *jin* poles over their brawny shoulders. They smiled at us despite blaring horns as we threaded our way until, nine miles from the Great Wall of China, everything stopped in the biggest roadblock I had ever seen.

I climbed out to investigate and concluded that we were in for a long wait. I gave myself a talking-to for showing the impatience I had sworn to control, but I had been on my way to the Wall for such a long time and it was finally so close. And I doubt if we can change our dispositions and the tempo at which we live our lives. My decision was made before I returned to the taxi. There I explained to the driver that I was going to walk, for him to come meet me if the traffic ever cleared.

What better way to reach the Great Wall than to walk it uphill, every step of the way, through a small mountain pass where Genghis Khan once rode his horse? I did not even break stride when I found the reason for the traffic jam, a jackknifed tractor trailer that had strewn tons of huge stones from its toppled flatbed. Two hours passed as I climbed, grateful in the heat and humidity for all those ten-thousand-meter conditioning runs. To occupy my mind, I computed the distance I had run in the last two years, and the answer came to three thousand miles. Then I saw the first blue-gray ashlars and it occurred to me that the jammed traffic had been no accident; this was how I was meant to reach it at last. I rubbed my hand on the ashlar lovingly, then climbed the steps onto the Great Wall itself and walked the five thousand meters that had been restored.

I shouted aloud, gazing up at the lookout tower. "You've been testing me, I know, but damn it, I've won. . . . I've won!"

I did not mind the stares and funny looks of Japanese, Chinese, and American tourists; somewhere along the endless road I had lost my inhibitions. By the time the taxi arrived I had already climbed to the lookout towers in both directions, east and west. There was a good restaurant and I had lunch with the driver. While he waited I walked the Wall all over again, all of which added up to twenty-one miles of walking for the day.

That three-mile stretch at Badaling is the showcase the Chinese want the world to see. It is far safer than the many hundreds of miles of unrestored Wall but it can still be hazardous for the traveler in poor health. That Sunday, there were a good many Americans there, some in typically questionable health hanging on to the steel-pipe handrails and pulling themselves along as they climbed, puffing and blowing. In the steeper places they sat to catch their breath. The weather did not help, being sticky and hot that late-summer afternoon.

The man in front of me looked as if he might be inviting a heart attack. He was much overweight, obviously an American, his face flushed and becoming more so with each step as he kept up with his wiry wife. We approached the steepest part near the western look-out tower, where you reach a flight of stairs chiseled out of granite, each step of the fifty-degree incline too short for most American shoes. That is what the man saw ahead of him. He stopped in his tracks, sighed audibly, and shouted a remark to his wife about the stupidity of it all. Then, with the lookout tower all but reached, he did such an abrupt about-face that we nearly collided. As I dodged around him I heard a loud "The hell with it!" and he plodded off downhill, his wife after him ranting and raving about having come all the way from Cleveland and not climbing to the top of the Great Wall.

Back at the American embassy, Ambassador Woodcock took me to see the foreign minister of the PRC, Huang Zhen, and glory be—I had my personal visa stamped in my passport on two pages. More than that, I was presented with the vital travel permit. By noon I was on my way to Beijing International Airport in an embassy car, headed for the far West where China presses up against the Pamirs, the Karakoram, and the Hindu Kush. My destination was Kashgar, the town on the Silk Road that I had visited briefly during my accidental entry into China a year and a half ago. The first leg of my thousand-mile trip was by air to Lanzhou.

I checked in with China National Aviation Corporation and joined the Chinese waiting for the flight. A boarding announcement came over the public address system, staccato yet singsong, as Chinese strikes my Georgia ears, and I waited until the line had formed before taking my place at the end. The Russian engineers had designed their airliner for people with short legs, so I was anxious to minimize my time aboard the uncomfortable Ilyushin. Suddenly a Chinese woman dashed up. She was pretty, dressed in the regulation blue cloth, her jet-black hair in what my mother would have called a Dutch-boy bob (the Chinese had invented spaghetti, the compass, and gunpowder—I would not have been surprised if they had also invented this hairstyle).

"Aren't you an American?" she asked.

I replied that I surely was. She picked up my heavy backpack with one hand and took my hand with the other, pulling me through the crowd to the head of the line. I dragged my feet and tried to relieve her of my heavy bag, which I finally accomplished. I told her in a friendly but loud tone of voice that I had been content to board last as befitted a stranger in a foreign land. She replied just as loudly that I was a soldier, pointing to my name and rank on the bag, then turned to address the crowd in rapid-fire Chinese. Passengers in the long line we had passed were smiling good-naturedly at me, some of them giving me the thumbs-up sign from my days in China in World War II. I heard the old shout of *Ding hao*, which means roughly "you are number one!" I had heard the words for "American" and "general officer" but I wondered what in the world else she had told them.

"You see," she explained as we climbed the boarding ramp, "they wanted you at the front of the line. You are guest of China— their guest too."

I tried to sit in my assigned seat but she tugged me into an aft section apparently reserved for VIPs. I offered her the window seat but she refused, saying she had to be free to move among her colleagues. They were college professors from the Institute of Applied Chemistry at Changchun, a large city in the Northeast, all on their way to Lanzhou to attend a seminar on the tung nut. She explained that she was an authority on tung oil, a very important resource in China, she assured me.

Before I realized it, I had been introduced to all the other professors as an American fighter pilot general who had flown for

China during the war. Naturally I was to blame for that. Fighter aces are not terribly modest and it has never taken me long to tell total strangers about myself. If she had singled me out to practice her English, she had another surprise coming, because I launched into a story on her own subject. It turned out to be the most interrupted anecdote I ever tried to relate because each time I finished a sentence she would translate it for all the others.

There were four squadrons in my 23rd Fighter Group, three of them dispersed over eastern China at fields such as Kweilin, Lingling, and Hengyang, while the fourth remained at our headquarters in Kunming. Every so often General Chennault would send me out to make tactical inspections, during which I would fly with the squadrons on their missions for two or three days. For some reason, each time I visited the 75th Squadron at Hengyang, I would find myself sticking to every chair I sat in; if I moved to another, that one stuck to the seat of my pants, the back of my shirt, and my sleeves. I raised a little hell about it and found out that every time it was announced that the group commander was to visit, the Chinese maintenance crews would swarm in to tidy up and paint. That included the tables and the bed I slept in.

I was highly honored but distressed by the physical aftereffects, because I always broke out in a rash that itched fiercely. By the time I returned home to Kunming, I was scratching all over. Doc Manget laughed and diagnosed my problem as hives. He saw the sticky residue on the back of my pants and shirt and needed no further explanation, already knowing the cause.

"Why, boy," he said, "all you have is a full-blown case of what we'd call poison ivy in Georgia. You see, the same caustic alkaloids appear in tung oil, which the Chinese use as a paint thinner. You've been sitting in it for days, long enough for it to develop into a case of hives."

It might not have been a nice story to tell elsewhere but the tung oil specialist and her friends made an attentive audience. Finally I revealed the ultimate cure, telling how I had scratched all summer until Doc Manget had sent to the States for an antitoxin called tincture of *rhus toxicodendron*, which is the Latin name for plain old poison ivy—presumably fighting fire with fire. In any case, the name was well known to these highly specialized professors; yes, they nodded, *rhus* was one of the chemicals in tung oil.

I could feel the change of pressure in my ears signaling that the pilot was letting down for a landing. It had been such an interesting "pickup" that I was sorry it was coming to an end. I wanted to know more about my traveling companion and asked if she was married.

"Oh, yes," she replied. "I have two children. My husband is soldier in People's Liberation Army stationed far away on Russian border, maybe thousand miles."

I asked if he was allowed to come home frequently to see his family.

"No," she said simply, "he never come home. When we marry, People's Republic of China allot us one child. We have two, so husband moved far away."

In Lanzhou the lady professor disembarked with her fellow faculty members. I waved and they waved back, friends joined by the lowly tung nut. I was shocked at her quiet acceptance of personal tragedy, the result of not complying with the national policy of birth control. Ever since, I have wondered if the Powers That Be have relented and permitted her husband to come home to his family.

After dinner at Lanzhou, I reboarded to find every seat filled with strangers who did not remotely resemble the Chinese. I had encountered the first of the minorities that inhabit the far West. Urumqi, our destination, is the capital of the Xinjiang-Uigur autonomous region, a new name—meaning "new marches"—for the old Chinese *Turkestan* of my high school geography. It is an enormous region comprising one sixth of China's total landmass, with a population of barely ten million, or less than ten percent of the country's billion inhabitants.

I diligently studied my map for company, feeling a bit lonely amid all those strangers whose dress and languages varied so greatly. What rescued me was that colorful *National Geographic* map that had accompanied the article "Journey to China's Far West" in one issue. The reverse had excellent artists' illustrations, portraits showing the various peoples of the region in action. There were the

Uigurs, Kazaks, Mongols, Kirghiz, Xibe, and Hui in native dress, often depicted with their children. The plane got very quiet and I realized that people were staring at me. No, at my map. Pretty soon I was mobbed in a friendly manner, the conversation constant even though I knew nothing of the three or four languages. Inquisitive, eager hands reached across from both sides of the aisle and from behind to point out to which ethnic group they belonged, the meanings of their pantomimed explanations startlingly clear. In minutes we felt we were bosom friends.

One of the older men, a Kazak, was head man of a village or commune in the Tien Shan, the high mountain range so prominently depicted on my map, and I knew he was important by the deference accorded him. He held back at first but was soon as animated and enthusiastic about the illustrations as the younger Kazaks. In his very few words of English he told me that his name was Abdullah Allazhan and invited me to come to his village, which we eventually located on the map. He pointed to the roof, then outside at the stars until I finally understood; he was telling me that the name of the body of water depicted near his village on my map was Sky Lake. When I realized, he took my hands in his and congratulated me.

Much as I would have liked to accept, I had to refuse because there would be an airplane waiting the next morning to fly me to Kashgar—or so I thought as we parted company on the ground at Urumqi. The China International Travel Service girl who met me said there was no air service to Kashgar, which she called "Kashi," and there never had been. She officiously added that in her two years as a travel guide I was the only foreigner ever to receive permission to venture into that closed military zone. She obviously felt some mistake had been made and was not well disposed to help me. The best she could do, she said, was book me passage on a bus to Kashgar.

After she left me at the Kunlun Hotel—the same one I had stayed in with my tour group—I studied my map from a different perspective. An airplane could have made the seven-hundred-mile journey in three hours; ground distance on roads that wandered all around the lofty mountains would surely extend the trip to over a thousand miles, an ordeal by bus I was not anxious to tackle until I had exhausted all other possibilities.

Then I dug the thick *Nagel's Encyclopedia Guide—China* out of my bag and learned that Urumqi in Uigur (pronounced *wee-gur*) was called Wu-Lu-Mu-Qi. It matched what Abdullah had told me; I gathered the Kazaks called it Wu-Lu-Mu-Chi, although I was not certain if they pronounced it in three syllables or four; I certainly could not argue with the name, though, because it was their capital.

CITS would have another chance to arrange travel more in keeping with my official permit; in the meantime, if it was not too late, I had decided to take Abdullah Allazhan up on his invitation. There were just too many stories I had heard about those mountains now to miss this golden opportunity. One had it that Genghis Khan's tomb was up there, protected by Mongols of a secret society. Most likely just folklore, but how was I ever to know unless I visited the Tien Shan? I knew, moreover, that the best horsemen in the world lived up there and I had visions of riding with them in the Celestial Mountains.

I found Abdullah having breakfast in the hotel and was cheered that the invitation was obviously still open—he met me with open arms, literally. It was a long distance to Sky Lake and I eyed our light-blue Mitsubishi minibus with distrust; that was, after all, the company that had built the Zero fighter I battled in the skies over China. As we climbed high over hairpin turns that reminded me of the Burma Road, though, I came to admire that Japanese vehicle. It was a tough 150 miles before we turned into a valley and Abdullah signaled me to get off.

From the very beginning I could not take my eyes off the scenery. A village of yurts lay before us and a crystal blue lake. Horses were everywhere, droves of them, never standing still but always seeming to run. Abdullah pointed to the snowcapped mountains forming the background and indicated on my map to be certain I understood. There was Bogda Shan at over 19,000 feet. Across to the west on the Soviet border was the king of the Tien Shan range at more than 23,000 feet. "Its name Mount Tomar, Russians say," Abdullah stated, "but our name Hantengri."

After I met Abdullah's wife, Moran, and children, we had

dinner in his yurt. It was a hemisphere, twenty-five feet in diameter, of thick felt over a wooden frame. The same four-inch-thick felt of yak fur also made the floor. There were a dozen pallets arranged around the walls and I imagined it would be very warm even at 7,000 feet with so many people sleeping in one room. How was a loner like me going to forget that there were other people around and be able to sleep? I need not have worried. At bedtime I was led off to another yurt—or *ger*, as Abdullah called it. Somehow I was isolated, given my privacy in the implicit but definite way of this foreign culture, and I slept well.

Kazak food was millet and lamb, the latter roasted over charcoal, with the finest melons I had ever eaten. I ate in Abdullah's *ger*, served by his wife, Moran. There were nine children but I do not think all of them were theirs. Some were possibly cousins or nephews and nieces, though I diplomatically did not try to find out. It was primitive but not in a derogatory sense; I could not have been accorded greater hospitality or more genuine friendship had I been a high official of Dzungaria, as I learned the region was called.

That first day with the Kazaks, Abdullah and I rode horses to the lofty shores of the most beautiful lake I had ever looked down upon. It was very aptly named Sky Lake; such was all I could think as I saw the reflections of clouds and sky in crystal water. That morning I also studied my host in his natural habitat—he had not fit on an airliner or in the hotel, but on his horse in the rugged mountains of Tien Shan he was magnificent.

Abdullah Allazhan stood five feet ten, slightly above average height for a Kazak. He had coal-black hair cropped short, ears that stuck out—the better to hear with, I thought—and skin like a Mongol, more golden than brown. A round face too strong to be handsome, but who looks for handsome men in the high passes of the Tien Shan? He was tough and masculine; he wore rough clothing, hand-spun and handmade by his wife, of thick blue denim "stone-washed" a thousand times, topped by a short-billed cap of the same material.

But it was the way he sat on his horse that set him apart from the rest of the world. He was part of his mount, the brain, so at home that you could see he had grown up there. A photograph I took shows him astride his quarter horse, Abdullah as tough as the crests of the Tien Shan behind him. On the sharp pommel of his saddle sits his one-year-old grandson, Yakub, already learning how to ride.

Kazaks ride very differently from the way I had been taught in cavalry instruction at West Point. They do not post as they trot their horses; they ride them at a full gallop, and they do not take their weight in their knees but put it all in their short stirrups. And what a saddle! Narrow seat with pommel and cantle so close together that it reminded me of being wedged between two shoehorns coming to a point at the horse. I endured those instruments of torture as I rode with the Kazaks and played their game for three days, and for a month afterward I was sore.

Abdullah understood when I told him I had been a fighter pilot. He explained it to his wife, moving his hands just as fighter pilots do when illustrating the relative positions of aircraft in a dogfight. He was obviously evaluating my riding skills as we rode up to Sky Lake, because soon afterward I was introduced to a fascinating and ancient game called "goat tussle."

The "ball" was a black goat submitted by a sponsor in this case my host, Abdullah. After being slaughtered by having its head removed, the animal was dumped in the middle of a playing ground between two groups of horsemen. At a signal every rider rode at a thunderous gallop, the first to arrive reaching down from his saddle to scoop the carcass up with his hand. Then off he plunged, with the others in hot pursuit, until another player caught up with him and a tug of war ensued. The ultimate victor was the rider who finally managed to take his prize to the top of a special yurt made of earth and stones with turf growing over the rounded roof twenty feet above ground level. It reminded me of a potato house or root cellar; whatever it was, I would have hated to try to ride a horse to the top, even with both hands on the reins, much less burdened with the carcass of a goat.

I have to stress the word *gallop,* because I never saw a horse walked or trotted during a game. I witnessed superb agility and skill as players routinely leaned out at a full gallop and touched the ground with their hands. In the games I played—if trying with all my might just to stay in my uncomfortable saddle can be called playing—I never once managed to touch the goat. Nevertheless, I take pride in the fact that I did stay on my horse every minute of the melee and was never "policed," as my classmates at West Point would have called it. Goat tussle is a primitive game, rough and cruel, not made for the meek, but playing it made my week.

The victor relished his success, holding the black goat's remains high overhead and waving them in triumph. Sportsmanship prevailed then as all the participants surrounded the structure upon which the victor's horse pranced, and cheered. Then the battered carcass was delivered to the winner's yurt, where his wife waited. It was drawn and quartered for roasting, and there followed another ceremony as everyone took part in a feast. I learned my visit was the reason for the games. Abdullah also assured me that good fortune came to all who feasted upon the prize. *"Buzkashi, buzkashi,"* he kept repeating, and thus did I finally learn what the Kazaks called it.

It seemed to me that I had heard of this game before in Afghanistan, that the Afghans considered it their national game, as, perhaps, the Mongols do too. I have tried to research this game since then, having heard rumors that it is the forerunner of polo. The only written description I have ever seen appears in the book *Tien Shans*, which I found in the Kunlun Hotel gift shop in Urumqi:

Sky Lake is at the foot of Mount Bogda where the immortals take their baths. An elongated depression from glacial erosion, it is 1,980 meters above sea level. Here the best horsemen in the world vie with each other in the game of Goat Tussle. A favorite traditional game among the Kazak, the Kergez, the Tajik and the Mongols, it is usually held during a festival or when the occasion calls for merry-making.

The book went on to say that there had been games in which as many as two thousand riders took part. There had been a score around me at the start, but by the third day—when word got out that there was a "tenderfoot" to watch—others came from far and wide. They wore their horses as fighter pilots wear their aircraft, viewing their mounts as we view our planes—as gunnery platforms, a means to an end. They also demonstrated their skills in other ways, speeding past me while standing tall on those tricky saddles, reaching down to draw ancient rifles from their scabbards. At a full gallop, they aimed quickly at small blocks of wood tossed aloft as targets and hit them—I saw the splinters fly. Then they reassembled and dashed past again to swing down beneath the bellies of their horses, disdainful of pounding hooves, their heads barely above the ground, after which they would pull themselves back into the saddle from the off side.

On a ride around the lake I had to come clean with my host and admit to him that I was allergic to the saddles. Mincing no words or gestures, I rubbed my *gluteus maximus* and grinned ruefully. He understood and from then on I resorted to taking walks. It was during one of these that I discovered the fairly modern buildings whose roofs of green tile I had seen from our minibus when we arrived in the beautiful valley. Closer inspection suggested a resort and I suspected it had been just that before the Cultural Revolution.

From there, across the lake I saw some yurts, a group of them suggesting another commune. My attention was drawn to a crowd gathered around a cloud of gray smoke. I set out to investigate.

Reaching the obviously happy group, I found men and boys roasting something over charcoal grates. They greeted me in friendship and I waved back and grinned, drawn to an appetizing smell like lamb. I gestured to indicate that I would pay for some of the food, trying to pay the man who seemed to be the chief cook, but he ignored the Chinese yuan and gathered a handful of skewers for me. He shook his head again at the money, smiling as he pointed me toward some pine trees where more people were eating the reddest watermelons I ever saw, ones with small white seeds. Before I realized it I was sitting eating the tasty lamb and washing it down with watermelon juice. Again they refused to take any money. They surely did not look rich and it took money to live anywhere, even Xinjiang. They did not look as though they belonged to the village I lived in. Did being the guest of Abdullah Allazhan extend this far?

I wondered all the way back to my isolated yurt, where my host told me that they were indeed part of his commune. They were hunters, and it was not lamb I had eaten but the rarest of big game,

*Ovis poli,* the Marco Polo sheep of the Tien Shan, Altai, and Pamir mountains.

My stay was over, and sad as the thought was, I had to leave my new friends to press on for Kashgar and the Silk Road. Again I tried to pay but Abdullah just laughed and put me in the blue van. I knew better after that than to offer money; I considered giving him my watch but what would he need it for? He was a communist, the first I had really come to know, and one of the finest human beings I had ever seen. More than that, he was my friend and I was his. Over final farewells I asked again how I could express my appreciation and he finally gave me an answer, mostly in pantomime. That picture I took of him with Yakub on the pommel of his saddle—he wanted a copy.

# 20

# KASHGAR, THEN ACROSS TAKLAMAKAN WITH THE UIGURS

CITS National Guide Jo Li-chen took even more pleasure than before in giving me the bad news. Despite the fact that my official permit specified air travel, I would have to go by bus if I insisted on visiting Kashgar. Oh, well, I concluded, perhaps I was due a bad week to compensate for the fascinating time I had enjoyed with the Kazaks of Sky Lake.

The thousand-mile-plus ride in the red bus lasted all day and all night, and it seemed an interminable journey before we finally stopped in front of a hotel in Kashgar. Judging by the countless large vehicles in all directions, this was "truckers' heaven." I went inside expecting the worst, but found a room and thankfully went to sleep.

It was mid-afternoon when I regained consciousness. I jumped out of bed, scolding myself for missing so much of the day in Kashgar. Here I was, back on the Silk Road and wasting time. From the window it was a different place from the Kashgar I had visited four years earlier. There was no blizzard this time to blow the smoke and fumes and dust from this desert outpost, which turned out to be a center of heavy industry. I could hear the pounding of great hammers and presses, and the very air was colored by noxious chemical fumes that had turned the surrounding countryside into a dustbowl. The effect was startling when the wind blew; now I understood the comment the bus driver had made about the "red wind of Kashgar." I could smell it, taste it, and now knew that it was what had been making me feel strange since my arrival.

When I went outside I realized that the surrounding terrain concentrated the pollution. My map confirmed the suspicion, showing mile-high Kashgar to be at the deep end of a U-shaped basin bordered by some of the highest mountains on earth. The Kunlun Shan lay to the south and the Tien Shan to the north, and closing the western side of the long channel between these ranges were the Pamirs. The enclosed waterless wasteland, known as Tarim Pendi or the Taklamakan Shamo, ran east a thousand miles.

As I walked along on my first exploration, I realized I had been fooled on the previous visit when heavy snow had called a temporary halt to the industry. I automatically associated high, wide-open desert with clean air, not the rusty redness of dust and grime and fumes and smoke trapped in this cul-de-sac. Blast furnaces were all around me producing steel and acrid smells; I could almost feel the molten metal. Chemical plants standing between the steel mills assailed my senses and forced me to cough. There were glass factories and rug factories and a locomotive plant, but worst of all, because it was the loudest, was the diesel works. I visited it out of curiosity that turned to fear as I heard the king of noisemakers at close range. Then I walked away to measure how far the din would carry—not blocks, but miles. Kashgar had become a Pittsburgh without any modern-day environmental controls or restrictions whatsoever.

The streets of this town on the Silk Road—streets I had romantically dreamed of treading since my boyhood—were clogged with such traffic as could hardly be believed. Uncontrolled conglomerations of vehicles, some belonging to another age, vied with camels, bicyclists, and pedestrians, everybody following his own rules. No traffic lights—just bedlam. I stared at one vehicle that reminded me of our Old West except that it was being pulled by loping camels instead of horses: a camel carriage.

Next day I continued my tour to determine how far the sound and fury carried, how far the fumes that caused my eyes to burn and my throat to scratch until I coughed way down deep, how far I could feel the strokes of the drop forges. When I left on a bus for Khotan on the third day, my mind turned to all the people that the industry had taken over and would, seemingly, destroy someday. I had counted a dozen different types of faces and dress, and they had studied me right back. If I represented another ethnic group, it meant thirteen distinct cultures mingled there on the Silk Road.

Khotan was a short run over the bone-racking roughness of the five-thousand-year-old road we navigated. It was the center of the silk industry and also, unfortunately, the end of the line of any organized transportation. From here to Jiayuguan, where I would meet the Great Wall at the Fortress Tower, I had to find my own way almost a thousand miles across one of the most challenging deserts.

Next morning I went to the bookstore, having long ago learned that if English is spoken anywhere in the boondocks, it is there. The young Uigur running the place really did speak English, and he confirmed what I had been dreading. "No camel trains anymore. Now many trucks, few camels."

There went my hopes of crossing the desert as Marco Polo had. Each time we passed the few caravans of camels on the road between Kashgar and Khotan, my pulse had quickened and my imagination raced. I knew the journey would take a month or more by camel, well beyond the expiration date of my travel permit, but I had dreamed of such a trip from childhood on. I consoled myself by purchasing a copy of the Red Book of Chairman Mao, which was on sale.

At breakfast I was doing my best between noodles and tea to read some meaning into the quotations of the Chairman, which I doggedly translated out of the Red Book with the help of my dictionary. I was so engrossed I failed to notice a man studying me from another table until at last I felt his eyes on me. I glanced up and nodded, out of courtesy, before returning to the Red Book. He did not respond or look away. After he finished his meal he stood and came over to my table, indicating one of the vacant seats. I did not understand what he said in Uigur but I pulled out the chair for him and shook his hand. He showed me he knew some English.

His name was Rhaman Khirip and he was a truck driver. Seeing me struggling with the Red Book had brought him into my life at just the right time. He had been a soldier in the Soviet Army during World War II, a truck driver then, too, he told me. Although I did not remotely suspect it when we met, he was to make possible my trek across the Taklamakan.

Rhaman fluidly recited some of his favorite sayings of Chairman Mao from memory and I asked him to explain one that went "To lose Yan'an is to win Yan'an!" He tried initially to explain its meaning but quickly changed the subject to his reason for coming over in the first place. To any Russian or Chinese addicted to tobacco, an American tourist meant the possibility of American cigarettes. His face fell when I told him I did not smoke, until I told him I had two cartons upstairs in my room which he was welcome to have.

In all my life I never smoked. Somehow I had always known that those bastardly little things wrapped in tissue paper really were "coffin nails," knew that they could kill you long before the surgeon general forced the tobacco companies to print warnings on every pack. I had even seen the lungs of addicts in autopsies—seeing them stained as black as coal, clogged with tar, should be enough proof for anybody. Yet I had brought six cartons along in my backpack because they were light, travel well, and are universal tender among smokers. Much as I hate cigarettes, I was very grateful to the tobacco industry of North Carolina as I handed over the remaining cartons of Camels.

We became excited when Rhaman realized that my desired course, which I traced on my map, was exactly the route traveled by the ten heavy Soviet trucks he commanded on regular runs to the railhead at "Chiayukwan"—to me Jiayuguan—which he also called "steel city." His convoy would be loaded with silk and ready to leave in just a few days. Just that simply, my passage across one of the most barren wastelands on earth was provided.

I honestly did not know if the cigarettes were adequate payment, and now understood that offers of payment were often insulting in this part of the world where they might cause the recipient to lose face. I was therefore in a quandary about what to give Rhaman

Khirip without offending him. I had heard, though, that it was all right to remove something from your person as a gift, so I took off the Rolex watch I had worn for years and presented it to him without saying anything about its being in return for any service. The watch might have been of no earthly use to Abdullah Allazhan, but it could certainly benefit my new friend, who lived by tight schedules.

Next day Rhaman took me to the garage where his ten trucks were being serviced for the journey. There I met some of the other drivers. The trip would take four to six days, I gathered, depending primarily on sandstorms in the desert. Before we left, he gave me a fascinating view of the five-thousand-year-old silk industry there in Khotan.

Marco Polo found silkworms here in 1275 and carried their eggs back to Venice in one of the pockets of his coat. As a Boy Scout, I had collected different species of caterpillars, raising them to maturity and waiting until they emerged as moths and butterflies from their cocoons. Spurred on by the history as well as my own special knowledge and interest, I visited the largest and oldest of the silk mills, where many of the wives and children of the Uigur truck drivers worked. The women did everything from feeding caterpillars to spinning strands of silk yarn to weaving the cloth. I was especially impressed by the children, who wore colorful pillbox hats covered with beautiful silk embroidery. Like all Chinese children, they were the most disciplined I had ever seen.

Rhaman Khirip had been born in Khotan and had grown up hearing stories about silk and its rich history. The name *Silk Road* was new in the last two hundred years, he told me. Before that it was called the Royal Road, because silk had been so expensive only emperors and their courts could afford it. Unlike other fabrics, it lived! Silk was and is the noblest of textiles, light and strong, cool and warm, pure, a soft and slightly golden color in natural form that, when dyed, takes on the luster of every hue in the rainbow. It protects without clinging and permits the skin to breathe. The thickest rug of knotted silk and the thinnest veil are everlasting. All from flimsy threads spun by the larvae of *Bombyx mori,* the mulberry spinner.

Other insects make silk thread but none is as suitable as that of *Bombyx mori,* which feeds only on mulberry leaves. Cultivated for five thousand years, this insect is dependent on man. The eggs laid by the female are minute, weighing less than a milligram, and may be kept for an indefinite time at low temperature. At the right moment, when mulberry leaves are available, a temperature rise to twenty-eight degrees Centigrade causes the eggs to hatch after ten days. In a month and after four moltings, the fully grown larvae are about six centimeters in length. They then spin their cocoons.

If left alone, dull-gray moths break out to mate and die in a brief lifetime. Cocoons used in production, however, are heated to kill the insect and dry the silk. They are then sorted repeatedly until all cocoons showing any imperfection have been removed. Those that are left are immersed in water heated to exactly the right temperature. If it boils, the cocoons fall apart; if too cool, they will not unwind. Those correctly treated are then brushed to remove the external threads, leaving a small ball on a hard core which is unwound in a technique going back two thousand years. Long ago the silk farmers also learned the principle of the crank and designed a winnowing fan driven by it. From the eleventh century on, Rhaman Khirip explained, there had been a silk winding machine using a foot pedal and a drive belt to unwind thread from the tiny cocoons.

All one morning I watched those little balls being unwound. The filmy thread, almost invisible and so fine I could not see it unless the rays of the sun picked it out, was as long as nine hundred meters. Five to seven filaments were twisted together to make a strand strong enough to be woven into silk cloth. By the time we were ready to leave I knew enough about the *Bombyx mori* to have qualified for a merit badge, the reason I had studied other caterpillars so many years before. I had also met all the other drivers and many of their families, and helped load twenty-odd tons of silk and gasoline drums. I felt more like a member of the crew, with a personal responsibility for that cargo, than a passenger.

No eight-hour drive, then a night's sleep, for silk caravans. I soon learned it was a flat-out run, day and night, with two drivers per truck taking twelve-hour shifts at the wheel or sleeping on the bunk behind the broad seat of the cab. Several times Rhaman mentioned we were in "bandit country." We had no guards and I saw no firearms anywhere, but guessed that being moving targets was our defense. Between oases we never stopped except for emergencies.

The caravan boss was of medium height and almost as wide as he was tall, with the biggest wrists I had ever seen—as big as biceps on most men. The only way I could account for them, corded as they were, were the violent jerks transmitted through the wheel. We threaded our way through twisting ruts almost as hard as concrete and the wheel did its best to twist out of his hands with pulsations as hard as a pneumatic hammer, but Rhaman Khirip never released his viselike grip. I watched his face, as intent as though he were driving at a hundred miles per hour even when we barely made walking speed. Only when the track straightened out would he relax a bit, saying over and over that someday there would be a paved road where we were.

"When?" I asked.

He just shook his head and wiped the perspiration from his face. Meanwhile, gravel slung from the tires rattled off the inside of the unpainted fenders. Every so often I would look back and report to the boss with a hand signal that all trucks were accounted for. That was when I discovered that making a circle with the thumb and forefinger, other fingers extended, means "okay" even in Uigur. On the second day, after the relief driver had driven his shift, we were on a smoother part of the Silk Road, out of those stony ruts. The boss nodded and I found myself taking a three-hour stint at the wheel. As though to tempt my nostalgia, we passed small caravans of camels every so often. I blew the horn and waved at them in salute and Rhaman waved also, for by that time I had told him of my boyhood ambition to travel the Silk Road on those "ships of the desert."

As I looked ahead through the sand-scarred windshield, I saw something ominous on the horizon. Could it be a dreaded sandstorm? Luckily, it never materialized. On the second day distant mountains rose out of the desert floor. By the next day they stood out dramatically. I drove another hundred miles before taking a turn on the bunk, where I managed to rest my eyes but could not begin to sleep in the heat and dust. I soon returned to my seat between the two Uigurs.

At an oasis where we filled our water cans, I found some Hami melons, the best melons in the world, I thought. I had been saving their seeds since Urumqi and Sky Lake for future experimentation back home. They constituted a remarkably healthy diet and those melon stops will be forever etched on my mind. I still have some of those seeds and am continuing to try to make them grow.

Then we reached A-K'u-Sai, marked by a sign chiseled into a great stone. I found the name on my map but there was no indication of a town. We stopped there on the crest of a hill to let our engines cool. Hot as the high desert was, standing there with the wind blowing through our radiators stopped the water boiling. All afternoon we had been flanking the Altun Shan, but right after that sign the road angled sharply north. I found the turn on my map and realized we had almost made it. Just sixty miles ahead lay Dunhuang and the Caves of the Thousand Buddhas.

On the fifth day we reached the mile-long cliff which held the famous caves, twelve miles out of the walled town of Dunhuang. It was mid-afternoon and one of the trucks had broken down, delaying it. I was driving and was about to pass when Rhaman touched my arm. He pointed to a guesthouse for visitors to the caves and explained as I braked that I could stay there while he towed the ailing truck back to Dunhuang for repair. So after 140 hours in that cramped cab I had a night in a room with a bed.

The guesthouse provided much more than a bed and meals after the thousand miles of Taklamakan desert; there was also a field office for China International Travel Service, and in it I ran into Chang Jin, a national guide I had met weeks ago with my travel group in Lanzhou. He recalled that I had wanted to see these caves, although visits had been restricted to archeologists. After dinner, Chang Jin took me back to CITS, where we found that my travel permit now made it possible for me to explore the caves. I was also permitted to rent a car and driver, and Chang Jin as my guide and interpreter, so after my visit we would all go by car back to Lanzhou, where they were based.

First, though, I had another visit to make. I asked to be taken into Dunhuang, where we found the garage so I could thank Rhaman Khirip. There I had a whole hour of good-byes with all the drivers. For presents I gave them postcards they wanted, showing cities in the United States, and one or two Hummel figures to pass on to the mothers of those small children with their richly embroidered pill-box hats. I had known the Uigurs just over a week but it seemed much longer; again I had found real friends.

When all the caves had been visited—and there were nearer two thousand than one—we set out in the car. The road to Jiayuguan for nearly two hundred miles lay along the ruins of Emperor Wu Ti's wall until it reached Yumen and the railroad to Urumqi. The remains of the mud wall, with a watchtower, were badly eroded and covered with drifted sand, but Chang Jin told me to take heart. Just ahead of us at Jiayuguan was the Tower Fortress at the west end of the real Great Wall of China. He remembered, moreover, that I had often talked about joining a camel train and he took pleasure in informing me of a nearby village where camel drivers lived with their animals. "Just be patient," he admonished. "In the morning I will make the arrangements."

At a hotel that night, I realized that another boyhood dream was about to be fulfilled, one that had refused to go away. I would ride camels along the Great Wall, even if only for a hundred miles, but I would not be content with just one or two; I would hire enough of those two-hump Bactrians to make my own camel train!

# 21

# MY CAMEL TRAIN

China—and therefore the civilized world—ended at Jiayuguan for centuries. The rammed-earth Great Wall built about 1370 by the Ming Dynasty ends there, too, on the Silk Road. Rising above this restored section of Ming Wall is a striking drum tower known fittingly as the Tower Fortress. There was no city at Jiayuguan before 1971, but immediately after the Cultural Revolution, iron was discovered in the Qilian Shan to the southwest and a town was created by decree. The first smelter was erected, fifty thousand workers were moved in, and a railroad was constructed to bring iron from the mines to the new "Steel City." Very soon Jiayuguan had a hundred thousand people.

Chang Jin took me to the Tower Fortress next morning to meet a middle-aged man in blue dungarees and a Mao jacket. He wore no insignia but I was certain by his bearing that he was an official of the People's Liberation Army. He seemed to know more about me than was stated in my travel permit, saying in passable English that he also had been a soldier in the big war, and I was surprised that he knew I had flown out of a base in Yunnan. After we shook hands he disappeared inside the Fortress Tower to return wearing a blue cap with the red star of the PLA. This he removed with a flourish and presented to me.

"I make you member People's Liberation Army!"

I thanked him, removing my baseball cap to put his gift on my head. I wore it from then on during my long trek to the end of the Great Wall.

My camel train awaited me, eleven Bactrian camels, each with a "puller" or driver. We spent the remainder of the day in the vicinity of the Fortress Tower taking pictures, with the ramparts of the Great Wall always in the background and me riding at the head of my spreading caravan.

It made for much starting and stopping, and was hard on the nerves. When I wanted to mount, instead of just climbing and settling myself between the two humps, I had to endure a lengthy and noisy ritual. The girl puller took in the slack on a line leading to the brass ring in the gawky beast's nose and called a long drawn-out "hhuurrhh!" The camel hated and despised this command, at first ignoring it as he continued to chew his cud. Following a more violent jerk on the line to his tender proboscis and a more insistent command, he stretched his long neck to the limit and gazed into the high heavens to emit a most plaintive cry of distress. Then, in final surrender, he plunged his front knees onto the rocky desert floor and slowly dropped from a half-crouch onto his stomach for me to climb aboard.

The ordeal of it all, the wailing and huffing, was bad enough but it was the wasted time that got to me. The breaking point was the sixth time; I knew that when in Rome you are supposed to do as the Romans do, but something in me rebelled. The hell with tradition, I thought, and took a running start at my standing camel. At full speed, I placed my hands on his high humps and vaulted, moving my hand to let my leg pass over the rear hump. It was simple, remindful of wall scaling in my Boy Scout days, and in one fluid motion I found myself snugly settled in among the soft camel hair. There had been no tugging on that tender nose, no shouting, no anguished wails echoing out across the desert.

The pullers and the PLA official who had given me the cap were shocked, but my camel seemed perfectly happy. In fact, when I grabbed his humps and vaulted onto his back, he acted as though he liked it; when I later slid off, it was clear he approved of the new routine. As soon as the indignity of crouching ceased, his dislike of me vanished. Hitherto, when my driver had forced him to drop to his stomach, he had bellowed at the sky and then twisted his neck a full 180 degrees to glare at me, long yellow teeth bared, and spit in my face. *Spit* is not the right word when a camel bathes you in its sticky regurgitated cud.

My journey along the Great Wall commenced in earnest the next morning. In the days ahead, the camel and I became friends. I took to stroking his neck as though he were a horse, and never again did he spit at me or glare with hatred in those green eyes. The worst part had been his doing his best to take a piece out of my backside with those huge teeth, and he never did that again either.

Human beings apparently accept some changes far less readily than camels, for it was obvious my actions confused the human element of my camel train. In 1985, word came back to me from tourists to Jaiyuguan who had been told about a "foreign devil" fighter pilot who had gotten on and off his camel in a ridiculous way—they were still laughing about me five years later!

Our course took us right alongside the dull-ocher Great Wall. This rammed-earth western expanse, baked brick-hard from centuries of exposure to sun and the elements, was badly eroded and now only fifteen to twenty feet high, as narrow as five or six feet on top. Every so often I would dismount and walk or run along the cracked crest, again to the surprise and delight of my pullers. I guessed my PLA official was there to keep an eye on me, but he proved to be a great assistant and expert photographer.

I took pleasure in rubbing my hands along the sides of the Wall, thrilled to be moving along its flanks although greatly disappointed by its condition. At times I dug small brightly colored pebbles from it to carry back home as souvenirs for young friends who had long believed in me and encouraged me to make this journey.

After two days we commenced to reach gaps in the ruins, short at first and then progressively longer until very little of the Great Wall remained to be seen. Then it ended dramatically at a dry river. We crossed it the next morning but failed to find more of the ruins until it was almost dark. It disappeared again on the fourth day and we all had a conference. The man in the Mao jacket showed me on my map that, except for isolated bits, little more existed of the ancient structure all the way through the Gansu Corridor to Lanzhou.

I had enjoyed the thrill of having my own camel train for over a hundred miles but it now seemed a good time to pay off the drivers so they could return to their village.

Chang Jin must have known exactly how far we could go with the camels, because he arrived late that afternoon with the car, and drove the PLA official back to the Fortress Tower before we headed on toward Lanzhou. We stopped frequently along the asphalt highway, the improved Silk Road, to visit remaining sections of the Great Wall marked on my map. At times we had to drive north off the highway along rough trails, frequently asking directions from the natives, before we found the ruins. They rarely lasted more than a mile but I would walk them and Chang Jin would meet me at the other end. Twice I discovered watchtowers, waiting for me but badly eroded. I traced them with my hands, feeling I was touching history.

After four days we reached a gap in the Wall north of Lanzhou. Here ran the railroad tracks over which I had journeyed with my tour group several weeks ago, and here was where I had dashed from one side of the train to the other in a vain attempt to see the Great Wall. No wonder I had seen only rocks and trees—this break in the ruins was five miles wide.

Chang Jin and I walked the top of the Wall, just where I would have been if the mayor of Lanzhou had not denied me permission, saying: "Nobody want to see broken-down Wall!" I could see the Yellow River—the Huang He—flowing east and then north, railroad tracks and Wall paralleling it. I knew they all ran northward until Yinchuan, where the Great Wall left to cut east across the horseshoe-shaped Great Bend of the Yellow River. My map told me the area enclosed by the thousand-mile-long bend was a desert region called the Ordos.

I would hire a car and go to Yinchuan, where I knew there was another gap in the Wall—that was where I had climbed a signal tower, searching unsuccessfully for my obsession. From there the car would take me east to follow the ruins across the Ordos, or so I thought as we returned to Lanzhou for the night.

# 22

# ESCAPE AT YINCHUAN

My plan went all to hell at sunrise. I hurried down to breakfast, only to feel my enthusiasm drain at the sight of tourists at every table. Just at that instant the girl from China International Travel Service caught me to say that, because of the crowds, there was positively no chance of finding a car for one lone foreigner. My hopes were blasted except for one daring contingency plan.

Ever since entering China, I had been studying the routine of train crews. My attention focused on the official who directed "foreign devils" to their isolated compartments and collected their tickets. This official, always a woman dressed in blue denim with a red star on her cap, knocked on your door as the train was puffing out of the station and carefully recorded in her logbook the serial number, point of departure, and destination indicated on your ticket. More significantly, she retained that ticket until you arrived at your destination, where she returned it and made certain you left the train.

For my emergency plan to succeed, no information could be taken down. Which meant holding on to that bit of paper no matter what, never letting her see it at close range. Then, with no record of my having boarded the train, I would be free to travel on my own with no national guide to prevent me from doing what I had to do.

China International Travel Service was most obliging when I explained that I had decided to terminate my journey because of the lack of rental cars at Lanzhou. I soon had a ticket and was cleared to depart on the Beijing Express. The Lanzhou railroad station was crowded with milling tourists, among them an American party waiting to board my train en route to the grasslands of Inner Mongolia. In order to fit right in and attract no attention, I removed my cap to reveal my gray hair and carried my backpack by its leather straps like a respectable suitcase. I also made sure my camera was very much in evidence.

When the train was announced I moved off ahead of the others, located my car, and showed my ticket to the woman at the steps. She glanced at it and held up three fingers to indicate my compartment, saying *"san"* in Chinese. I climbed aboard, running as soon as I was out of sight, and ducked into my compartment. Once inside I locked the door, pulled the shades, and changed clothes quickly, until within two minutes I could almost pass for Chinese—blue denim from head to toe, camera hidden in my soft blue combination suitcase-duffel bag, now worn as a backpack, the blue People's Liberation Army Cap pulled down over my hair, and dark sunglasses to hide my round eyes. After one quick glance in the mirror I unlocked the door, looked in both directions, and walked casually out of that VIP car toward the rear of the train.

However egalitarian "People's Republic" might sound, Chinese citizens do not enjoy the relative luxury accorded foreigners. Their rudimentary accommodations are at the rear of the train, often consisting of hard seats or no seats at all. I increased my pace through the filling train until I reached that section and slumped to the floor with an audible sigh, knees up and head down as though I had been carrying that pack for miles and miles.

I had entered another world. Chinese, dressed similarly to me, placed their bundles in racks above the hard seats behind me. It was not long before the train jerked into motion and I felt relief from all the tension.

When I calculated that seventy-five miles lay behind us, I knew we were passing through that wide gap in the Great Wall at Ching-T'ai; later I felt the train turn eastward from its northerly course, heading for the Yellow River bank just before reaching Chungwei, where we had walked along the Great Wall just yesterday. As more hours dragged by, I was aware that we had turned with the river to begin the final run north into Yinchuan.

By then darkness had closed in on the train compartment where I had sat for two hundred and fifty miles, barely moving other than to adjust my tired body. Although not near a window and unable to study my map—which would have been a dead giveaway—I was not worried about knowing when to get off, because Yinchuan, right on the edge of the Alashan Desert, is a large town for Inner Mongolia. Before we arrived, there would be movement, the waking of children, the gathering of bundles, so I leaned against the wall and trusted to such signals to alert me. There was just one tense moment barely twenty miles from my destination when a man in the white uniform with red piping of a security officer came through the door. To my relief he passed to the next car back, but returned shortly. He said something to a child before going forward again.

Near midnight the train slowed. I saw that a crowd had already gathered with belongings ready, so I joined it, ready for the most dangerous moment of my plan. When we stopped I walked off, keeping as many people around me as possible. Another white-uniformed security police officer stood by in the station, but he did not stop anyone to ask for identification.

I could tell by the stars that we were walking east. Knowing I would not have the opportunity to study my map all day, I had long since familiarized myself with Yinchuan and its environs. The railroad station lay some six miles west of town, which we reached on foot in two hours with me right in the midst of the largest group, not talking, to all appearances just another tired worker coming home.

Entering a hotel—the first one I saw—I went to the desk with travel permit and passport in hand, my sunglasses and hat off so as now to appear a typical "foreign devil." The clerk did not even look at the papers but asked a question in Chinese or, more likely, Mongol. I took a chance and nodded and he handed me a key. I never even had to sign my name. The next day I realized that he must have asked if I were part of the tour group that had just arrived at the hotel. My luck had held again.

Next morning, over rice cakes and tea, I met one of the Japanese tourists. In a mixture of pidgin English and pidgin Japanese, we talked about his itinerary and I learned they were traveling from Yinchuan to Yulin along the route of the Great Wall. Because of illness among my new friend's fellow travelers, there would be a few vacant seats on the bus. I had been prepared to set out on foot but there was no real point walking along the rammed-earth Wall, which was undoubtedly badly eroded. The distance to Yulin was nearly three hundred miles and from experience I suspected that for at least half that distance there would be no Wall at all.

Just that simply, I joined the Japanese tour and was out of Yinchuan before any of the security people could begin to investigate a lone foreigner who might have left a train before it reached the destination on his ticket. Of course my actions were forbidden by CITS, which was a government agency. The government-run railroad might not even know I had been on the train, as no ticket had been collected; for all they knew I might just have missed it.

With great confidence, therefore, I displayed my map aboard the Mitsubishi bus to show where I had been along the Great Wall—all of which produced much spirited discussion. The Japanese became interested in the ruins too; frequently we would stop, line up in front of the weathered mud structure, and take pictures. As I suspected, it was badly eroded but my enthusiasm was nonetheless contagious.

We reached Yulin and the Zhenbei Terrace of the Great Wall at mid-afternoon. It was the best-preserved section we had seen, so we explored it, after which my Japanese friends helped me to find a hotel. As they drove away in a cloud of dust toward Yan'an, their destination that day, it seemed that from every window of that bus two or three arms were waving.

Leaving the hotel early next morning, I realized I was on my own again and it would behoove me to keep a low profile as, dressed like a Chinese, I set out at a rate of three miles per hour. I planned to keep close to the Great Wall and as far from the dirt highway as possible, but the ruins lasted no more than two miles.

When all semblance of the Wall disappeared I moved closer to the highway. Widely scattered traffic moved in both directions, toward the Yellow River and away from it. All the vehicles were trucks, not automobiles. I paid them no heed, refusing even to look in their direction, as my entire objective was to invite no question.

The Ordos is a hot, dusty, desolate area with scattered villages, typically of mud houses. The loess soil was strange to me, brownish-yellow and very deep. I had heard that it was very rich if only water could be brought in. Blown in from the Gobi and other deserts over millions of years, the loess was responsible for the peculiar color of this earthen portion of the Wall—what remained of it! The few times that I found traces of the Great Wall, no matter how ruined, I veered off to follow them. This procedure continued all that first day out of Yulin until I reached a riverbed with a little water in it. As the sun was just setting, I decided to make camp there, accepting the contact with water as a good sign in the desolate country.

I let my backpack slide to the ground and looked around. There was no village in sight and the highway was far off to the right, several miles. Squinting into the glare I made out two mud houses of the same yellowish-brown earth as the Great Wall. That habitation reminded me of melons, my weakness in China, so I set out, leaving my pack behind. When I reached the two-room house, I found a man drawing water from a shallow well. Around his home were crops, chickens, and a pig or two fenced in by a waist-high sunbaked mud barrier. With friendly waves I approached, saying in my best Georgia-accented Chinese, "Melon, please."

What I said apparently meant nothing to him, so I gestured toward the melons growing in the garden and held up some Chinese paper money to indicate that I would pay. By then several curious children and a woman had appeared. I had some colored candy like peppermints sealed in clear plastic which I offered for the children, but he would accept nothing. Stopping what he had been doing, he reached down to pull a melon from the vine and handed it to me. Again in my best Chinese, I tried to thank him and retreated to my camp.

I built a fire with a few pieces of wood that burned well, much like our western greasewood. Obtaining water from the river, I placed my pan on the fire and made tea. That, slices of melon, and homemade oatmeal and chocolate chip cookies from my pack were my supper out there in the Ordos. Afterward, I pulled out my ground cloth and had no trouble sleeping after all the miles I had walked.

The ruins of that rammed-earth Wall ran out on me again the next day—just totally disappeared—and for two more days I never saw a sign of the Great Wall on the eastern end of the Great Bend in the Yellow River. A few of those yellowish hills of loess rose out of the haze and dust as I walked near the curving empty road. The first town I reached, named Shenmu, was at the very edge of a desert marked on my map as Mao-Wu-Su Shamo. I knew that *shamo* meant desert and wondered if the first part of the name stood for Chairman Mao. The word *mao*, however, means many things in Chinese and I could not be sure.

I walked sixty miles before reaching Shenmu and had two more days of walking after that, always a little uphill, it seemed. Everything considered, it was far from the inspiring journey I had imagined in my dreams. I could not help thinking about that Chinese boy leading his three camels along the Great Wall. Way back when I had first seen that photograph in the magazine, I had resolved, come hell or high water, that I would walk the same route. Now I had walked it for days and days, and had seen nothing but dried mud eroded to nothing. My only consolation was that the rammed-earth Wall had just about run out and I was nearing where the real Great Wall still stood, made of everlasting masonry blocks called ashlars.

Just before sunset on the fourth day I reached the Yellow River at the town of Fuku. My walk of 125 miles added to the distance traveled with the Japanese had brought me across the area framed by the big bend of the Huang He again. There was a fairly new bridge across the river there that led to the town of Baodeh on the far side; I was tempted to take the easy route and cross on that bridge, but the fairly heavy traffic was made up entirely of Army trucks. To me that meant security officers somewhere nearby, so I passed it by in favor of an old ferry two miles farther upriver that was propelled by pulling on a rope in the water.

Three more days I walked east before I reached another town, and still no sign of the Wall. In olden days it had served as an east-west barrier against enemies to the north, but other sections of wall, many running north-south, had also been built to separate feudal states. My map indicated that up ahead I would meet one such section, repaired in the Ming Dynasty. I arrived there at noon on the fourth day after leaving the Yellow River and the sight made me leave the road for a closer inspection. My adrenaline was flowing, because this wall was made of blue-gray ashlars.

This section was like the Wall I had flown over decades before, so much higher and wider than those wasted mud structures behind me that the sight made me cheer out loud. I took a heavy twenty-penny nail from my pack and, with a rock for a hammer, roughly chiseled my name in Chinese characters, and the year "1980." The restored Wall at Badaling has been similarly covered with graffiti—to such an extent that my resolution to add my own name had come at first sight. As long as I can remember, I have objected to defacing trees or walls (the saying from my youth comes to mind: Fools' names, like their faces, always seen in public places), but I felt finally reaching the Great Wall justified establishing once and for all that I had been there. I gave one last admiring glance at my name in Chinese, proud that the phonetic translation looked just like a man running—which, by the gods, I thought most appropriate.

My pilgrimage led me onward. In less than an hour I reached a fork in the road where traffic increased, and at about the same time I heard the shrill whistle of a train and the rattle of cars along a track. Almost before I realized, I had found a railroad and I saw a busy line with long freight trains hauling pulverized coal. There is only one rail line in that part of northern Shanxi; I had reached the main line from Taiyuan which runs north to my destination of Datong.

The road ended at the rails, so I turned north. There was another town, Shuoxian, not more than twenty miles ahead, a distance I could make in four hours. As the trains passed I found myself tempted to climb aboard—or "hack it," as we used to call it in Georgia when I was president in high school of a group called the Hobo Club. I resisted the temptation, knowing I would be blatantly tempting fate. Why risk having to explain why a foreigner with an authentic travel permit was stealing a ride on a coal car of the People's Republic of China?

I did not have far to walk. For the first time since I had begun my trek, a truck stopped. It was such a surprise that I did not react at all; surely it had not stopped for me! The driver and his passenger sat there, neither calling nor gesturing. Glancing up, I saw several passengers in the otherwise empty cargo space. I also saw that it was a military vehicle, a khaki-colored People's Liberation Army six-by-six with large numbers stenciled on the front and rear. But standing there in the highway was embarrassing, so, gathering my wits and courage, I climbed over the tailgate. The vehicle jerked into motion before I sat down.

Taking stock of my situation, I studied the three passengers, dressed similarly to me in blue denim. None of them could possibly be security people. I saw no uniform in the cab, nor had I been accorded any special attention. My companions and I just sat there with no sign exchanged between us as we bumped along the road toward Shuoxian. They appeared tired and unconcerned, so that was how I tried to look. All was well and I was gratified that my disguise had worked, but as I recovered from the dread I could not resist reaching up to feel for my vital papers where I carried them in a waterproof plastic envelope.

We entered town and slowed, made a few turns, then bumped to a stop. The driver leaned out of his cab to call something in Chinese that brought my fellow passengers to their feet. As they climbed down over the tailgate, they repeated something that sounded like *shih-shih*. I went over the tailgate to the ground, too, calling out in a friendly tone those same words of thanks. As I stood adjusting my backpack, I looked for the others with whom I had shared the ride but they were already walking away, so I set off in search of a hotel.

Shuoxian was a large station on the double-track railroad between two of the largest industrial centers in Shanxi Province. I was certain there would be a real hotel with a bath so I could clean myself up before arrival in Datong. Locating it took a while, because I could not ask any questions without giving up my disguise. The hotel turned out to be near the railroad station, which posed a problem, as stations in China seemed to be full of uniformed security guards.

I had been planning to cover the remaining eighty miles to Datong by train, but how could I explain how I had got from Lanzhou to where I was? No, I would not take a chance so close to Datong. I would rather walk. As the desk clerk spoke a little English, I inquired about renting a car to take me to see Wan Li Chang Cheng. He smiled knowingly and replied that he would arrange for one in the morning. What time did I wish to leave?

The accommodations were good and I was more than ready to visit the dining room I found. Better yet, there was a short bathtub in my room. A refreshing bath, and being able to wash my clothes after all those miles walking the Ordos and the near-desert east of the Yellow River, made me bold by morning. Why hire a car just for a short trip to the Great Wall, why return to the hotel at all? I would drive all the way to Datong, detouring the forty miles to see the Wall on the way.

Studying my map that night, I was excited to find that the nearest section of Wall was at Yao-tze-Shen, a name I cannot forget because I flew over it several times in my P-51 Mustang during World War II. Yes, we would trace the main line of the Wall from Yao-tze-Shen all the way to Datong!

All this I had decided by the time my driver met me at breakfast. When we reached the Great Wall it was at the very junction I remembered where one arm comes up from the south and intersects the main line. There were the equally spaced lookout towers that I had followed during the war toward the Yellow River and as far west as the Zhenbei Terrace at Yulin before turning away to refuel at Xi'an. In one of these well-preserved towers, I once again chiseled my name in Chinese in an ancient room that might once have been an armory. We then drove along the wall some 160 miles over a rough road without ever seeing another car or truck.

Once in Datong, the driver located from my description the same hotel I had stayed in during my frustrating earlier trip with the tour group. China International Service was there, as were my old Chinese friends in the office who remembered me. A strange fact came to light when I cashed an American Express traveler's check to pay the driver who had brought me from Shuoxian to Datong: Somewhere along the way since I had escaped the train at Yinchuan, *I had lost two whole days of my life.* With utmost confidence I signed and dated my check, only to be informed that I was wrong. The women at the exchange desk tried to tell me in Chinese, finally resorting to pointing at the calendar. It was not Thursday—as I was certain it was—but Saturday. Ever since then I often go back in my mind and over my map, searching for those two days. I check and recheck each night that I spent in Yinchuan, Yulin, and those I slept by ruins and open ground in the Ordos, but no matter how I search I have never yet come up with an explanation for those missing two days.

# 23

# HOUSE ARREST AT DATONG

With three thousand miles of China and nearly all of the trail of Marco Polo behind me, I was ready to follow the Great Wall on toward Beijing. My travel permit was valid all the way. While visiting the U.S. embassy to get final approval from the People's Republic of China, I would visit the Marco Polo Bridge and bring to a successful conclusion one of the ambitions of my life—retracing that thirteenth-century Venetian's route. Then, final travel permit in hand, I would press on to the eastern end of the Great Wall at Shanhaiguan (as Shanhaikwan is now spelled), where it meets the Yellow Sea.

That was what I told China International Travel Service that first morning, after a good night's sleep. All they had to do was clear me on to Chang-Chia-K'ou, which the Mongols call Kalgan. I was rested and raring to go, happy that nothing had been said about my getting off the train at Yinchuan. Perhaps my change of itinerary had not even been noticed?

But in response to my request, I was told my clearance had not yet arrived from Beijing and I would have to wait. Three days later I was still waiting, bored and ever more apprehensive about that train that had long ago arrived at my destination—and I had not been aboard. The fourth morning as I reported to CITS, I distinctly heard the interpreter repeat my name into the telephone. That brought me to full attention. Worse still, a visitor dressed in the white uniform of the security police was waiting for me; the instant I stepped in the door he rose and came my way.

So began my worst days in China, days that stretched interminably into a week. The interpreter informed me that my travel permit and passport were to be surrendered. I explained that they were in my room, whereupon the three of us set out immediately. All the way up eight flights of stairs, under surveillance by the police, I had visions of having to leave China in disgrace. What worried me the most was that I might embarrass the U.S. embassy, which had trusted and assisted me in procuring my travel pass.

In my room I quickly located and presented my documents to the security officer. He went over them meticulously with the interpreter while I unfolded my almost worn-out map and stood by, ready to show the route I had followed across the Ordos from Yinchuan. But time stood still as for what seemed an eternity the policeman studied every word on both my passport and travel permit. Through it all I never asked a question, nor was one asked of me. After this session, they both rose and left the room, the security officer with my documents. At the door, the interpreter told me to please remain there until he returned.

As dramatically as that, I felt the weight of the world settling on me. By evening it was no mere albatross around my neck—it was one of those Great Wall ashlars. Well, there was no use sitting there feeling sorry for myself. Now that the initial shock had worn off and I realized I had not been formally arrested, I began to look forward to the questioning. Everything could be explained so simply but for the language barrier. To pass the time, I sat down and wrote out my itinerary, day by day, from Lanzhou and Yinchuan across the Huang He to Yulin, and finally to Datong. In the narrative I even left it doubtful as to whether I had been on the trek across Mao-Wu-Su Shamo for eleven or thirteen days, because I was not certain. This was the first time I had itemized the journey in story form, and the more I reviewed it, the more innocent it all appeared to me.

The interpreter from CITS returned alone and we had lunch together in the dining room. Afterward, he said, the security officer would be back to see me. I asked questions but all I could determine was that telephone calls had been made to the Office of Foreign Affairs, People's Republic of China, in Beijing. I told him about the narrative I had written.

Some of my doubts vanished later that afternoon when the interpreter returned with the security officer, for the soldier had brought me a red can of Coca-Cola. The first thing that crossed my mind as the cold drink touched my lips was that if they were planning to lock me up and expel me, surely they would not be comforting me with a soft drink! Then the questions began, the primary one being what had happened to my ticket from Lanzhou to Beijing? I handed it over to the questioner, who quickly compared it with a serial number in a telegram he consulted.

While he was making notes, I began quietly telling the interpreter how I had moved back in the train at Lanzhou, trying to make him see how innocent that was, even if I did change my itinerary and get off the train at Yinchuan. All I had wanted to do, I told him three times, was see a part of the Great Wall that I had never seen. In the midst of my explanation, he interrupted the security officer and translated what I had told him. To my surprise, the man in uniform stopped what he was doing and began measuring distances on his own map.

Then it came to me. That area where he was making such careful measurements was the rocketry range north of Linho in Inner Mongolia. What was more, it was not too far from Yinchuan and barely sixty miles west of the railroad tracks. This man, and those individuals in charge of the internal security of the PRC, were not concerned with a tourist who had missed a train; they were investigating a possible spy.

Next the security officer asked about the different crayon colors I had used to depict my route. "Walking in red," I explained, "riding camels in green, and trucks in blue."

His concern centered on the wavering line along the Silk Road. That represented my joining the truck caravan, and sure enough, at the east end of the Taklamakan Desert we had passed far south of an area I knew was restricted to foreigners. It was a vast and remote dry lake bed called Lop Nor. I had read about it—all that had been released—and knew it was where the Chinese tested their nuclear missiles.

I had not been to Lop Nor, had not even been interested as we crossed Taklamakan hundreds of miles away, but were I investigating the ramblings of a retired general who maintained that he was doing research to write a book, the circumstances would strike me as suspicious too. My unused train ticket to Beijing had without doubt triggered alarm within the government of the People's Republic of China that I might be a CIA agent engaged in espionage.

Question followed relentless question, throughout which I tried to answer patiently and display confidence. I pulled from my bag some of the most important pieces of correspondence from my years of asking for permission to make this journey. Chief among them was the letter from the U.S. embassy that had finally produced that vital travel permit, and a copy in Chinese. While the officer read that, I gave the interpreter my handwritten narrative.

We reviewed my daily progress well past the dinner hour, when I thought back to that twenty-penny nail I had taken from my pack to chisel my name in Chinese characters on the Great Wall. That part of my story the interpreter had to explain several times, after which the security man glanced up at me with the hint of a smile. There are untold thousands of such ideographs covering the balustrades of the restored Wall at Badaling; evidently such graffiti is a custom even among the orderly Chinese.

All along I had felt the need to leave my mark. In the less-permanent rammed-earth western reaches of the Great Wall—along the route of march from Jiayuguan—I had even tried leaving footprints in the sun-dried mud ruins. Once I reached masonry, I could not resist periodically adding my imprint to the ancient ashlars, and those places where I had done so were marked on my map with red X's. My second graffito had been posted the day I rented a car at Shuoxian and came sixty miles to Yao-tze-Shen; I left others as my driver and I drove on to Datong.

Along the way there was a magnificent place I recognized, having seen it first from the cockpit of a P-51 fighter many years before. Spectacular from on high and never to be forgotten from the ground, it is a gap in the Great Wall between two walled cities named Yu-lin-Ch'eng and Yuyu. Both had red X's on my map.

The entire affair was becoming an endless test of my endurance. The conversation droned on in a strange singsong tongue until it sounded less and less clear; at times certain concepts simply defied literal translation. One evening both my companions departed to a late dinner, leaving me hungry and confused. Beyond my fatigue, though, I felt new resolve growing within me. I had just reached the most spectacular part of the Great Wall of China—I had to go on!

I was later to learn that telephone calls had been made to hotels in Yinchuan, Yulin, and Shuoxian. Investigators interrogated the driver of the car I had hired, security police visited the ruins of the Great Wall where I had first carved my name, and my story was corroborated in countless other ways. Had I known, I would have worried more, because I had not mentioned the Japanese tour group; their giving me a ride was the only omission from my otherwise factual account, one made to spare them any troubles arising from their kindness.

My first thought when I was awakened very early the next morning was that I was finally being arrested. Without explaining, the interpreter told me to pack enough gear to be away from the hotel all day; I was to accompany the security officer and him on an investigation. After a hasty breakfast, and with a lunch for the three of us prepared at my request by the hotel, we boarded a khaki-colored vehicle of the People's Liberation Army. As to our destination, no hint was given. I did not ask any questions, confused as I was, because for days I had learned the hard way that questions led to endless translations and no answers. How I wished I had studied Chinese enough to be able to lay it on the line, say how long I had been striving to be here. All I wanted to do was travel the Silk Road and see the Great Wall, ruins and all; I had no desire to learn military secrets and had been in no forbidden areas!

To my surprise, as we drove away from Datong both my Chinese companions became relaxed and pleasant. The one in the white uniform lost his officiousness behind the wheel of the jeep, although I remained wary of him. Sitting up front beside him, I soon realized he was following the line marked on my map, due west out of Datong along the road I had been over the week before in my hired car. I glanced over and saw on the map that we were approaching one of the red X's marking lookout towers where I had left my name.

Lord, I hoped it was still there! Had I really put one there? Everything seemed uncertain after the browbeating I had been through for a whole week. My red X up ahead was right where the Great Wall touched the border of Inner Mongolia, exactly one hundred kilometers from Datong. The road was good, the sky blue, and the Chinese jeep purred smoothly along while I tried to keep up some light conversation. My carving my name put me in mind of the "Kilroy Was Here" story from World War II, where GIs had left the autograph of a nonexistent soldier all over Europe. But it would have had to be translated for the security officer and I had endured so much of that for a week that I decided not to try. Maybe the Chinese did not understand such jokes, did not have the same sense of humor.

At precisely twelve noon we reached the Wall. As we climbed out of the jeep, I anxiously studied the tower and breathed a sigh of relief as I recognized it. Here was also the very place we had parked my hired car. The security officer led the way up stone steps and I found myself wishing that I had not left my camera behind at the hotel. The top floor of this well-preserved Ming tower had a stone storage room for weapons or perhaps a barracks for soldiers. As we entered the ancient armory, whose walls had loopholes instead of windows, I saw it immediately but I held back, restraining the urge to run over and point it out.

My Chinese escorts quickly spotted my three characters in a vertical line amid graffiti going back perhaps to the Ming Dynasty. The security officer studied it and asked through the interpreter how I had learned to carve my name in Mandarin. I took out one of the Chinese business cards I'd had made in Beijing and handed it to him. He looked from it to the wall. Then, for the first time since I had been apprehended, he shook my hand, saying in a good imitation of my Georgia-flavored English, "Kilroy is here!"

Oh, how I longed for my camera back in my baggage. What a photograph that moment would have made!

We then sat down to our happy lunch—bean curd and sprouts flavored with aromatic seeds, plus rice cakes for dessert.

Afterward we drove north some twenty minutes into Wei-Lu-Pau, another place I had described visiting in my narrative. I cannot forget flying over this spot during the war, because here the highway makes an S-turn through a gap in the wall, traversing it three times. There cannot be another place in China where such an event occurs. Then we drove on into the walled city of Fengchen and turned south to follow the railroad line into Datong. It was already night when we reached China International Travel Service, where all my travel documents were returned to me.

# 24

# WALKING THE GREAT WALL WITH GENERAL LEE

Just as he had promised, the security officer was waiting for me the next morning. After a warm greeting he introduced me to another Chinese named Li, who was dressed almost like me in blue denim. This man was no civilian; I had been a soldier for fifty years, too long to be fooled by another professional soldier. His name was pronounced like my middle name, so I immediately thought of him from that moment forward as "General Lee." Estimating his age from his looks was deceptive: Sometimes he looked to be in his thirties; at others, as old as I, although there was not a strand of gray in his hair.

My bag was placed in the back of another Chinese jeep. Mr. Li climbed in next to it, while I sat up front with the same security officer I had been dealing with for more than a week. I had no idea where we were going—for all I knew, after the stunts I had pulled, it was back to Beijing under Mr. Li's watchful eye. But we went north instead of east toward the capital. I pulled out my map to see where we were headed and Mr. Li leaned forward to speak to me for the first time. His English was surprisingly good. No wonder the interpreter had not come along.

"General, I now become your guide. You want to see Great Wall, you see Great Wall. People's Republic of China want you to."

He pointed to my map. "We go ahead thirty-five kilometers, meet Chang Cheng here."

I looked at the route indicated and wondered if the jeep could follow the Great Wall up the high mountain slopes ahead. The Wall disappeared as we climbed; when it came into view again, the driver turned right, as Mr. Li indicated. Almost immediately our road became no more than a trail, forcing the jeep into four-wheel drive. In that manner we bumped and rattled along until I had trouble hearing what the guide was shouting at me.

The blue-gray expanse of Wall drew closer and more distinct with each passing minute until I could distinguish the lines of ancient mortar holding the individual ashlars together. Mr. Li told me we were at 4,000 feet and nudged my shoulder to point up at the top of the mountain, which was not too far above the point where the Great Wall crested.

"Seven thousand feet at the peak," he said.

The struggling jeep could go no farther on a trail that steepened and faded to nothing, no track at all, as boulders merged into one solid barrier. We stopped with a groaning of gears that marked a stall in four-wheel drive.

"From this point," Mr. Li stated in the sudden silence, "we are on our own."

When we unloaded I noted that he had brought a backpack similar to mine. Most likely he planned to see if this crazy foreigner really could walk long distances along the Great Wall as he claimed he had been doing. I understood enough Chinese to know he was telling the security soldier to meet us somewhere to the east, at a town called Min-Chien-Feng. That would not be for several days and I gathered the exact time would depend upon me. As it was uphill all the way, my suspicion was that Mr. Li was about to put me to the test.

How times had changed from my last week. Here I was guided by a Chinese general who appeared to know more about the Great Wall than any professor of history. Had they finally decided to trust me after that week-long investigation? Had they come to accept that my project merited their help? The U.S. ambassador had said as much in the letter they had read, but much had happened since then.

We began with a lesson in mountain climbing. It was not long before I came to the conclusion that Mr. Li was a professional in this field also. Though the highest altitude we reached was little more than 6,000 feet, it might as well have been three times that, considering the difficulty of the terrain. With my guide in front setting a stiff pace, we walked the top of the Great Wall just as I had always dreamed, but the walkway had succumbed in places to the erosion of time, forming a mass of disintegrating masonry like the moraine of a lost glacier. When we came to such spots and began to slip and stumble on granite sharp enough to cut leather boots, let alone our tennis shoes, Mr. Li would lead us down to circle the rubble on a goat or cattle path at ground level until we could climb back up to a firmer footing.

At sunset we reached a lookout tower in good condition and Mr. Li dropped his pack. He stood in silence and looked around. The sun was a fiery ball over the gray dragon of the Wall, part of which we had just climbed. I caught my breath as the sun seemed to touch the very tower I had visited the day before, when I was still under suspicion. Way out the other way, toward the east, the Wall ran on and on. The startling magnificence of the view filled me anew with wonder that such an incomprehensibly vast engineering project could have been carried out centuries ago, in such inhospitable terrain.

I understood by Mr. Li's actions that this was where we were to spend the night and I guessed that he had been here before, perhaps many times. He unpacked a pot and trivet, knew just where to find water close by, and was soon making tea. The source of heat was new to me, a sort of Chinese Sterno. Thus we had a simple meal that included my homemade oatmeal and tollhouse cookies, and we bedded down inside that ancient tower of the Great Wall of China. In the wildest stretches of my imagination I had never even dreamed of such a lodging place.

My education in Chinese history and engineering began at first light. Mr. Li led me around the watchtower, pacing off distances and explaining to me how Ming engineers had constructed the foundation by digging parallel trenches twenty-five feet apart into the solid granite mountainside. These trenches were then filled with great granite ashlars cut to roughly four meters by one meter by one-half meter, and identical stones were then cemented together above-ground to complete the visible portions of the Wall. With such a base, it was no wonder our lodging tower was still standing after six hundred years.

In this student-teacher relationship we traveled together for eleven never-to-be-forgotten days. Only one night was spent in a hotel, but I preferred the others, perhaps even the one when we endured a cold drenching rain in an eroded cavity of the Great Wall that I will always think of as the Great Pothole.

The night at the inn on the bank of a river turned into a celebration. It was not the room or the bed or the hot food, but rather washing myself and my clothes, and having them dry again that put me in such high spirits. While there, "General Lee" told me about the river outside which had a bearing on Marco Polo. Strange as it sounded, it flows southeast toward Beijing, 140 miles away, but never arrives. Long ere that, it is shunted west by the rough terrain and becomes known as Yung-Tung Ho, or "muddy river." The fascinating thing is that this swiftly flowing stream gathers so much silt in the canyons of Hebei Province that it becomes absorbed and just disappears, and all that remains a few miles west of Beijing is a dry riverbed. It is here that there stands the structure I was longing to see: the Marco Polo Bridge.

The general queried me often about my war years in China, noting that the area we were now in had been occupied by the Japanese then. I told him of my long P-51 flight westward over the Great Wall, starting where it begins at Old Dragon Head on the Yellow Sea, and we discussed my sighting the five giant Chinese characters I had spotted on the gate tower at Shanhaiguan. Mr. Li understood completely, explaining that China had considered itself in antiquity the only world there was, with Beijing the center. The gate at Shanhaiguan was thus, indeed, the "First Gate in the World."

Some nights he talked about the Long March, describing events most vividly, and I knew he must have been here with Mao, al-though he never said so. For our meal on the final night we had a melon he had been carrying in his pack for days—just for the occasion, he said. I had saved the last plastic bag of my homemade cookies, although I was ashamed of their condition. They looked like pulverized crumbs. I explained how I had baked them, and the beating they had taken in thousands of miles of travel by plane, train, camel, truck, and on foot. To make a joke I said, "That's the way the cookie crumbles," uncertain Mr. Li would know what to make of this subtly philosophical Americanism.

We discussed the dark-green mountains to the north, and Ku-Pei-K'ou a hundred kilometers to the east across rough terrain. The tower there, I told him, had been an important checkpoint for me on my flights during the war. Then I asked "General Lee" about a story I had heard of an Army unit that had torn down some three miles of the Great Wall at Gubeikou to build new barracks, only to have the Ministry of Internal Affairs order the barracks torn down and the Wall restored. Mr. Li verified the report, explaining that the Communist Party of the People's Republic of China maintained a strict policy of preserving cultural treasures.

Several days before, I had expected Kalgan to be as far as Mr. Li would guide me. Beijing was close and I needed to detour there for a last travel permit to allow me to follow the Great Wall to the Yellow Sea. But no jeep waited for us in Kalgan and my guide showed no surprise as we followed our ancient trail eastward another seventy-five miles. The day after our announced last night and the shared melon, we finally stopped within view of three walled towns; here the Great Wall branched in two, forming a distinct Y that I had seen from the cockpit of my P-51 Mustang many years before. It was somehow fitting at this dramatic juncture that we now also go our separate ways. Thus my unforgettable journey with "General Lee" along the Great Wall of China came to an end.

As the security officer drove us back to Kalgan, my new friend handed me a letter that was sealed and addressed in Chinese. "When you reach Ku-Pei-K'ou," he instructed me, "present this to the commander of the military garrison. His name I do not know but he will know me. When he reads this he will also know you and your mission. I am certain that he will assist you."

In the train station Mr. Li escorted me aboard the Beijing Express and sat down with me, and I noticed that he held on to my ticket. We sat discussing our adventures until the Chinese equivalent of "all aboard" sounded, when he jumped up and hastily shook my hand. I could not help laughing as he presented me with my ticket, letting him know that I realized he was preventing me from slipping off this train the same way I had left the one at Yinchuan.

"That's the way the cookie crumbles, Bob!" he shouted back as he hurried to get off the train.

# 25

# KU-PEI-K'OU
# TO OLD DRAGON HEAD

While I waited in Beijing for the U.S. embassy to obtain my final travel permit, I visited the Marco Polo Bridge. I spent the day photographing this thousand-foot marble span, admiring its arches, pillars, and sculptured lions. The day passed as I walked back and forth over the dried mud bed of the disappearing river "General Lee" had described to me, my mind lost in recollections of my own half-century following Marco Polo's trail.

The bridge marked the end of Marco Polo's journey to Cambaluc, his name for Beijing. For me it marked the fulfillment of a lifelong obsession beginning with a motorcycle ride from Europe to Asia Minor in 1932. It was no more than 5,000 miles back to Venice in a straight line, but the way I had come—and probably Polo, too—it had been some 7,700 miles. If I had not walked all the way—as had the Venetian, his father Niccolò, and his uncle Maffeo—they in turn had not had to cope with modern-day border problems.

In spite of all the frustrations and obstacles, I had completed one of my ambitions. With the necessary document in hand I set out to complete another, traveling by hired car to Ku-Pei-K'ou for the final stage of my adventure with Wan Li Chang Cheng. When I reported to the local PLA commander, Captain Chu, he read Mr. Li's letter and immediately informed me that I would not need my car; the military would support me during the remainder of my quest to travel the entire length of the Great Wall of China. "General Lee" had not gone out of my life at all, it seemed, but was still here helping me. The local garrison commander indeed knew of him; twice I heard Captain Chu refer to him as "Tiger Li" and I wondered all the more about my remarkable friend.

The town of Ku-Pei-K'ou was small and high in the mountains, hardly more than a military outpost and almost a part of the Great Wall itself. My old navigation checkpoint, the lookout tower, was far more impressive from the ground than it had been from the air, a fortress smaller than the one at Jiayuguan but no less spectacular. Captain Chu called it *guangcheng* as he drove me around in a jeep or a weapons carrier on interesting side trips, one of which was to show me the section of wall restored after having been torn down to build military barracks. We walked along the reconstruction for almost a mile.

I was taken by truck to the very spot where Mr. Li and I had spent our last night together, and walked the seventy miles back to Ku-Pei-K'ou in three days. Now just 170 miles remained before the Yellow Sea and the end of my long journey. Captain Chu tried hard to get me to cover the distance in a supply truck sent weekly to Qinhuangdao (formerly Chinwangtao), a large seaport near Shanhaiguan, but I was adamant about doing it myself. Reluctantly he bade me farewell and wished me good luck, apparently wondering why anyone would choose to walk when he could ride in a truck. Every time I reached a gap where a road crossed the Wall, one of Captain Chu's PLA trucks would be there waiting for me just in case I had changed my mind.

Day by day I made a good twenty-eight to thirty miles. My goal was drawing near, the realization of a lifelong dream, and suddenly it came to me that I did not want it to end. I was now exactly a hundred kilometers—a bare sixty-two and a half miles—from Jiaoshanguan, the Horned Mountain Pass, from which high ground I would look downhill to the ocean. The most I could stretch that out to was three days.

I had been hurrying every step of the way; that was life for me, the way my motor ran, never walking when I could run. Now I found myself doing everything possible to delay the end, examining the Wall, stopping to take pictures when there was nothing to justify the shot. Yet no matter how I dragged my feet for a few minutes, I was soon back to my normal cadence—faster and faster. With excitement I searched for Jiaoshanguan as I topped each rise; it was there that I had long since decided to spend the final night, not caring if I slept, just as long as I could look down the few remaining miles to the Yellow Sea.

It came unexpectedly. Sure enough, there was the glint of the ocean. Night was falling and it was risky walking on top of the Wall among all those eroded shards of stone. I let my backpack slide to the ground and stood taking in the view, feeling a part of this ancient gray dragon of weathered masonry I had traveled so long. It was an old friend.

Lights began to flicker in the distant city of Shanhaiguan. I could make out the gate tower at the north end of town, at which I had dived in my Mustang before climbing for where I now stood. Long after I had settled down for the night and lay there wrapped in my ground cloth, I found myself torn between feelings of victory and regret. Sometimes I crawled out of the bedroll and made my way precariously to the top of the Great Wall just to look around. The lights flickered like fireflies.

Suddenly my thoughts turned to Kitty Rix. It had been almost nine years since her death and I suppose my loneliness was the reason I kept doing all these strange things. I had her on my mind the rest of the night; each time I shut my eyes I saw her face and wondered what she would say if she knew where I was. Along with seeing her, I imagined I heard many times her last words to me. I had leaned down that last night of her life, putting my ear close to her lips to hear what she whispered.

"Scotty, I know you had to do all those things you did. It was *your* way and I understood, I understood."

Before sunrise I set out down the mountain. Hurrying the dawn was foolish in that shadowed terrain but I had not slept and was impatient. Amid the rubble and the steep slope, I came close to falling several times. How stupid to come so far, then break some bone in the last ten miles!

It was full daylight when I neared level ground, the Wall all ruins until I crawled through a barbed-wire fence and came to another rebuilt section. Lasting only a mile, it led me to the fort at Shanhaiguan which had also been restored. There, as if waving a welcome, were the five ancient characters, each tall as a man, that had so long fascinated me.

*Tian, Xia, Di, Xi, Guan,* as my friend Li had read them out to me. The First Gate in the World.

Just past the fort and gate tower, the Wall faded out. Then came the coastal highway. Beyond that the Wall was just a raised pathway of hardened earth with gray stones protruding. I walked the two miles, then two steps, then the last one to the edge of the parapet at Old Dragon Head. On the beach far below, waves washed over ancient ashlars that had once been part of the Great Wall of China.

I took off my blue cap and waved it at the far bluer sky, then ran, shoes and all, down sand dunes from Old Dragon Head into the welcoming waves of the Yellow Sea.

# 26

# Flying Tiger
# Returns to China
# to Honor Former Boss

I did not see that headline in an August 1980 issue of *The New York Times* until after I returned to Beijing. While talking with fellow wartime pilot George Bush at the embassy cocktail party in his honor, I had mentioned in front of a reporter my intention of returning to Kunming and setting up a memorial to General Claire Chennault.

"Oh," the reporter had exclaimed, "I hardly think the Chinese will permit that. The regime has changed, you know."

Something in my determination must have convinced him that I was serious, because that newspaper story appeared in many countries. I knew nothing of it, of course, as I traveled the Silk Road and then followed the Great Wall from end to end. All the way, performing this duty before I left China was never far from my mind.

General Chennault had known great adversity in life, and far too little of the acclaim he so richly deserved. My mission now was to leave near our old base some expression, some tangible tribute, to his genius, his determination, his refusal ever to quit, and most of all to those special qualities and strengths that utterly won the loyalty of pilots lucky enough to fly for him. I would put up a lasting memorial on behalf of those pilots, and in a larger sense on behalf of both the Chinese and American peoples. No matter the politics of the Generalissimo, General Chennault had fought for China and I had fought for General Chennault.

As I walked down the airline ramp at the new airport at Kunming, it was like a reunion with the Old Man. Is there any wonder that the first place I looked was at the broken mountain peak to the west? That was Xishan. There were tears in my eyes as I saw it. It had been a favorite place of Chennault's where he used to take me when we had secret plans to discuss, or when he wanted to talk to me as an apprentice rather than a junior officer. He had told me of the ancient earthquake that had shattered this mountain west of Yunnan-fu (the old name for Kunming), had made half the face of Xishan fall a mile into the great lake beneath. Up there, by the grace of God, I would place the memorial.

The unwanted publicity worried me; had it perhaps already made it impossible for me to quietly fulfill my mission? The white uniform of a security police officer shook me up in the airport but he made no move to detain me. Then a young man introduced himself as Zhao Jufang, a guide from the China International Travel Service. He would be my interpreter and guide while I was in Kunming.

In the car I tried to carry on an innocent conversation that would not reveal my purpose, yet would produce information. I needed to know if you could still drive up the back side of Xishan to the Taoist temple that had been there, and where there was an expert stonecutter? On the positive side, Zhao Jufang had obviously been briefed about me and he knew about Chennault and the Flying Tigers.

Kunming had changed so dramatically that I did not recognize a single familiar landmark. There had been a wall completely around the city of a million people—how could an entire city wall disappear? Zhao explained that it had been replaced during the Cultural Revolution with the wide Dongfengxi Boulevard on which we were driving. I asked about the old airfield we had used, our *fiejishan*, but he had not heard of it, nor did he know anything about Hostel Number One, where the Flying Tigers had lived. He shook his head and I shook mine.

At the Jade Lake Hotel, I set about trying to find out, ever so

carefully, if any of those Chinese who worked with us in the 23rd
Fighter Group were still around. I also tried to locate a stonecutter
but did not even know the term for one in Yunnan. I pulled out the
scroll of heavy rice paper on which a scholar of calligraphy had
drawn the Mandarin characters for:

GENERAL CLAIRE LEE CHENNAULT
FLYING TIGERS
WE, YOUR MEN,
HONOR YOU FOREVER

The Chinese characters would be chiseled from the top of the
stone down the center, and the date would follow. At lower left in
much smaller characters there would appear:

THIS TRIBUTE IS FROM YOUR MEN
CERTIFIED BY GENERAL ROBERT LEE SCOTT
ENDORSED BY GENERAL MERIAN COOPER

My search for a stone artisan began on my first sightseeing tour
of modern Kunming. I had forgotten, if I ever knew, that it had been
founded during the Han Dynasty in 109 B.C. My idol Marco Polo
had visited here—a full thousand miles south of the Great Wall—
when it was the kingdom of Da Li. Our old airdrome was not gone,
but was an active military airfield and closed to foreigners. I was
especially eager to visit it because some of my men were buried
nearby in a Buddhist cemetery. Less than forty years had made an
incredible difference.

On the fourth day of being chauffeured around under courteous
but close supervision, we were joined by another Chinese man,
most likely a general officer. No matter how long I had been retired,
I was finding that sooner or later I was "checked out" by a military
person of equivalent rank. This general was dressed in the usual blue
denim trousers and Mao jacket, like any civilian, and was most
friendly and knowledgeable. He told me with pride that I was to be
shown the Taoist temple on the mountain as I had requested. The
tour rekindled many memories of trips with Wang Chauffeur always

at the wheel in that old Studebaker staff car that had once been strafed on the Burma Road. There were the very old trees where we had walked when discussing missions Chennault would have led, had he been young enough. Sometimes we climbed the famous helical tunnel, 371 steps chiseled out of solid mountain by generations of patient monks. At the top was Dragon Gate, not a gate at all but a parapet high above the lake, from which we could see our airdrome ten miles away.

Those steps had not changed, anyway. I stopped, felt their chisel marks with my hands. At the top the general pointed out important landmarks including the new airport. I asked if the old *fiejishan* was still operational and he nodded. I told him I had to return there before I left, as eight of my men were buried there.

It was a special afternoon, somehow like coming home. Everyone was friendly and relaxed, and I did not feel watched. On the way back down, the unexpected happened. Our driver jammed on his brakes in the middle of a hairpin turn and brought us to a skidding stop amid a cloud of dust. I saw nothing on the road, but by then the driver was talking excitedly in a staccato of Chinese so fast I did not even get the gist, much less the words.

"General Scott," Zhao Jufang said, "driver Han Tsui say he just realize who you are. His father work for you in big war, drive car for you. Your chauffeur!"

It was possible, although I usually drove my own jeep. There were times when, returning from combat, I would be met by base vehicles. Then, too, somebody used to bring my jeep across the field to me. His father, Han Tsui said, had told him a great deal about his days with the American fliers before he died during the Cultural Revolution. He knew the name of Chennault's chauffeur and had a good answer for every one of the other questions I put to him. There was a general feeling of shared experience, a bond that made the remainder of the trip all the more pleasant.

By the next day I had no doubts that dramatic changes had occurred in my status. For almost a week my requests to visit the airfield had fallen on deaf ears; now I was invited to visit by an Air Force colonel in full uniform who came in a PLA jeep. Nostalgia overtook me as we drove past the same scarred eucalyptus trees and cultivated fields that I had driven past a thousand times myself. Familiar sights, sounds, and smells tugged at my heart as we entered the gate, the sentry saluting. I saluted back from force of habit.

On the field, though, not a single building or tree looked at all familiar. Gone was the six-thousand-foot runway of stone and mud grouting that I had watched thousands of Chinese women and children build with their bare hands. Running in the same direction— toward the lake—was a broad concrete ribbon of modern runway. I caught myself looking to Xishan for orientation; only the mountain was the same. The greatest disappointments were not finding any sign of the house where I had lived with Chennault and others, and the total disappearance of the Buddhist cemetery with the graves of eight of my men.

I was distracted from my search every time a Chinese jet fighter took off or landed, standing there spellbound as the MiG-19s descended in flat power-on approaches that ended in hot landings with drag chutes popping open to stop the heavy aircraft.

Having been an instructor and check pilot for too long, I found myself mentally at the controls, evaluating the performance of the MiG-19s, which the Soviets sold the Chinese back when they were friends. Each takeoff was an experience; they needed every inch of the runway to become airborne and were obviously underpowered, a problem compounded by Kunming's 6,000-foot altitude. In almost five thousand hours of jet time I had flown a number of "ground loving" jets—for example, our Republic F-84Es at Fürstenfeldbruck, Germany, in the early 1950s—and there was no doubt in my mind that this MiG was a real *dog*. The high point of the visit, nevertheless, came when the base commander took me to the flight line to meet all the Chinese fighter pilots. I was surrounded within seconds by eager young fliers communicating in the international language of fighter pilots, hands following each other in graceful simulations of aerial maneuvering.

They invited me to sit in the cockpit of a MiG while several of them stood on the wings and leaned over the canopy rails to point out features and give me my "cockpit checkout." They all knew about the Flying Tigers and many brought copies of a large magazine with a pictorial history of the AVG. Because I had not been one of the original Flying Tigers, my picture was not there but that did not stop them from wanting me to sign anywhere. What an honor for me, and how wonderful to learn that Chennault and his American Volunteer Group were finally being recognized as having fought for China, regardless of which regime!

About the same time as my visit to the airbase, I was taken to the best stonecutter in Kunming. All I had to do was note how busy he was and see the quality of his work to know that he was the artisan for the task. As soon as the general had introduced me, I showed him the pattern for calligraphy and he dropped what he had been doing to set to work. I had initially planned on a modest stone I could transport myself, picturing a slab of marble roughly two feet by three, and two inches thick. Now I learned that, while a slab that size could have been sandblasted at any memorial works in the United States, it would be much too thin and would shatter here, where work was still done by hand the old way, with a hammer and chisel. When we found the right stone for General Chennault's memorial, it turned out to be forty-two inches tall, twenty-two inches across, and six inches thick. It was a beautiful piece of granite, native not just to the region but to Xishan itself, part of the cataclysmic rockfall from that forgotten earthquake that had shattered the mountain.

I visited every day to watch it being carved. Its weight by my best estimate was just over half a ton and I wondered how I could possibly move it up to the top of the mountain if it took six of us just to lift it off the ground. The audience grew every day as the artisan worked, all of us admiring the glowing tribute to General Chennault as it took shape—it looked so good in that ancient script, an expression of our love and respect as everlasting as the stone itself.

Ever since the driver of the car had remembered that his father had been my chauffeur during the war, he had been on my side all the way. He had evidently stimulated a similar enthusiasm in others who had not forgotten that Kunming had been the home of the Flying Tigers, because when the moment came to transport the memorial to its resting place, there was no lack of muscle. We tenderly lifted the half-ton of polished stone in its protective padding to the bed of a four-wheel-drive truck, and drove it slowly up the back side of Xishan to where the road ended at an altitude of 9,000 feet. The final distance was covered with the use of a "drag" similar to the travois once used by American Indians, except that we pulled it ourselves instead of using horses. Reaching the end of the steep slope, we carefully rolled the stone forward; taking off the padding, we slipped it snugly into a niche of rock in the broken face of Xishan so that the calligraphy faced straight toward our old airfield ten miles across shimmering Lake Dianchi. The monument had fit so perfectly into its new home that it was just as if nature had prepared the spot and been reserving it a very long time.

We made some final adjustments with small stones, everyone trying to help, not one of my helpers wondering why we were going to all the trouble. I had the comfortable feeling the Old Man knew I was there, as well as the Chinese he had known well and regarded so highly. Before we went back down the mountain to Kunming, I stood at the memorial and saluted General Claire Lee Chennault just as though he were there.

# EPILOGUE:

# GOALS, THE PAST, AND THE FUTURE

I now happily serve as chairman and chief fund-raiser of the Heritage of Eagles Campaign, a nonprofit organization fostering the development of the superb new Museum of Aviation. Located at Robins Air Force Base in central Georgia, this museum—which is being opened in stages—differs from most by *teaching* as well as displaying. It already has sixty aircraft ranging in size up to the B-52, and I hope to fly a P-40 to the field as soon as we locate one for the collection.

The Museum of Aviation stresses the value of the past as a tool by which to explain military aviation's future. In its role as a teaching museum, it is considering such displays as an F-15 Eagle—a multi-million-dollar first-line fighter of today—that has been "exploded" to reveal its high-tech wonders and electronic miracles.

Why are such machines necessary, a schoolchild might well ask? I would answer that having such weapons ready is the best way to make sure they will not be needed or used. I would say that if we did not have the proper state-of-the-art weapons, chances are the next generation would indeed have to fight yet another war. I would explain about the early days of World War II when we were losing all over the world; how it took two dangerous and costly years to get into service critically-needed aircraft of the right kind like the P-51 and B-29.

As these words are being written, I am in the process of moving back to Georgia. Whatever the merits of Horace Greeley's advice, I have to paraphrase Walt Whitman and say that the farther west I have gone, the worse I have felt. It took me years to catch on. Then one day I flew *east* to the Museum of Flight and heard a fine lady by the name of Peggy Young tell me what it was, and I was hooked; I had found my ultimate purpose in life. I am now back in the Cherokee rose state to stay, near my hometown of Macon where—so many years ago—I jumped off the roof of the tallest house in town in a homemade glider.

The Museum of Aviation only came into my life recently; it was not many years ago that I lacked the sense of purpose and satisfaction it brings me. After coming home from China, victorious over my dual obsessions, I went through the worst period of my life, and found out how very much I need goals. Big ones, too, because I never did learn how to do anything at less than full throttle.

Anyway, my adventures had run out by 1982 when I made the worst mistake of my life by shutting myself away to work night and day on this book. I gradually became worse than bored until, as the year came to a close, I knew something was very wrong with me. I could not sleep and the thought of food—even breakfast, my favorite meal of the day—made me ill. As a teen-age Merchant Marine sailor I had never been seasick even in North Atlantic storms. As a flight instructor, I had never known airsickness in all my years of teaching aerobatics. Now my force-feedings left me nauseated.

I no longer bounced out of bed, awakening to sunrises full of plans, expectations, and promises. A fog had rolled in and with it came fear, cold and stark. I have always worked to remain in good physical condition and all medical tests failed to find any problem. Then they sent me to the last department, Psychiatry.

I had *reactive depression*. As a psychiatrist explained it, I had lived a full and productive life only to become a recluse in my self-made prison. I learned then that depression is a disease; for me, accustomed as I was to boundless good health, it was the worst sickness I have ever known. In these more enlightened times, help is finally available in some measure for the millions who suffer from depression. Just recognizing it as a disease that can be treated has been a major step.

Where would I begin finding new goals, new directions down life's road? I began by hearing again the sound of jet airplanes passing over my house. Climbing to the roof, I watched F-15s and F-16s, and dreamed back to the world of a fighter pilot that had been mine all those years. I gloried in the versatility and beauty of the new airplanes as they climbed vertically into the blue, envious of every young man flying them.

Watching was soon not enough; I had to see them close up, rub my hands over their sleek contours. So I visited my old command where my ID as a retired general cleared me to the flight line of the 311th Aircraft Maintenance Unit. There I became a privileged character, walking around with the crew chiefs and young test pilots, and I was really living again when they invited me to climb the ladder and sit in the cockpit of a General Dynamics F-16 Falcon.

CRT displays—color television screens—replaced the primary instruments, and the central control stick I was used to had given way to a side stick controller on the right-hand console. The throttle was still on the left, but far down toward the cockpit floor to keep high G's from pulling your hand away. Noting the heads-up display (HUD) and countless other technological changes over the quarter century since I had retired, I sat spellbound; such places as this had been my office, the only one I had really liked.

I saw how far out of date the F-84s, F-100s, and F-104s I had flown were. None of the mechanics who labored around me could have been born when I was in my glory, flying the best fighters of the day in combat over China; most not even when I commanded Luke Air Force Base twenty-seven years ago. How could they be expected to understand me?

A crew chief climbed the ladder when I was putting in my "cockpit time" one day, dreaming I was flying again. For a moment I thought he was going to tell me that I had overstayed my welcome, but he invited me into the hangar to have a cup of coffee with the other mechanics. There on the wall they showed me one reason they had been so patient with me; in a framed poem called "Remembering the Forgotten Mechanic" was the line "And think of our wartime heroes, Gabreski, Jabara, and Scott. . . ."

Just sitting in F-16s did not cure my depression for long—the urge grew with each day that passed actually to fly the "Ultimate Falcon." My nickname for the F-16 came from memories of my first military airplane, the Curtiss O-1G Falcon I flew at Mitchel Field, New York, in the early 1930s. Surely more than fifty years stood between that crude, fabric-covered biplane and this futuristic marvel, the most sophisticated fighter in the world?

"Say, Jim," I asked the 58th TFW's commanding officer, Colonel James Record, "how about an old bold fighter pilot like me with thousands of hours of jet time getting a ride?"

He dashed my hopes immediately. There was a regulation forbidding anyone over the age of sixty from flying in a USAF fighter and I was already sixteen years over the limit. I had tried to fly the F-15 Eagle a few years before and had been turned down. This time, driven by the specter of depression, I decided to go right to the top and write General Charles Gabriel, the USAF chief of staff.

It helped that General Gabriel was a fellow fighter pilot, the only one ever to reach his exalted office. To him I bared my soul, stressing my thirty thousand hours of flight time—much of it in jets—and my excellent physical condition. Throwing modesty to the wind, I also mentioned God Is My Co-pilot, the first of my fourteen books, still much in demand after forty years and which still influences young Americans to choose the Air Force as a career.

Reader's Digest added weight to my request by asking me to write an article for them on fighter pilots, their wives, and their aircraft. It was to be a love story combining reminiscences of my many "affairs" with fighter planes with observations about the marital stresses confronting today's generation of military flier.

Ten days after I told all this to General Gabriel, word came down that I was to be indoctrinated in the F-16. I reported the next morning to Dr. David Schall, a flight surgeon and rated F-16 pilot. I had a flight physical every six months anyway because I still occasionally flew World War II airplanes—now called "warbirds" or "antiques" at air shows—and expected a cursory check lasting fifteen minutes. What followed were four hours of grueling medical examination, from checking my teeth to putting me in a pressure chamber. Thank heavens my fighter pilot's eyes had remained sharp over the years. It was beginning to look as if orders had come down through channels, saying: "Find something wrong with this guy."

"General," Dr. Schall told me, "I just hope I am as healthy as you when I reach your age. But blooming health or not, you are seventy-six years old. Every little blood vessel in your brain will be subjected to nine G's in the F-16; it one breaks, that's a stroke. That's why I have to be so careful."

Being pronounced qualified for flight took me next to the high-tech F-16 simulator, where I spent hours mastering new techniques. I had to learn to fly with a side stick controller that did not move. All you had to do was touch it and the aircraft moved in the direction from which the pressure came. I had already heard of "fly-by-wire" technology, where computers interpret your input and fly the airplane, but fifty years of habit is hard to break; I kept trying to move that controller *and* coordinate with the rudder. In the simulator, that was fatal. The "plane" banked steeply, then just sat there quivering as though not knowing what to do. What was happening, the instructor told me, was that I was telling the computer something it did not understand—it had already added exactly the right amount of rudder to coordinate the turn, and there I was trying to add more.

The first day I mentally wrote myself a pink slip, thinking how the world had changed, but the next day I caught on and did not hate myself so much. All you had to do was *think* where you wanted the fighter to go, visualize in your mind's eye the maneuver you wanted it to execute, and the F-16 would do it. I practiced over and over, seeing the value of flying the simulator before being entrusted with a real F-16 costing the taxpayer almost twenty million dollars.

I graduated to a day of equipment fitting: flight suit, G-suit, helmet and oxygen mask, all the way to flight boots. The G-suit had yards of heavy zippers and fitted like a corset from the ankles to above the waist; on hard pull-ups it inflates to force blood back up to the brain and keep the pilot from blacking out. Next came an afternoon of "egress training" in a cockpit mock-up where I practiced leaving the ship in a ground emergency such as an explosion in the axial-flow turbine. I discovered that the pilot does not wear his parachute anymore; it is already in the seat so he just clips himself to it with D-rings.

July 19, 1984, was the great day and I was out of bed and

ready to go before sunrise. By six A.M. I was at the 310th Tactical Fighter Squadron being briefed on our simulated combat mission. To my joy I realized my flight would be far more than a takeoff and landing to get rid diplomatically of a retired fighter pilot. My check pilot was the squadron commander, Colonel Rick High, a veteran of aerial combat in Vietnam. We and another F-16 would take off at 8:00 A.M. with max fuel—over ten thousand pounds—plus full ammunition for our 20 mm guns.

Pride surged through me when I saw my name emblazoned on the waiting F-16. I made a walk-around inspection with Rick and admired the sleek silhouette of a technological marvel a thousand years beyond my Mitchel Field Falcon. We climbed up and Rick High checked me out once more on the rear cockpit controls and emergency procedures.

Just then word came that General Gabriel wanted to speak to me on the telephone. Good Lord! Ten days getting ready for this moment—no, ten years—and now something has happened to cancel the flight. I fumbled with the buckles and ran down that ladder expecting the worst.

"Glad I caught you, Bob," the Air Force chief of staff said. "They told me you are checked out and ready. Good luck, happy landings!"

I breathed again. "Thank you, sir."

Busy General Gabriel was gone. As I stood there holding the phone I heard the voice of his deputy, General Lawrence Skantz. "Remember, Bob," General Skantz added, "when you finish your flight in the F-16, don't forget to give it back to the Air Force!"

I returned to the ship before something else could intervene. As we buckled in, Rick fed the critical data into the computers: how much fuel on board, what the armament consisted of, course and altitude for the legs to and from our targets at the Gila Bend Firing Range. . . . I caught myself already talking to this streamlined titanium jewel that came so close to perfection, and hoped the F-16 pilots had wives as understanding as mine had been.

My reverie broke as the engine came to life, screaming its readiness to the world, and I understood why Rick had insisted that I wear ear plugs under my helmet. With the turbine running we checked to see that our G-suits inflated properly and that our regulators would automatically go to 100 percent oxygen in the event of an emergency. Rick then called that the canopy was coming down and I made sure my hands and arms were out of the way. Sealed inside, we gave the signal to pull the chocks and were on our way.

Our two-ship flight carried the code name Viper. By that name we were directed by the tower to runway zero three. Thrust from the eager engine was instantaneous and, hardly needing afterburner, we broke ground after 2,500 feet to climb vertically at 400 knots. I shouted in pleasure and remembered to say thank you to the very skies just before Rick gave me the controls.

My career flying fighters from second lieutenant to general had accustomed me to a veritable explosion in science, but nothing I had known prepared me remotely for the Falcon I now controlled with my right hand. Sheer power, smooth as glass, from an axial-flow fanjet engine I had only read about. We climbed steeply over the White Tank Mountains west of Luke and I found myself desperately trying to master the new technique I thought I had learned in the simulator, but all those years of moving stick and rudder simultaneously were hard to forget. Rick finally had me adjust my rudder pedals all the way forward, out of the way. "You won't need them again," he advised me, "until we're on the ground and you want to taxi."

I purged my mind of old habits and forced myself to apply only the lightest of pressures, just "thinking" the F-16 around, and oh, what coordinated smooth turns it made! By the time I had figured it all out we were at the target range and Rick took over again. I "followed him through" on the controls, looking over his shoulder at the heads-up display which gave primary flight data, how many G's we were pulling, even where the rockets would impact if we fired them, all without taking my eyes off the targets on the desert floor. Rick made the first simulated attack on salvaged trucks and tanks with bold red stars, using the constantly computed impact point (CCIP) firing system. I then made the second attack.

We abandoned low-level operations and rocketed up through billowing clouds at 25,000 feet per minute—also indicated on the

HUD—as Rick explained how with our radar we could follow the other F-16, which broke off to simulate a MiG. We tracked it from thirty miles out, identified it, and "shot" it down. Rick explained that the computer interpreted aircraft radar signatures, then generated blips on the HUD display that told the pilot what friendly or enemy fighter he had encountered.

We tracked the ersatz MiG repeatedly until our fuel level told us to head for home—again all brightly displayed on the HUD. After we flew back in formation and the other F-16 landed, I postponed the inevitable by asking Rick to demonstrate the most thrilling of maneuvers I had yet seen these high-tech jet fighters perform: the closed circuit landing. Colonel High started a standard touch-and-go, went to full throttle and "burner," and rotated into a vertical climb as the airspeed hit 400 knots. It was an Immelmann off the deck, a half loop with us coming out of burner on our backs at the top, followed by a half roll and a tight turn to another perfect touch-and-go.

It was the fastest trip around the landing pattern I have ever made, perhaps forty-five to fifty-five seconds. I tried the second and almost forgot not to use the rudder, that distraction making me come out of burner late. By my third try, though, even my check pilot liked it. By then I was not giving any conscious thought to the side stick controller; it had become second nature to "think" the airplane where I wanted it.

My third "closed pattern" brought my dream flight to an end. Rick had me taxi where the tower directed us, not to the ramp from which we had left but to a maintenance hangar where there waited a blue Air Force van. A female airman gave us ice-cold towels for our heads when we took off our "brain buckets" and we went to a debriefing room where a videotape of everything we had done—or failed to do—was critiqued. The recorded HUD display eliminated all guesswork with a real-time record of the entire flight: where I tried to level off at 40,000 feet and overshot to 46,000—every move we had made was all there.

Back at our departure point, twenty-five or thirty young pilots waited for us. The commanding officer formally presented a photograph of me buckling into the F-16, framed in Air Force blue and gold with the patches of the 58th Tactical Fighter Wing and the 310th Squadron. Colonel Rick High bestowed upon me a certificate stating that I had been awarded the ultimate experience, a nine-G workout in the world's finest fighter.

I stood before those young fighter pilots feeling grateful for the life I had led. My generation had passed the torch to this new breed, had moved along to make room for better men still. I searched for words of thanks as my hand strayed to the breast pocket of my flying suit for something I had placed there, my "dog tags" from World War II which I had brought for old time's sake. With those stainless steel discs on what was left of the clear plastic necklace, my prying fingers found the little gold locket Kitty Rix had sent me for Christmas in 1942.

In my mind's eye I could see the minute photographs inside of her and then two-year-old Robin Lee. My fingers traced the old Army Air Corps winged-propeller insignia on its cover, feeling the words that reminded me of so many things.

OUR HEARTS SOAR WITH YOU,
OUR LOVE AWAITS YOUR LANDING.

# INDEX

RD 5 T